Ice Cream
and
Ice Cream Desserts

≫≫-≫≫-≫≫-≫≫-≫≫-≫≫-≫≫-≫≫-≫≫-≫≫-≫≫-≪≪-≪≪-≪≪-≪≪-≪≪-≪≪-≪≪-≪≪-≪≪-≪≪-≪≪-≪≪

470 TESTED RECIPES
for Ice Creams, Coupes, Bombes,
Frappés, Ices, Mousses, Parfaits,
Sherbets, &c.

BY
L. P. DE GOUY

≫≫-≪≪

DOVER PUBLICATIONS, INC.
New York

This Dover edition, first published in 1974, is an
unabridged republication of the work originally
published by Hastings House in 1938 under the
title *Ice Cream Desserts for Every Occasion*.

International Standard Book Number: 0-486-22999-8
Library of Congress Catalog Card Number: 73-88333

Manufactured in the United States of America
Dover Publications, Inc.
180 Varick Street
New York, N. Y. 10014

Author's Foreword

⫸⫸⫸⫸⫸⫸⫸⫸⫸⫸⫸⫷⫷⫷⫷⫷⫷⫷⫷⫷⫷⫷⫷

Does ever a day go by that the homemaker doesn't ask herself, "What shall I make for dessert?", or, "How can I serve and dress up my frozen dessert?"

If she wants easy, economical, ever-popular answers, she will turn to ice cream, or a parfait, an ice, or a sherbet. All these will she find in this book, which suggests frozen delicacies that are not only delicious to eat, pleasing to the eye, cooling and refreshing, but supply marvelous food values—protein energy units, vitamins, calcium, phosphorus, and other valuable minerals—for the enjoyment and health of her family and guests.

Thousands upon thousands of American housewives are today making their own ice cream at home and, with the aid of modern freezing equipment, can produce the most delectable frozen delicacies.

Here are hundreds of these recipes for all kinds of ice cream desserts, for every day and for special occasions. You can depend upon every one of them. Many are new. Many are old time favorites. They have all been tested, checked and rechecked. Every measurement, every step has been thoroughly considered and approved so that the result may be triumphant.

For this serviceable book, the author, a practical professional chef, has selected ingredients easily found and available on the markets throughout the United States.

To the American homemaker this book is happily dedicated.

L. P. DE GOUY

New York, N. Y.
August 3rd, 1938

Contents

SECTION I

General Information

EATING AND DRINKING TO KEEP COOL

God and the doctor we alike adore,
But only when in danger, not before.
The danger o'er, both are alike requited.
God is forgotten and the doctor slighted.
JOHN OWEN, English epigrammist (1560–1622)

BOTH the external temperature and the internal body heat influence digestive processes. The effect upon the system of the temperature of food and beverages is also a matter of important consideration. Hot food and beverages in cold weather, cold food and beverages in hot weather, are instinctively resorted to by almost every one, although this is, no doubt, as much due to mental association and, perhaps, a temporary agreeable sensation of the temperature in swallowing as it is to any decided influence exerted over the body temperature.

One of the three "R's" of nutrition that we all learned a way back in school is that food is fuel which the body uses like a furnace to generate heat. And, like a furnace we can control the generation of unnecessary amount of heat, especially in Summer, by the proper selection of food and beverages.

Strange as it may seem, iced foods and beverages with ice in them actually make the body feel even hotter, by making it slave overtime to bring the temperature of these iced foods to the degree

[3]

where the digestive juices can act upon them; so ice cream, sherbets, and in fact any kind of frozen dessert, should be eaten very, yes, very slowly, so that they may become well warmed in their passage to the stomach.

In Summer, midday and dinner meals should contain or rather include one hot food or drink, for it is a known fact that if cold food and beverages make the body generate more heat, hot food and beverages are the signal for the body to get busy, throw off its stored-up heat and cool off. Of course, one should eat lightly of cooling foods.

THREE TYPES OF ICE CREAM

There are three general types of ice cream: French ice cream, which is a rich egg yolk custard and heavy. American ice cream, which is a less rich custard with or without flour or cornstarch, and cream or cream and milk. Philadelphia ice cream, which is a thin cream, or cream and milk and no eggs.

I   MAKING ICE CREAM—
FUNCTIONS OF INGREDIENTS USED

The most important ingredients used in ice cream making are:
MILK, which gives body to the mixture, the solid substances in milk holding air bubbles and preventing crystallization. The milk should always be scalded.
EVAPORATED MILK, which may be substituted for sweet milk for richness, having the same properties and action as sweet milk. It is not necessary to scald it before using.
CONDENSED MILK, giving the same results as sweet and evaporated milk, plus richness of texture and certainty of sweetness.
CREAM, which gives richness, smoothness, since its butter fat contents prevent crystallization.

[4]

EGGS, acting as a binder, leavening, thickening, stabilizer, and giving texture as well as flavor.

SUGAR, giving sweetness and at the same time preventing crystallization.

GELATINE, acting as a stabilizer, and holding ice crystals apart.

MARSHMALLOWS, acting like gelatine, being a gelatine themselves.

FLAVORINGS, have no effect on the freezing.

FRUITS, being solids, retard the freezing process, and thus should not be added until the mixture is half solid or half frozen.

NUTS, acting in the same manner as fruits.

STARCH, be it flour or cornstarch, is a stabilizer because it holds the ice crystals apart.

Milk should always be scalded to reduce its water content and concentrate its protein. Evaporated and condensed milk used in ice cream making need not be scalded for the simple reason that their protein has already been concentrated during the manufacturing process, the butter fat is evenly distributed or emulsified.

The amount of sugar should be carefully measured as too sweet a mix will delay the freezing.

Cream should be added when half beaten, or to a fluffy texture, the consistency of boiled custard.

Gelatine and marshmallows should be always dissolved.

Ice cream to be smooth, that is, free of crystals, must be frozen quickly, so the control should be set in the coldest position, and, as soon as the mixture is frozen, the control should be turned back to normal, lest the ice cream become too hard.

An important point to be remembered is that all the ingredients used in ice cream making should be chilled thoroughly before combining them.

If water is used in the recipe, the mixture should be beaten when it is frozen to a stiff mush, as this will break up any crystals that may have formed.

2   HOW TO USE A HAND FREEZER

There are many patterns of ice cream freezers that are well constructed and inexpensive. They are sold by the size, a No. 2-quart freezer giving you two quarts of the frozen cream or ice.

See that the crank is oiled and the whole apparatus clean. Have ready cracked ice and rock salt, usually in the proportion of 1 part salt to 3 parts of cracked ice (snow may be used.) Shavers or mallet or machines come for cutting the ice, but it is easy to pound or crack it in a strong bag or burlap. Set the freezer can in place, which should be well-chilled, put around it the ice and coarse rock salt alternately, shaking down and packing firmly. Have the ice cream mixture cool, pour it in, having the can not more than ¾ full, to allow for expansion. Put on the lid, cover with ice and salt, wait 5 short minutes, and begin to turn the crank. Open and stir down once or twice, being careful to keep out the salt, lest the cream mixture may be spoiled. Now take out the crank before the cream mixture is too stiff. Pack the cream firmly down in the can, or mold, if desired (see "How to mold ice cream"). See that the melted water is removed from the pail, put in more ice and rock salt, and leave for at least two hours.

If ice cream is granular, too much salt was used in freezing, or the can was too full, or the crank was turned too rapidly. The turning of the crank should be slow and steady to insure a smooth, fine-grained mixture. After frozen to a mush (about 10 minutes) crank should be turned more rapidly until it turns with difficulty, showing that mixture is frozen solid. After packing the finished product, cover with newspapers or heavy carpet.

3   HOW TO USE A REFRIGERATOR

Most desserts such as mousses, parfaits, and in fact almost all frozen desserts, which merely require packing in salt and ice, can be easily made in a mechanical refrigerator without stirring. But, as there are many different makes of this useful apparatus, it is wise to always consult the booklets issued by manufacturers for exact information about using each make of mechanical refrigerator. However, whatever the make, you should be always certain that the temperature of the refrigerator is sufficiently low for freezing. The motor may be set correctly for proper and correct refrigeration, and yet, not low enough for freezing desserts. A temperature control feature obviates any disappointment and allows temporary adjustment.

4   TABLE OF WEIGHTS AND MEASURES

Accurate measurements are absolutely necessary to insure the best products. The experienced artist may be capable of measuring by sight, but the average cook will profit by using definite amounts. A standard measuring cup, spatula, tablespoon and a teaspoon are the essential equipment. As a rule, all measurements are level. Dry ingredients should be sifted or broken, then measured. Semi-liquids should not be rounded in the cup or spoons, unless otherwise indicated. Solids should be packed in the measuring cup, then leveled with a spatula or a straight knife blade.

Terms used and their equivalent

A few grains		is equivalent to		less than ⅛ teaspoon
60	liquid drops	"	"	1 teaspoon
3	teaspoons	"	"	1 tablespoon
2	tablespoons	"	"	1 liquid ounce
4	tablespoons	"	"	¼ standard cup

[7]

General Information

8	tablespoons	"	"	½	standard cup		
16	tablespoons	"	"	1	standard cup		
1	standard cup	"	"	½	pint		
2	standard cups	"	"	1	pint		
4	standard cups	"	"	1	quart		
16	standard cups		"	1	American gallon		
	(4 quarts)	"					
2	cups liquid	"	"	1	pound		
8	quarts	"	"	1	peck		
4	pecks	"	"	1	bushel		
31½	gallons	"	"	1	barrel		
105	quarts	"	"	1	barrel		
2	barrels	"	"	1	hogshead		

Dry Ingredients

Flour and confectioner's or powdered sugar should be sifted before measuring. The measure of chopped and ground materials will vary slightly depending on the fineness of the grind and how they are packed into the measuring utensil. All measures level full.

Almonds—4 cups	equal	1 lb.
Apricots (dried)—3 cups	equal	1 lb.
Barley (pearl)—2 cups	equal	1 lb.
Beans (limas)—2⅔ cups	equal	1 lb.
Bread crumbs (stale)—1 cup	equal	8 oz.
Bread crumbs (stale)—2 cups	equal	1 lb.
Butter—2 tablespoons	equal	1 oz.
Butter—2 cups	equal	1 lb.
Cheese (freshly grated)—4 cups	equal	1 lb.
Cheese (dry grated)—8 cups	equal	1 lb.
Chocolate (grated)—4 tablespoons	equal	1 oz.
Chocolate—16 squares	equal	1 lb.
Cocoa—4 tablespoons	equal	1 oz.
Cocoa—¼ cup	equal	1 oz.
Coffee—4⅓ cups	equal	1 lb.
Corn (canned)—2 cups	equal	1 lb.

[8]

Corn meal—3 cups	equal	1 lb.
Cornstarch—3 cups	equal	1 lb.
Cranberries—5 cups	equal	1 lb.
Currants—2¼ cups	equal	1 lb.
Eggs—9 medium-sized	equal	1 lb.
Figs (whole, dried)—2½ cups	equal	1 lb.
Flour (all-purpose)—4 tablespoons	equal	1 oz.
Flour (all-purpose)—4 cups	equal	1 lb.
Flour (Graham)—4½ cups	equal	1 lb.
Flour (pastry)—4 cups	equal	1 lb.
Flour (wheat)—3⅞ cups	equal	1 lb.
Hominy (blanched)—1 cup	equal	6 oz.
Macaroni (uncooked)—4 cups	equal	1 lb.
Meat (chopped)—2 cups	equal	1 lb.
Oatmeal (uncooked)—2⅔ cups	equal	1 lb.
Oats (rolled)—4¾ cups	equal	1 lb.
Peaches (whole, dried)—3 cups	equal	1 lb.
Pecan (kernels)—3 cups	equal	1 lb.
Prunes (whole, dried)—2½ cups	equal	1 lb.
Raisins—2 cups	equal	1 lb.
Rice—1⅞ cups	equal	1 lb.
Rye (meal)—4⅓ cups	equal	1 lb.
Spinach (cooked, squeezed)—2½ cups	equal	1 lb.
Sugar (granulated)—4 tablespoons	equal	1 oz.
Sugar (granulated)—2 cups	equal	1 lb.
Sugar (brown)—2⅔ cups	equal	1 lb.
Sugar (confectioner's)—3½ cups	equal	1 lb.
Sugar (powdered)—2½ cups	equal	1 lb.

Water

Simmering	equals	180–182 deg. F.
Boiling	equals	212 deg. F.
Freezing	equals	32 deg. F.
Greatest density	equals	39.2 deg. F.
Zero Centigrade	equals	32 deg. F.
100 Centigrade	equals	212 deg. F.

5   SIZE AND CONTENTS OF CANNED FRUITS OR VEGETABLES

No. 1 can equals 1⅓ cups   No. 3 can   equals 4   cups
No. 2 can equals 2⅖ cups   No. 10 can   equals 13¼ cups
No. 2½ can equals 3⅗ cups   No. 1 can milk equals 1⅓ cups
      1 No. 1 can evaporated milk yields 3 cups whipped cream

6   CANDY CHART

Thread stage	236–238 deg. F.	Icings, fillings, toppings
Soft ball stage	238–240 deg. F.	Fudge, Penoche
Firm ball stage	248–250 deg. F.	Caramels
Hard ball stage	268–270 deg. F.	Taffy
Crack or brittle stage	288–290 deg. F.	Butterscotch
Hard crack stage	300 deg. F.	Clear hard candies

7   ALCOHOLIC CONTENT OF MOST COMMONLY USED FLAVORINGS
(*Variable according to brand*)

Almond extract	35%	alcohol	Pineapple extract	82%	alcohol
Lemon extract	84%	alcohol	Rum flavoring	12%	alcohol
Orange extract	82%	alcohol	Sherry flavoring	14%	alcohol
Peppermint extract	78%	alcohol	Vanilla extract	40%	alcohol

8   HOW TO WHIP EVAPORATED MILK

". . . . Milk has been called by its enthusiastic proponents the modern elixir of life. Without dealing in superlatives, it can indeed be said that milk is the most nearly perfect of human foods, for it is the only single article of diet which contains practically all of the elements necessary to sustain and nourish the human system. . ."

—DR. SAMUEL J. CRUMBINE

Pour the indicated quantity of evaporated milk into top part of double boiler. Heat with the lid off over boiling water until hot. Add to the hot milk granulated gelatine, which has been soaked in cold water (see table of proportions below). Stir until dissolved. Pour into chilled bowl and chill until icy cold before whipping. Whip until stiff with rotary egg beater; then sweeten to taste or as directed.

IMPORTANT.—Do not remove the film of milk solids that forms on top of the hot milk. It will whip up just like the rest of the milk.

The bowl should be large, from 3½ to 5½ inches, according to amount of milk to be whipped.

If you use a cooking thermometer, you will find that the temperature of the milk is about 150 deg. F. when sufficiently heated, but not boiled, and about 45 deg. F. when thoroughly chilled.

Follow this table for proportions of milk, gelatine and water. Soak the gelatine in the cold water for 5 minutes:

MILK	GELATINE	WATER
½ cup	¼ teaspoon	1 teaspoon
¾ cup	½ teaspoon	2 teaspoons
1 cup	½ teaspoon	2 teaspoons
1½ cups	¾ teaspoon	3 teaspoons

Another simple method for whipping evaporated milk is as follows: Place an unopened can of evaporated milk in the freezing compartment of refrigerator for at least one long hour. Empty into a well-chilled bowl and whip. This takes but a few minutes. Or, pour a can of evaporated milk into one of the ice trays of the electric refrigerator and set the control for quick freezing. When partly frozen, that is when in a mush, whip in the ordinary way.

There is yet another method similar to the one mentioned at the beginning of this section, but without the use of gelatine and which is as follows:

Pour the amount of evaporated milk called for into top part of a double boiler and heat over boiling water to scalding point. Do not discard the film of milk solids that forms on top of the hot milk. It will whip up just like the rest of the milk; stir it in, then chill the milk by placing it in a pan containing either cracked ice or very cold water. Then chill in refrigerator and whip in the usual way; or, place the unopened can of evaporated milk into a saucepan and cover with very cold water. Boil 5 long minutes, after boiling actually begins. Cool in running cold water, chill and whip in the usual way. *The main point to remember in whipping evaporated milk is that the milk must be thoroughly chilled,* either in refrigerator or the can placed in a large bowl and surrounded and covered with cracked ice.

9   HOW TO WHIP TOP OF RICH MILK

By taking the cream from the top of a bottle of rich fresh milk, which has stood for 48 hours, adding ¼ teaspoon lemon juice and beating with a rotary beater for two or three minutes, the thrifty homemaker can have a perfect bowl of whipped cream with no thought of failure. Whipped cream made like this, and added to any recipe, calling for whipped cream either for refrigerator or hand freezer ice cream, eliminates any fear of crystallization.

10   HOW TO USE GELATINE
TO ADVANTAGE IN FROZEN DESSERTS

Gelatine, which we use so much today, is very useful, may be purchased in all sorts of flavors, and is used to stiffen many other desserts besides the simple, clear, chilled jellies. Gelatine has become a practical necessity in every home kitchen, as it combines well with almost any kind of cooked or raw food with the exception of fresh pineapple which contains an enzyme (derived from the Greek word "en", meaning "in", and "zyme", meaning "yeast"; or together "in yeast"), which prevents gelatine from setting. If you wish to combine fresh pineapple with gelatine, always scald the pineapple, both fruit and juice. When using canned pineapple this is not necessary, as the pineapple has already been cooked.

11   HOW TO TINT WHIPPED CREAM

Whipped condensed milk, or milk top of heavy cream may be tinted with vegetable liquid or paste coloring. Fold liquid coloring, a few drops at a time, into the whipped mixture until the desired shade is reached. If using paste coloring, mix a small bit of paste coloring with a few drops of milk and add gradually to the whipped mixture.

12   HOW TO CRYSTALLIZE MINT LEAVES

Mint leaves, when crystallized, afford a fine decoration to ice cream and the like. To crystallize mint leaves, proceed as follows:
Wipe fresh mint leaves, remove from the stems, and brush each leaf with egg white beaten until stiff, that is, until it holds its peaks. Now dip in ⅓ cup of granulated sugar flavored with 4 or 5 drops of oil of spearmint. Place closely together on a fine wire cake rack

[13]

covered with wax paper and allow to stand in a very slow oven (225 deg. F.), door open, until dry. If the mint leaves are not thoroughly coated, the process may be repeated.

13   HOW TO BLANCH NUTS

Nuts, added to ice cream mixture before freezing, add a crunchy delicate flavor. Almonds, English walnuts, and pistachio nuts are blanched in the same way. Cover the nuts with boiling water, and allow to stand 2 or 3 minutes. This is called "to blanch" in culinary terms. Drain, put in cold water, rub off skins, and dry on clean towels.

To blanch filberts, cover with boiling water, let stand 6 or 7 minutes, drain, remove the skins with a sharp knife.

14   HOW TO MAKE
PRALINE POWDER FLAVORING

Praline powder, often called for in flavoring ice cream as well as cakes and frozen desserts, may be made at home without any trouble at all. Blanched almonds, pecans and walnuts, as well as pistachio nuts may be used. Proceed as follows:

1 cup granulated sugar   ¼ scant teaspoon salt
1½ cups chopped nut meats

Caramelize granulated sugar as indicated for recipe No. 368, into slightly buttered or olive oiled pan; cool, and when cold put through food chopper, then pound well, and pass through a very fine sieve. This will keep indefinitely in an airtight container, kept in a dry place.

15   HOW TO MAKE SPUN SUGAR

To be used as a garnish for ice cream and certain frozen desserts.

2 cups granulated sugar   ⅛ teaspoon cream of tartar
1 cup cold water   ⅛ teaspoon salt

Boil without stirring, all the above ingredients which have been stirred previously until thoroughly blended before placing the saucepan over the flame, to 310 deg. F., or until syrup spins a very long thread. Quickly place the pan in the larger one containing cold water. The purpose of doing this is to stop further boiling. Then return to hot water, and do not allow to boil. Place 2 pieces of wooden bars across chairs about 3 feet apart, and spread wax paper on the floor beneath. Dip sugar spinner in syrup and wave very swiftly back and forth over the bars. Gather up the spun sugar from time to time and form into nests or pile on cold platter.

If syrup gets sugary, melt over the flame for a small moment. Spun sugar softens very quickly in warm weather, so keep it in a dry cool place. You may color the spun sugar, according to taste, using vegetable coloring.

16   HOW TO MAKE CARAMEL SYRUP

Caramel syrup often called for in ice cream making as well as certain desserts is made as follows:

1 cup granulated sugar   ½ cup boiling water

Caramelize granulated sugar as indicated for recipe No. 363, then add boiling water very slowly, stirring constantly, and cook, over a low flame for 10 minutes.

17 HOW TO MAKE NUT BRITTLE

Candy brittle added to ice cream, adds a tang and delicious crunchy flavor. To make it, proceed as follows:

1 cup granulated sugar   1 cup coarsely ground blanched almonds

Caramelize granulated sugar, add coarsely ground (or finely chopped) blanched almonds, turn mixture into a slightly buttered or olive oiled pan, cool, then grind or pound fine. Put through fine strainer or sieve. Keep indefinitely in an airtight container kept in a cool, dry place. For plain brittle omit the nut meats.

18 HOW TO FLAVOR COOKED MIXTURE FOR FROZEN DESSERT

In ordinary desserts, cakes, pies and the like, why does the recipe say "add flavoring last"? Because these food extracts, or cordials, or liqueurs, or fruit juices change under heat, and lose a large share of that flavor, taste or perfume. Thus, in making a cooked mixture for frozen desserts, if you add the flavoring and cook it with the mixture, the result would be that the flavor of the added flavoring would be almost lost. So, always add the indicated flavoring last, after removing mixture from the fire and it is slightly cooled.

19 HOW TO MAKE LEMON AND ORANGE BASKETS

Cut two pieces from each lemon or orange, leaving what remains, in shape of basket with a handle. Scoop carefully the pulp, using

[16]

a sharp knife first, then a spoon, being careful not to pierce the walls. Then place baskets in ice water until ready to use or fill. You may scallop the edge of the baskets, using a very sharp knife. Grapefruit baskets are made in the same way. These baskets are very attractive and may be used to serve fruit cocktail, fruit coupes, and any kind of frozen dessert or ice cream and its derivatives.

20   HOW TO PREVENT
      CUSTARDS FROM WHEYING
          (See recipe No. 192)

21   FRENCH NOUGAT CANDY
          (See recipe No. 205)

SECTION II

Bombe Recipes

✷ ✷

22   WHAT IS A BOMBE?

IN THE old school of cuisine, bombes—a French name, meaning
"bomb," used to be made exclusively of a cooked, then frozen
syrupy custard (egg yolks and light sugar syrup) composing the
lining of the mold; then the selected ice cream, mousse, or parfait,
to which whipped cream was added was used as a filling. Today,
thanks to progress in culinary things, as well as time-saving demands, bombes may be made of one, two, three or even four frozen
mixtures, in which whipped cream may be incorporated, such as
mousse, parfait, Italian meringue, or even a Bavarian, Spanish, or
Charlotte cream mixture may be indiscriminately used in their
making, either as lining of the mold or filling it.

Many delicious combinations, such as Lemon ice and Pineapple
ice cream; Chocolate ice cream and Orange ice, etc., may be made
in bombe shape; in fact almost any kind of cream mixture, even
Frozen custard, may be used in conjunction with or without ice
cream, or frozen derivative.

23   HOW TO LINE, FILL AND FREEZE
A BOMBE MOLD

The mold should be thoroughly chilled. This is very important, for the lining or filling which will be put in is frozen itself, and if the mold is hot, it will soften the mixture, thus requiring more time to set, with a chance of having both mixed in. Now put mixture in by spoonfuls, spreading as evenly as possible with the back of a chilled spoon or case knife until lining layer is about ½ to ¾-inch thick. Then, put in filling or fillings in center, also by spoonfuls, overflowing the mold; cover with a buttered paper or a buttered, double cheese-cloth or muslin, then adjust the cover hermetically set, and spread, for further precautions, a little butter around the seam of the cover. The mold or molds, or it may be individual paper cases, may be decorated with odd pieces of fresh or candied fruit, or nut meats. Individual paper cups, plain or fancy, are placed in freezing compartment and left for at least 2 to 2½ hours or until serving time. If both mixtures are frozen, pack as you would for a frozen mixture made in a hand ice cream freezer.

Bombes, like ordinary food must appeal to the appetite, and food like bombes that makes an attractive appearance is always the most tempting. The very simplest garnish will have a decided effect upon the appetite and is within the reach of every homemaker and hostess. Ingenious homemakers will plan bombes, in fact any kind of food, and serve them with a beautiful look, a mysterious appearance, full of good promises, as well as an eye-appeal.

The varieties of bombes are so great, that only imagination is the limit, so the author has confined himself to giving all the necessary information, leaving the homemaker to decide which mixture will combine well, according to her budget.

24 HOW TO MAKE DECORATED AND DECORATIVE ICE CUBES AND ICE BLOCK

This is an easy, economical and attractive way to decorate frozen desserts, of molded ice cream, mousses, parfaits, or bombes. Here are a few suggestions:

ICE CUBES.—Put in each compartment of refrigerator pan, a nut, a candied cherry, a red or green maraschino cherry, an almond which has been blanched, which may be shredded, even tinted; a piece of ginger, a pinch of shredded grapefruit, lemon or orange peel; one large or two small fresh mint leaves; a small piece of any kind of candied fruit or fresh fruit; a small fresh flower, such as sweet pea, lily of the valley, violet, nasturtium, daisy, or a few rose leaves; a fresh strawberry, or raspberry, or blackberry, or goose-berry; a few grains of stemmed or unstemmed red, black or white currant, etc., according to imagination, availability or occasion; then fill with water and freeze.

TINTED AND DECORATED ICE CUBES.—Variety in color . . . and flavor too, is the spice of life. Colored (tinted) and deco-rated ice cubes add charm. Chilled ice cubes, either for your bev-erages or for decorative purposes, such as for frozen desserts, or molded cream, may be made by freezing canned fruit juice, such as pineapple (not a fresh one, unless cooked, then cooled), orange, lemon, grapefruit, or any kind of canned or fresh fruit juice, single or compounded, in the cube tray of the refrigerator. For fancy didoes, you may put one of the above mentioned items in the fruit juice, when nearly frozen, and let it freeze into the middle of the cube, which after being used for decorative purposes may be placed into the water glass, if desired.

ICE BLOCK.—For a large block of ice, plain or colored to be used as a setting onto which to set molded frozen dessert, or any kind of molded ice cream, or even fresh fruits, as a center piece, when placed over a tray, fill large refrigerator pan with water, which may be colored according to fancy or occasion with a few drops of vegetable coloring, until the desired hue and effect is attained. When nearly frozen, decorate either with: a wreath of candied fruit or holly, if for Christmas; heart-shaped small candies or plain, cooked cranberries, if for Valentine Day; white lilies if for Easter; small hatchets made of cranberry gelatine or plain red gelatine, if for Washington's Birthday; and so forth. These little nick-nacks are simple, easy to make and do not cost much, yet they appeal to the guests.

SECTION III

Coupe Recipes

➤➤➤ ➤➤➤ ➤➤➤ ➤➤➤ ➤➤➤ ➤➤➤ ➤➤➤ ➤➤➤ ➤➤➤ ➤➤➤ ➤➤➤ ⫸⫸⫸ ⫷⫷⫷ ⫷⫷⫷ ⫷⫷⫷ ⫷⫷⫷ ⫷⫷⫷ ⫷⫷⫷ ⫷⫷⫷ ⫷⫷⫷ ⫷⫷⫷ ⫷⫷⫷

". . . . Wouldst thou enjoy a long life, a healthy body, and a vigorous mind, and be acquainted also with the wonderful works of God, labor in the first place to bring thy appetite to reason. . . ."

—BENJAMIN FRANKLIN

25   WHAT IS A COUPE?

THERE is a subtle distinction between a fruit cocktail, a fruit cup and a frozen cup. Fruit cocktail is essentially an appetizer; whereas fruit cup is often served as a dessert, and a frozen cup, usually composed of fruit and ice cream, attractively dressed, is also a dessert. The origin is French and is an ice cream served in a large special glass similar to that called "champagne coupe," or sipping glass, in the form of a tulip. Sometimes a cordial, a brandy or liqueur is added to the mixture, but only when ready to serve, thus permitting the entire perfume of the liquid to be inhaled at leisure. Obviously, then a fruit cocktail is usually less sweet, smaller in quantity and more simple than the fruit cup; while a frozen cup, or "Coupe" in French, is daintily served and, of course, sweet. The top may be garnished with whipped cream forced through a pastry bag and tube, candied fruits, chopped nuts, candied flowers, such as violets, roses and the like, chopped candy, jam, candied orange, lemon, or grapefruit peels, mint leaves, and even fresh fruit, raw or cooked.

26 CEYLON LEMON ICE CREAM COUPE
(Serve 1)

Cut a slice of canned pineapple into small cubes, combine with equal amount of cubed banana, and sprinkle with a scant teaspoon of kirsch. Allow to stand 15 minutes. Then place the fruit and juice into a champagne coupe; place in center a scoop of lemon ice cream and garnish with shredded assorted candied fruit soaked in a very little rum and well-drained. Serve at once.

27 COUPE ADELE
(Serve 6)

Finely grind 1 lb. dried figs and chill thoroughly. When ready to serve, place two tablespoons of fig puree into each champagne coupe; top with a scoop of strawberry ice cream and garnish with whipped cream forced through pastry bag and tube, which has been sweetened to taste and flavored with ground pistachio nuts. Serve at once.

28 COUPE BABY'S DREAM
(*Rêve de Bébé*)

Garnish as many champagne coupes as required with a small scoop each of pineapple and raspberry ice cream. Between the two ice creams, arrange a line of small fresh strawberries, which have been rapidly washed and hulled, then soaked for 15 minutes in orange juice. Garnish each coupe with a small border of whipped cream, sweetened to taste and flavored with a few drops of vanilla extract. You may, if available, sprinkle over the whipped cream, which has been forced through a pastry bag with small fancy tube, a few crystallized violets. Serve at once.

29 **COUPE CLO-CLO**
(Serve 1)

Garnish center of a chilled champagne coupe with a large scoop of vanilla ice cream to which has been added a teaspoon of chopped glazed chestnuts, which have been soaked in a little maraschino liqueur, then thoroughly drained. Top with a whole glazed chestnut and surround the ice cream, leaving the whole chestnut uncovered, with whipped cream flavored with well-drained strawberry puree, using equal parts of cream and strawberry puree, and forced through a pastry bag with a fancy tube. Serve at once.

30 **COUPE DOLORES**
(Serve 1)

Garnish center of a chilled champagne coupe with a large scoop of vanilla ice cream; then flatten with a spoon dipped in hot water. Over the ice cream, arrange a layer of drained, canned red cherries (*you may, if desired, combine green and red maraschino cherries, also well-drained instead of canned cherries*). Cover entirely with whipped cream, sweetened to taste and flavored with a few drops of lemon extract, forced through a pastry bag with a small fancy tube. Serve at once.

31 **COUPE EMILIA**
(Serve 1)

Garnish half full a well-chilled champagne coupe with pineapple cubes (canned) mixed with a little plain whipped cream. Chill one hour. When ready to serve, top with a tablespoon of vanilla ice cream using a rounded tablespoon dipped in hot water, so as to imitate an egg. Surround this egg with whipped cream, sweetened to taste and flavored with one or two drops of almond extract, then tinted with a drop of red vegetable coloring or beet juice, forced through a pastry bag with a small fancy tube. Dust the ice cream only with a little ground pistachio nut meats. Serve at once.

32 COUPE GANELIN
(Serve 1)

Garnish a well-chilled champagne coupe with a large scoop of vanilla ice cream. Cover entirely with mashed raspberries; make a border of whipped cream sweetened to taste and flavored with a few drops of vanilla extract, and top center with a large fresh strawberry. Serve at once.

33 COUPE GOURMET
(Serve 6)

2 squares grated sweet chocolate	2 tablespoons powdered sugar
2 egg yolks, fresh and unbeaten	2 egg whites, stiffly beaten
¼ cup heavy cream	6 scoops chocolate ice cream
blanched, chopped almonds (optional)	

Combine chocolate, egg yolks and heavy cream and whip, using rotary egg beater, until stiff and mixture holds its peaks; then fold in powdered sugar alternately with stiffly beaten egg whites. Divide mixture into 6 well-chilled champagne coupes; place in center of each coupe a scoop of chocolate ice cream, and dust (optional) with blanched chopped almonds. Serve at once.

34 COUPE HAVANA
(Serve 6)

2 cups honeydew melon, chilled then cubed small
1 rounded tablespoon powdered sugar
⅛ teaspoon salt
1 teaspoon lime juice
1 cup mashed, sweetened strawberries
6 scoops vanilla ice cream
1 cup whipped cream

Chill honeydew for at least 48 hours; peel and cube small; sprinkle with sugar, salt and lime juice. Divide mixture among 6 well-chilled champagne coupes. Place in center of each coupe a scoop of vanilla ice cream; cover the entire surface of each coupe with mashed sweetened strawberries, and surround with a border of whipped cream, sweetened to taste and flavored with a few drops of vanilla extract, forced through a pastry bag with a small fancy tube. Serve at once.

35 COUPE IMPERIAL
(Serve 1)

Fill, half-full, a well-chilled champagne coupe with wild strawberries (if not available use small fresh strawberries) sprinkled with a little orange juice. Place in center a scoop of vanilla ice cream, and decorate, pyramid-like, with whipped cream sweetened and flavored to taste.

36 COUPE JACQUELINE
(Serve 1)

Half-fill a well-chilled champagne coupe with small cubes of fresh pineapple, soaked in a little brandy for 30 minutes and thoroughly drained. Over this place a thin layer of sieved, cooked and cooled dried apricots. Top with a small scoop each of pineapple and apricot ice cream, side by side, and between the two ice creams, arrange a line of well-chilled, nice raspberries, which have been rapidly washed, hulled, then soaked for 15 minutes in orange juice. Garnish with a border of whipped cream, sweetened to taste and flavored with a few drops of maraschino liqueur, forced through a pastry bag with a small tube. The whipped cream may be tinted a delicate pink, if desired, or the whipped cream may be divided in two equal parts, each part tinted to taste. Serve at once.

37   COUPE JACQUES
(Serve 1)

Garnish a well-chilled champagne coupe of two scoops of ice cream, one of lemon ice cream and the other of strawberry ice cream, placed side by side in the coupe. Between the two ice creams arrange a tablespoon of mixed fresh fruits, cubed very fine, and marinated in a little kirsch. Garnish with whipped cream, sweetened to taste and flavored with a few drops of vanilla extract, forced through a pastry bag with a small fancy tube. Serve at once.

38   COUPE LOUISETTE
(Serve 1)

Place in a well-chilled champagne coupe a large scoop of vanilla ice cream; flatten the top with the round side of a spoon, dipped in hot water; place on top of the vanilla ice cream a brandied peach, of which the stone has been removed, and a walnut kernel has been substituted. Surround the coupe with a border of plain whipped cream, forced through a pastry bag with a tube, and dust the whipped cream with orange flavored sugar. Serve at once.

39   COUPE MERVEILLEUSE
(Serve 1)

Place in a well-chilled champagne coupe a generous scoop of vanilla ice cream; cover with a layer of strawberry ice cream, scooped with a teaspoon dipped in hot water, and between each space of the strawberry ice cream, arrange fresh stewed cherries, well-drained. Cover the entire surface of the coupe with whipped cream, sweetened to taste and flavored with a few drops of vanilla extract. Dust with chopped glazed chestnuts. Serve at once.

40   COUPE PELL-MELL
(Serve 6)

If fresh fruit is used, it should be sweetened to taste and allowed to stand at least 2 long hours in a refrigerator.

1 pint vanilla ice cream	Shredded, blanched almonds
1 pint mixed fresh or canned fruit (prepared fruit for fruit cocktail)	Chocolate Mint Sauce
	½ cup heavy cream, whipped

Prepare the fruit and chill. Prepare chocolate sauce as follows:

½ cup cocoa	⅛ teaspoon salt
1 cup cold water	1½ teaspoons vanilla extract
2 cups granulated sugar	½ teaspoon essence of mint
2 tablespoons butter	

Stir cocoa over direct heat with the water until smooth and thick. Add sugar and salt and stir until dissolved. Boil 3 long minutes, remove from the fire, and add vanilla and essence of mint (you may substitute ½ teaspoon more vanilla extract for essence of mint, if desired); stir in butter, and when cold, store in an air-tight jar and keep in refrigerator until wanted. May be served hot, when reheated, with hot or warm dessert, and will keep very long in refrigerator.

Here is how to serve this delicious and economical coupe: Divide the pint of vanilla ice cream equally among 6 well-chilled champagne coupes; likewise with the fruit; then pour over two tablespoons of chocolate sauce; sprinkle each coupe with blanched, shredded almonds, and surround each coupe with a border of plain whipped cream, forced through a pastry bag with a small fancy tube. Serve at once.

41 COUPE PEPITA
(Serve 1)

Place in a well-chilled champagne coupe a scoop of vanilla ice cream; with a teaspoon dipped in hot water, flatten the ice cream and place over it a fresh peach which has been poached in a light sugar syrup, then well-chilled. Pour over the entire surface 2 tablespoons of slightly melted red currant jelly, and top with a fresh or canned, or maraschino cherry. Serve at once.

42 COUPE ROSE
(Serve 1)

Place in a well-chilled champagne coupe 3 tablespoons of mashed raspberries combined with 1 tablespoon of crumbled macaroons. In center of this mixture, place a scoop of rose ice cream made as indicated for recipe No. 263, Rose Ice Cream. Cover with two tablespoons of canned, well-drained pineapple, and garnish with

[29]

whipped cream (unsweetened and unflavored) forced through a pastry bag with a small fancy tube. Serve at once.

43 COUPE SABAYONNE
(Serve 6)

Beat 6 fresh egg yolks until thick, with 6 tablespoons of maraschino liqueur. Place over direct heat (low flame), and cook, stirring constantly from the bottom of the pan, until mixture is of the consistency of mayonnaise. Allow to cool, and when cold fold in the stiffly beaten egg whites of 6 eggs. Chill well (about 2 hours) and when ready to serve, place a small scoop of vanilla ice cream in 6 well-chilled champagne coupes, and cover entirely with the sabayon cream. Stick in the cream a dozen (in each coupe) of small sticks of blanched almonds. Serve at once.

44 COUPE SUZETTE
(Serve 1)

In the bottom of a well-chilled champagne coupe, place two tablespoons of whipped cream, sweetened to taste and flavored with a few drops of vanilla extract. Place a scoop of pistachio ice cream in center, and sprinkle all around the ice cream 2 tablespoons of cleaned, rapidly washed, and well-drained raspberries. Over the berries sprinkle a scant tablespoon of kirsch; top the entire surface with plain whipped cream (unsweetened and unflavored), forced through a pastry bag with a small fancy tube, and dust the entire surface with a tablespoon of maraschino cherries (green ones) chopped fine and squeezed through a clean cloth. Serve at once.

45   COUPE VERNEUIL
(Serve 1)

Mash ½ dozen of large, ripe, well-washed, hulled fresh strawberries and combine with equal amount of sweetened, unflavored whipped cream. Chill well. When ready to serve, place
the strawberry-whipped cream mixture in bottom of a well-
chilled champagne coupe; place in center a scoop of macaroon
ice cream; sprinkle with chopped pistachio nut meats; and cover
the entire surface with whipped cream sweetened to taste and
flavored with a few drops of vanilla extract, forced through a
pastry bag, in pyramid shape, that is pointed in center. Top with
a large, nice, fresh strawberry. Serve at once.

SECTION IV

Frappé Recipes

❀❀❀❀❀❀❀❀❀❀❀❀❀❀❀❀❀❀❀❀❀❀❀

". . . . Beloved jollity was the offspring of wisdom and of good living. . . ."
—TAVERN MOTTO IN OLD WILLIAMSBURG

46   WHAT IS A FRAPPÉ?

THE word "FRAPPÉ" is French, meaning "chilled" or "iced". Frappés may be classified with water or fruit ices and are not as rich as ice cream, parfait or even sherbet. A frappé mixture has the coarsest texture of all the frozen family desserts, resembling coarse rock salt. It is much used as a frozen mass in many punch bowls, frozen cup beverages, etc. They are usually served either in parfait or sherbet glasses, and often topped with whipped cream.

Frappés are frozen to a mush in a hand freezer or in refrigerator tray. If a hand freezer is used, equal parts of ice and rock salt should be used. Any kind of fruit, canned or fresh, cut into small pieces may be added to a frappé, if desired.

The following recipes serve 6 unless otherwise indicated.

47 ## APRICOT FRAPPÉ
(Hand freezer or refrigerator tray)

Drain a can of apricot; cut into small pieces. Let stand into a strainer. Prepare a sugar syrup with 1½ cups granulated sugar and 2¾ cups of water, cooked 5 minutes after actual boiling. Strain through a folded cheese-cloth or a piece of muslin; add cup apricot; cool and freeze in hand freezer until firm.

48 ## COFFEE FRAPPÉ I
(Hand freezer or refrigerator tray)

To 4 cups of freshly made strong coffee, add 1 generous (rounded) cup of granulated sugar; stir until sugar is thoroughly dissolved. Cool and freeze in hand refrigerator, using equal parts of ice and rock salt. Serve in parfait glasses with a topping of plain whipped cream forced through a pastry bag with a fancy tube.

49 ## COFFEE FRAPPÉ II
(Hand freezer or refrigerator tray)

1 quart hot extra strong freshly made coffee	¼ teaspoon salt
	½ generous teaspoon vanilla
3 cups granulated sugar	1 egg white, stiffly beaten

Combine sugar, salt and coffee (hot) and stir until sugar is thoroughly dissolved. Chill; then add vanilla extract and stir in stiffly beaten egg white. Freeze in hand freezer, using equal parts of ice and rock salt. Serve in frappé glasses, which have been well-chilled, and top with a rosette of whipped cream.

50 ## CHOCOLATE FRAPPÉ
(Rich mixture. Hand freezer or refrigerator tray)

1 quart hot scalded milk
2 squares unsweetened chocolate
   melted over hot water

¾ cup granulated sugar
¼ teaspoon salt
1 teaspoon vanilla extract

Pour hot scalded milk over melted chocolate; stir in the sugar and salt and cook, stirring frequently until mixture reaches the boiling point. Allow mixture to simmer for 5 minutes. Cool, add vanilla extract. Chill and freeze in hand freezer using equal parts of ice and rock salt. Serve in frappé glasses with a topping of plain whipped cream, forced through a pastry bag with a small fancy tube, and top (optional) with a roasted peanut, or an almond, or a toasted cashew nut.

51 ## CRANBERRY FRAPPÉ
(Hand freezer or refrigerator tray)

1 quart hot cooked cranberry
   pulp
2 cups granulated sugar

Juice of a small lemon
Grated rind of a small orange

Combine and stir well the hot cranberry pulp and sugar. Cool; add lemon juice and orange rind. Chill and freeze in hand freezer.

52 ## GRAPEFRUIT JUICE FRAPPÉ I
(Hand freezer or refrigerator tray)

3 cups grapefruit juice
1 cup boiled, cooled water

⅛ teaspoon salt
1¼ cups granulated sugar

¼ cup orange juice

[34]

Combine grape fruit, water, salt and sugar and boil 3 minutes. Add orange juice, chill and freeze in hand freezer, using equal parts of ice and rock salt.

53   GRAPEFRUIT JUICE FRAPPÉ II
(Rich mixture. Hand freezer or refrigerator tray)

2½ cups granulated sugar	⅔ cup orange juice
3 cups cold water	2 tablespoons unstrained lemon
Grated rind of ½ lemon	juice
Grated rind of ½ orange	1 tablespoon rum
2½ cups grapefruit juice, unstrained	

Combine water, sugar, orange and lemon rind in a saucepan; bring to a boil, then allow to boil for 5 short minutes. Strain through a double cheese-cloth or piece of muslin. Cool. When cold, add grapefruit, orange and lemon juice (unstrained) and rum. Chill; then freeze to a mush in hand freezer. Serve in frappé glasses, which may be topped (optional) with a maraschino cherry. Any other liqueur or cordial may be used, using the same amount as that of rum, if desired.

54   ITALIAN FRAPPÉ
(Hand freezer or refrigerator tray)

2 cups granulated sugar	Grated rind of 1 orange
3½ cups cold water	1 cup orange juice
1½ cups grapefruit juice	½ teaspoon grated lemon rind
½ cup lemon juice	1 teaspoon of brandy

Make a syrup of sugar and cold water and boil 5 minutes. Add grapefruit juice, combined with orange and lemon juice and rind of orange and lemon; stir well and cool, then chill.

[35]

When well-chilled add brandy, and freeze to a mush in hand freezer, using equal parts of ice and rock salt.

55   PEACH FRAPPÉ

Proceed as indicated for Apricot Frappé, No. 47, substituting canned, well-drained, cut small peaches for apricots. Freeze as indicated.

Pineapple, prunes, and in fact any kind of fruit may be prepared in the same way.

56   PINEAPPLE FRAPPÉ

1 cup granulated sugar	2 cups ice water
2 cups cold water	2 cups canned, drained crushed
Juice of 3 small lemons	pineapple

Make a syrup with cold water and sugar, and cook 5 minutes. Remove from fire, cool a little and add combined crushed pineapple and lemon juice. Cool, and when cold strain, then add ice water. Freeze to a mush, in hand freezer, using equal parts of ice and rock salt. If fresh fruit is used, more sugar is required.

57   RASPBERRY FRAPPÉ

Proceed as indicated for Cranberry Frappé, No. 51, substituting raspberry pulp for cranberry pulp. Operate exactly as directed.

58   STRAWBERRY FRAPPÉ

Proceed as indicated for Cranberry Frappé, No. 51, substituting strawberry pulp for cranberry pulp. Operate exactly as directed.

SECTION V

Ice Recipes

Any of the following ice recipes may be developed and made into sherbets by the simple addition of two stiffly beaten egg whites, or, if desired, and for economy's sake, 2 level teaspoons of granulated gelatine which have been softened for five minutes in one tablespoon cold water, then softened over boiling water. The recipes serve 6 unless otherwise indicated.

59   WHAT IS AN ICE?

THE word "Frappé" is French, meaning *"chilled"* or iced. The mixture thus prepared has the coarsest texture of all the frozen desserts, resembling coarse rock salt, and is used chiefly as a frozen mass in punch bowls, etc.

Ices, Water or Fruit Ices desserts, are similar to sherbets. They are made of water mixture (or fruit mixture) of coarser grain than a sherbet. Nothing but juices and flavored water and syrup are used. Ices are more granular than the sherbets, and are usually served in well-chilled sherbet glasses. A hand freezer or refrigerator tray may be used in all of the following recipes.

60 APRICOT ICE

For effect, you may serve ices in orange cups, if desired.

2 cups boiling water
½ cup granulated sugar

1 cup apricot juice
2 tablespoons unstrained lemon juice.

Add sugar to boiling water, and cook for 5 minutes. Add apricot juice and unstrained lemon juice, stir well and cool. Freeze either in refrigerator or hand freezer as indicated for Parfaits No. 357. Serve in chilled sherbet or punch glasses.

61 APRICOT ICE CUBES

The following is not exactly an ice. The cubes resulting from the freezing may be served as a garnish for molded mousse or parfait, or ice cream, or served with cold beverages. Peach, pear, plum, prune and in fact any kind of fruit pulp may be prepared in the same way.

1 cup of dried apricots
¼ cup granulated sugar

3 cups cold water

Wash apricots, let soak for 30 minutes, drain, reserving 3 cups of the water and cook until tender (about 35 minutes), adding sugar for the last 5 minutes' cooking. Sieve the fruit. There should be 4 cups of pulp and juice. Strain, cool and pour into refrigerator tray to freeze.

62   AVOCADO ICE

In the following recipe honey is substituted for sugar. This cooling ice may be served with almost any kind of roast, in small sherbet glasses.

Peel and seed 2 avocados; remove the seed and force through a sieve or strainer. To the pulp, add ⅓ teaspoon salt, the juice of 3 limes, 1 tablespoon of unstrained lemon juice, the grated rind of half lemon, and ⅓ cup of strained honey. Mix thoroughly. Pour into refrigerator tray and freeze 3 long hours, stirring once when mushy.

63   BLACKBERRY ICE

2 cups boiling water
½ cup granulated sugar

1½ cups blackberry juice
2 tablespoons unstrained lemon juice

Proceed as indicated for Apricot Ice No. 60.

64   BLUEBERRY ICE

2 cups boiling water
½ cup granulated sugar

1½ cups blueberry juice
2 tablespoons unstrained lemon juice

Proceed as indicated for Apricot Ice No. 60.

65   BLUEBERRY ICE MAINE STYLE

1 pint blueberries
1 cup granulated sugar
½ tablespoon granulated gelatine

1 cup boiling water
½ cup unstrained lemon juice
1 egg white, stiffly beaten
½ cup cold water

Sprinkle a little of the sugar over the well-washed blueberries and force through a sieve. There should be 1 cup of juice. Add cold water to juice making 1½ cups of liquid. Soak gelatine in 2 tablespoons of cold water; add boiling water to which has been added the granulated sugar. Now combine blueberry juice mixture, add lemon juice and stir in the stiffly beaten egg white. Freeze in either refrigerator tray, or hand freezer, following the directions of recipe No. 2 or No. 3, accordingly. Serve in chilled sherbet glasses.

66   CANTALOUPE ICE

2 cups ripe cantaloupe pulp and juice	¾ cup granulated sugar
1½ cups cold water	3 tablespoons unstrained lemon juice

Make a syrup with water and sugar and allow to boil 5 long minutes. Add cantaloupe pulp and juice to which has been added the unstrained lemon juice. Freeze in either refrigerator tray or hand freezer, following the directions of recipe No. 60. Serve in chilled sherbet glasses.

67   CHERRY ICE

2 No. 2 cans sour pitted red cherries	½ cup unstrained lemon juice
¼ cup granulated sugar	1 tablespoon granulated gelatine
	1 egg white, stiffly beaten

Drain cherries and measure 2 cups of the cherry juice, then boil for 5 minutes. Soak granulated gelatine in lemon juice for 5 minutes. Chop 2 cups of the cherries and stir in the softened gelatine mixture, then add to the hot cherry syrup. Stir well. Cool. When cold rub mixture through a sieve, and pour into freezing trays of refrigerator. When frozen to a mush, turn mixture into a large bowl and beat well, using an egg beater, folding in at the same time the stiffly beaten egg white and the remaining whole cherries. You may mold, or place in refrigerator tray and freeze until firm (about 3 hours) stirring every 30 minutes until set. Delicious.

You may use equal amounts of sour cherries and maraschino cherries if desired.

68   CIDER ICE I

1 quart cider   ½ cup unstrained lemon juice
1 cup unstrained orange juice   1 cup granulated sugar

Combine all the above ingredients and stir until sugar is thoroughly dissolved. Freeze in hand freezer, using equal parts of ice and rock salt. Serve in chilled orange cups or in red apple cups. Very appropriate for Thanksgiving Day.

69   CIDER ICE II

To 3 cups of cider, add 1 cup each of water and orange juice and 1 cup granulated sugar. Freeze to a mush in refrigerator and serve in either scooped large red apples, orange cups or chilled sherbet glasses.

You may, if desired, add ¾ cup of peeled, cored, cubed raw apples just before setting in refrigerator tray.

70   CITRUS FRUIT ICE

1¾ cups cold water   1 cup each of orange juice and
   ¾ cup granulated sugar   grapefruit juice
            2 tablespoons of lemon juice

Boil water and sugar and all the fruit rinds for 5 minutes. Strain; chill, then add orange and grapefruit juice. Freeze to a mush in either refrigerator tray or hand freezer. Serve in chilled parfait glasses.

71   CHRISTMAS CIDER ICE

2 tablespoons granulated gelatine
¼ cup cold water
2 cups strained applesauce

2 cups sweet cider
½ cup granulated sugar
1 tablespoon lemon juice
A few grains salt

Soak granulated gelatine in cold water for 5 minutes, and soften over hot water, then add and stir well the applesauce, cider, lemon juice and salt. Mix well. Pour into refrigerator tray and freeze to a mush. Serve into scooped small red apples. Fasten a sprig of holly to each apple. Very appropriate to serve with almost any kind of roast.

72   COFFEE ICE FRENCH METHOD I

Grind enough roasted coffee so as to have 5 tablespoons (more if a stronger mixture is desired) place in a hot saucepan, and pour over 2 cups of boiling milk; cover and allow to infuse for 20 minutes. Strain through a fine muslin cloth; add 1 cup of sugar syrup made of equal parts of water and granulated sugar. Chill, then freeze to a solid mush in hand freezer, using 3 parts ice and 1 part of rock salt. Serve in chilled sherbet glasses, topped with a rosette of whipped cream.

73   COFFEE ICE FRENCH METHOD II

Proceed as indicated above (recipe No. 72) and when ready to freeze, add 1 tablespoon of good cognac. Freeze as indicated and serve likewise.

[42]

74 **CRANBERRY ICE I**
(Very appropriate for Thanksgiving or Christmas)

Have ready 1 pint of fresh cranberries, washed and cooked 10 minutes in 1¼ cups of water, or long enough to soften the berries, and force through a sieve. Cool while preparing the following mixture:

1 teaspoon granulated gelatine	¼ cup orange juice
¼ cup cold water	½ cup granulated sugar
⅓ cup white corn syrup	2 tablespoons lemon juice
¼ scant teaspoon salt	

Sprinkle gelatine over cold water and allow to soak for 5 minutes. Bring corn syrup and sugar to the boiling point, stirring often, then add the soaked gelatine, stir and cool slightly. Combine this with sieved cranberries, orange and lemon juice and salt. Stir well, and allow to chill. Freeze in refrigerator tray, stirring every 15 minutes. Then freeze to a smooth mush. Serve in chilled, scalloped paper cases alongside of the roast.

75 **CRANBERRY ICE II**

4 cups cranberries	⅛ teaspoon salt
2½ cups granulated sugar	½ cup orange juice
3½ cups boiling water	¼ cup lemon juice

Pick and wash cranberries. Combine sugar, water and salt and boil for 5 long minutes; add washed cranberries and cook 10 minutes longer, over a low flame, or until berries are softened. Rub through a sieve, cool, then add combined orange and lemon juice. Chill, then freeze in refrigerator tray to a solid mush. (About 2 hours.) Serve in sherbet glasses.

76   CRANBERRY ICE III

4 cups cold water   2 cups granulated sugar
2 cups cranberry juice   2 tablespoons lemon juice
                Grated rind of half orange

Cook enough cranberries so as to make 2 cups of cranberry juice (pulp and liquid). Stir in sugar and dissolve thoroughly. Then add lemon juice and grated orange rind and freeze in refrigerator tray to a solid mush. (About 2 hours.)

To add flavor, you may add ½ cup softened small seedless white raisins, if desired, or softened currants.

77   GRAPE JUICE ICE

3 cups cold water   2 cups bottled grape juice
1½ cups granulated sugar   ¼ cup lemon juice
⅛ teaspoon salt   Grated rind of half orange

Make a sugar syrup with water and sugar, boiling it for 5 long minutes; remove from fire and add grape juice, salt and grated orange rind. Cool, then add lemon juice. Chill, then freeze to a mush, in hand freezer, using 6 parts of ice and 2 parts of rock salt. Serve in sherbet glasses which have been chilled.

78   HONEYDEW MELON ICE

1 large honeydew melon   ⅛ teaspoon salt
  Juice of a large lemon   ¾ cup sherry wine
2 cups cold water   1 egg white stiffly beaten, or
1 cup granulated sugar   ½ cup heavy cream, whipped
                Mint leaves

You may serve the ice either in the scooped honeydew, in scooped red apples, or in chilled orange basket.

[44]

Peel or scoop out melon; force pulp through a sieve, and sprinkle over lemon juice. Stir well. Make a sugar syrup with cold water, sugar and salt, allowing it to boil 5 minutes. Cool slightly, and add sieved honeydew pulp mixture and sherry wine. Stir well, then fold in either the stiffly beaten egg white or the whipped heavy cream. Freeze in refrigerator tray until firm, that is, to a rather solid mush, stirring every 30 minutes.

79   LIME ICE I

2 cups cold water
⅔ cup granulated sugar
½ cup unstrained lime juice
A few grains salt

A few drops green vegetable coloring
2 egg whites, stiffly beaten

Make a sugar syrup with water and sugar, and allow to boil for 10 minutes. Add unstrained lime juice; cool, then add enough green vegetable coloring to attain the desired hue. Freeze to a mush in refrigerator tray; remove from refrigerator and scoop into a well-chilled bowl, then beat with rotary egg beater until mixture is very light. Then, fold in the stiffly beaten egg whites and salt; return to freezing tray and allow to freeze for 3 to 4 hours. Serve in well-chilled sherbet glasses, topping each glass with a crystallized mint leaf.

80   LIME ICE II

(Very appropriate with almost any kind of roast on Saint Patrick's Day.)

1 package lime-flavored gelatine
⅔ cup boiling water
½ cup granulated sugar

½ cup cold water
3 cups pale ginger ale
Orange baskets No. 19

[45]

Dissolve lime-flavored gelatine in boiling water. Make a syrup with granulated sugar and cold water, allow it to boil 5 minutes; then add the dissolved gelatine, and cool. When cold, add pale ginger ale. Freeze in refrigerator tray for at least overnight. When ready to serve, fill orange baskets, made as indicated for recipe No. 19 and serve at once.

81   LEMON ICE I

Make a syrup with 2 cups of granulated sugar and 4 cups of cold water, allowing it to boil for 5 minutes. Remove from the fire, cool slightly, add ¾ cup of lemon juice and freeze in hand freezer, using 3 parts of ice and 1 part of rock salt. Serve in well-chilled sherbet glasses, or in orange baskets, if desired.

82   LEMON ICE II

½ cup lump sugar (tablets)   1 cup hot water
4 medium-sized thin-skinned   2 cups cold water
   lemons   ¾ cups granulated sugar

Rub entire surface of lump sugar (tablets) over rind of lemons which have been washed and sponged until dry. Over this lemon-flavored sugar lump, pour ½ cup of lemon juice, combined with the hot water, stir until sugar is thoroughly dissolved, then add the cold water, into which has been stirred the granulated sugar. Strain and freeze in hand freezer, using 3 parts of ice and 1 part of rock salt. Serve in sherbet cups which have been well-chilled.

83   MARASCHINO ORANGE ICE

4 cups boiling water   2 cups orange juice
2 cups granulated sugar   ¼ cup lemon juice
          1 cup maraschino cherries, chopped very fine

Make a sugar syrup by boiling water and sugar for 10 minutes. Cool slightly, then add orange and lemon juice, cool, and freeze in hand freezer, using 3 parts of ice and 1 part of rock salt. When partially frozen, that is, to a mush state, add chopped red or green maraschino cherries, using color according to occasion (for instance, for Valentine's Day, use red maraschino cherries, and for Saint Patrick's Day, use green maraschino cherries), and finish freezing until solid. Serve in chilled sherbet glasses.

You may omit maraschino cherries and flavor with a tablespoon or two, according to taste, of maraschino liqueur, operating exactly as indicated above. (No. 82.)

84   MINT ICE

(Very appropriate to serve with lamb or mutton course)

1 quart cold water	3 tablespoons dried mint leaves
2 cups granulated sugar	A few drops of green vegetable
Juice of two medium-sized	coloring
lemons	

Make a sugar syrup with water and sugar and allow to boil for 5 long minutes. Quickly pour over crushed mint leaves. Allow to infuse while cooling, then strain, and add lemon juice and a few drops of green vegetable coloring. Freeze either in refrigerator, or in hand freezer, using 3 parts of ice and 1 part of rock salt. Mold, if desired, into small paper cases, using a teaspoon, dipped in hot water, or serve in small chilled sherbet cups.

85   ORANGE ICE I

It may seem strange, but I seldom strain orange juice, used in cooking, either for hot, cold or frozen dish. To do so, means that only the water-soluble material of the fruit is used, and I have learned while studying for my degree of dietitian, that there is a good deal of nutrient food value, notably vitamin A and iron, in the suspended particles of pulp which are discarded. The result, especially when a clear crystal product is desired, may not be clear enough, yet it is advisable to leave the pulp, or at least, if straining is wanted, to use a coarse strainer.

2 cups granulated sugar	2 cups orange juice
4 cups cold water	¼ cup lemon juice

Grated rind of 2 oranges

Make a syrup with cold water and sugar, and allow it to boil for 5 long minutes. Cool slightly, then add orange and lemon juice and grated orange rind. Cool, strain and freeze in hand freezer, using 3 parts of ice and 1 part of rock salt. Serve in chilled orange baskets, or in chilled sherbet glasses.

86 ORANGE ICE II

2 cups cold water	Grated rind of 1 orange
1 cup granulated sugar	1 small bottle maraschino
Juice of 12 oranges	cherries
Juice and 1 lemon	

Make a sugar syrup with cold water and sugar, and allow to boil 5 long minutes. Cool, then add orange and lemon juices, grated orange rind and coarsely chopped maraschino cherries, using either red or green, according to occasion, which have been thoroughly drained and slightly squeezed through a clean towel. Freeze either in refrigerator tray, or hand freezer. If using the latter, use 3 parts of ice and 1 part rock salt. Serve in well-chilled sherbet glasses.

You may serve into cantaloupe, casaba or honeydew melon which has been thoroughly chilled, cut in quarters, or halves, according to size; or, you may combine two ices, for example: equal parts of lemon ice and equal parts of orange ice, if desired.

87   PINEAPPLE ICE

¼ cup granulated sugar   ½ can canned crushed pineapple
½ cup cold water   1 egg white, stiffly beaten
½ cup cold water   3 tablespoons granulated sugar
                  ¼ cup lemon juice

Combine the ¼ cup granulated sugar and first ½ cup of cold water, stir until sugar is dissolved, and boil for 3 long minutes. Cool to lukewarm, then stir in the second ½ cup cold water, combined with lemon juice, crushed pineapple and half of its juice, and stir well. Freeze to a mush either in refrigerator, or in hand freezer (if later method is used, use 3 parts ice and 1 part of rock salt. Remove from refrigerator, or hand freezer when mushy; break up with a fork, and add, folding gently the stiffly beaten egg white, into which has been folded the 3 table-spoons of granulated sugar. Return to refrigerator, or hand freezer, and freeze until firm, but not icy. Serve in orange cups, or chilled sherbet glasses.

88   PLUM ICE

4 cups cold water   2 cups sieved, cooked plum pulp
2 cups granulated sugar   Juice and rind of 1 lemon
                A few grains salt (⅛ teaspoon)

Make a sugar syrup of water and granulated sugar, allowing it to boil for 5 minutes. Cool; then stir in the plum pulp to which has been added the juice and rind of 1 medium-sized lemon and a few grains of salt. Freeze in hand freezer, using 3 parts of ice and 1 part of rock salt, until very mushy. Serve in chilled sherbet glasses.

89   PRUNE ICE

Proceed as indicated above (Recipe No. 88), substituting cooked, cooled, sieved prunes for plum pulp. Freeze and serve as indicated.

90   RASPBERRY ICE I

Several methods are used to make this refreshing and delicious ice which are as follows:

4 cups cold water	2 cups of raspberry juice
1⅔ cups granulated sugar	2 tablespoons lemon juice

Make a sugar syrup with cold water and sugar, and allow it to boil for 5 minutes; cool, then add raspberry juice, made from enough mashed (raw) raspberries, then squeezed through a fine muslin, then add lemon juice and strain again. Freeze in hand freezer, using 3 parts of ice and 1 part of rock salt. Serve in either orange baskets, or in chilled sherbet glasses.

91   RASPBERRY ICE II

1 quart picked raspberries, run under cold water faucet, then sponge dry	1 cup granulated sugar
	1 cup cold water
	2 tablespoons lemon juice
⅛ teaspoon salt	

Raspberry ice when prepared in this method will retain its tempting natural color.

Sprinkle sugar over well sponged raspberries; cover and allow to stand for at least 2 long hours. Then mash and squeeze through double cheesecloth or fine muslin cloth. To this juice,

[50]

add water which has been mixed with lemon juice and salt, and freeze in hand freezer, using 3 parts of ice and 1 part of rock salt. Serve in well-chilled sherbet glasses.

92   RASPBERRY ICE III
(Using canned raspberries)

2 cups cold water	⅛ teaspoon salt
Sugar to taste	2 cups raspberry juice

2 tablespoons of orange or lemon juice
½ teaspoon grated orange or lemon rind

To the juice drained from canned raspberries—there should be two cups—add water to which has been added enough granulated sugar to taste, the amount depending on the brand or sweetness of fruit, and salt and orange (or lemon) juice and rind. Freeze in hand freezer until mushy, using 3 parts of ice and 1 part rock salt. Pack in salt and ice, and allow to stand at least 2 hours before serving in sherbet glasses.

93   RASPBERRY AND BLACK CURRANT ICE

1⅓ cups granulated sugar	1⅓ cups black currant juice
4 cups cold water	(fresh)
⅔ cup raspberry juice (fresh)	1 teaspoon grated lemon rind

⅛ teaspoon salt

Make a sugar syrup with sugar and water, and let it boil for 5 minutes. Cool slightly, add combined raspberry juice, black currant juice, grated lemon rind and salt, strain, and freeze in hand freezer, using 3 parts of ice and 1 part of rock salt. Serve in chilled sherbet glasses.

94   RASPBERRY AND RED CURRANT ICE

Proceed as indicated above (Recipe No. 93) substituting red currant juice for black currant juice. Freeze and serve as indicated.

95   RASPBERRY AND STRAWBERRY ICE

Proceed as indicated for recipe No. 93, substituting raspberry juice for black currant juice. Freeze and serve as indicated.

96   RHUBARB ICE

Proceed as indicated for recipe No. 87, substituting cooked, sieved rhubarb for crushed pineapple. Freeze and serve as indicated. (More sugar may be added, if rhubarb is too sour but remember that too much sugar prevents freezing.) It is advisable to proceed exactly as indicated, using the exact amount of sugar and top each sherbet glass with sweetened, but unflavored whipped cream, forced through a pastry bag with a small fancy tube.

97   STRAWBERRY ICE I

Strawberries must be fresh. In general, the freshness is indicated by the firmness and perfume. Berries that are not fresh, or are over-ripe take on a dull, lustreless appearance. They are sometimes shrivelled or shrunken, and very likely, wet or leaky. Damaged and leaky strawberries can usually be traced by a stained box.

When buying strawberries, or in fact any kind of berries, look for the berries which have a fresh, clean, bright appearance, with a full solid red color throughout. It should be free from mois-ture, dirt and trash, and the cap should always be attached to the berry.

In washing strawberries do not allow the faucet (cold water faucet) play on them. Put them into a bowl of cold water and then lift them out of the water with fingers somewhat apart to act as strainer. The sand and soil on the berries will settle to the bottom of the bowl. It is for that reason that you should not pour the water off the berries. Unless they are quite dirty, two such rinses are usually sufficient. Then allow them to drain, placing them into a colander. Do not keep berries too long in refriger-ator, their flavor and perfume will suffer. This applies to any kind of berries.

1½ cups granulated sugar	2 cups strawberry juice
4 cups cold water	2 tablespoons lemon juice
¼ teaspoon salt	½ teaspoon grated lemon rind

Make a syrup with water and sugar, and let it boil 5 long minutes. Cool slightly, then add remaining ingredients. Chill, then freeze in hand freezer, using equal parts of ice and rock salt. Serve in chilled sherbet glasses.

98   STRAWBERRY ICE II

Follow the directions as indicated for recipe No. 91, Raspberry Ice II, using strawberry juice instead of raspberry juice. Freeze and serve as indicated.

99   TEA ICE

Tea experts prize very highly tea that becomes cloudy when ice or a chilled liquid is added to it, because, they say "it is often indicative of quality, especially body." The chemical reason for this cloudiness, lies in the precipitation of the caffein and tannin in the tea in the form of caffein tannate. This caffein tannate content is the element which makes tea vitualizing and cooling. It varies in different blends of tea but the average has been found to be one part caffein to three parts tannin.

When tea that has been brewed in boiling water is chilled, the tannin in the caffein tannate content turns cloudy. This has nothing to do with the taste or refreshing quality of the tea but does detract from its clear, sparkling appearance. There are ways to avoid this. The homemaker has to select a brand of tea containing the smallest possible amount of tannin. A number of such blends are on the market, made for exclusive use in making ice tea. The smaller amount of tannin in these iced tea blends reduces imperceptibly the tang which is most appealing to connoisseurs of a good cup of tea but assures a clear, sparkling drink.

Another way to avoid cloudiness, without using a special ice-tea blend, is to use the cold water method, a method indorsed by all tea experts:

Use two teaspoons of tea for each glass of water. Allow the cold water to remain on the tea leaves in a glass, china or pottery container for from twelve to eighteen hours or, still better, overnight. Strain liquid from the tea leaves before serving. This method saves ice and a quantity of iced tea can always be available, because you may place the brew in the refrigerator.

Tea made by this recipe will not cloud because the tannin in the leaves is not as soluble in cold water as the caffein and other properties. It will carry the same bouquet and stimulating qualities as a hot brew.

Now for the delicious TEA ICE, which may be made in many varieties of taste, by the simple addition of a tablespoon of your favorite cordial or liqueur, except whiskey, which does not blend very well, and does not give the best results, yet makes a tasty ice. For each pint of ice mixture:

3 cups of tea prepared with cold   1 cup cold water
   water method   1 cup granulated sugar
           2 tablespoons Cordial or liqueur (optional)

Make a sugar syrup with cold water and sugar, and allow it to boil for 5 long minutes. Cool, then combine with chilled ice tea and freeze in hand freezer, using 3 parts of ice and one part of rock salt, until mushy, if liqueur or cordial is to be added. If not, when mush is obtained, pack and allow to stand for 2 hours.

100   WATERMELON ICE

2 cups watermelon pulp and   ¼ teaspoon salt
   juice   3 tablespoons lemon juice
½ cup cold water   1 cup cold water, or 1 cup of
¾ cup granulated sugar   Yukon Club Lime, dry

Force pieces of watermelon through a sieve, and measure 2 cups of pulp and juice. Combine the ½ cup cold water and sugar and make a sugar syrup, allowing it to boil 3 long minutes. Cool, add watermelon pulp and juice, lemon juice and water or Yukon Club Lime, or still better, 1 cup of dry ginger ale. Mix well, then freeze in hand freezer, using 8 parts of ice and 1 part of rock salt. Turn evenly until mixture is frozen; drain off water, remove dasher, repack in 4 parts ice and 1 part rock salt. Allow to "ripen" 1 long hour before serving. Serve in chilled sherbet glasses.

For effect you may serve this doubly cool and refreshing dessert: Cut chilled watermelon into slices 2 inches thick in diameter. Remove as many seeds as possible. Scoop out a little melon from the center of each round, which has been cut with large biscuit cutter, with a teaspoon and fill with the watermelon ice.

SECTION VI

Ice Cream Recipes

INCLUDED among the ice cream recipes in this section will be found some of the most desired ones, those greatly praised and talked of by travelers to Europe, in order that American home-makers may use them in their daily menus. Among these ice cream recipes the homemakers will find delightful party ice cream recipes, as well as everyday frozen desserts to fit the most modest budget.

Many of the recipes herein contained are the frozen dessert lore of all parts of the United States as well as of all parts of the world, yet made in this country.

These recipes are practically known to the author who has tested, made and served all of them during his 45 years of practical experience as chef in some of the leading hotels, restaurants and private families in America and Europe.

Certain elaborate and costly ingredients and those difficult to obtain in America for home use, have been eliminated or substituted by others less complicated and easily obtainable at lower cost.

Recipes and formulas have been adapted to serve an average family of six persons, unless otherwise indicated.

Measurements may be increased or modified in corresponding proportions to meet the requirements. The homemaker is allowed free scope to bring her innate talents into action, to suit the

[56]

tastes of her family or guests in accordance with her individual taste and economic status, while always recognizing that measurements should be exact and that frequently the cheapest products are the most expensive in the end.

Lastly, let me reiterate, recipes and formulas should always be carefully read over first before beginning to operate, also that ice cream, as soon as dished, should be served immediately.

For more information how to use hand freezer as well as mechanical refrigerator, see No. 2 and No. 3 under "General Information".

101 ALMOND ICE CREAM
(French method. Hand freezer)

To a quart of vanilla ice cream made as indicated for recipe No. 286, Vanilla Ice Cream French Method, add, when ice cream begins to stiffen, ½ lb. blanched, finely chopped or coarsely ground almonds, and 2 or 3 drops of oil of almond, or ¼ generous teaspoon almond extract; then, continue freezing until mixture is stiff. Pack or mold in 3 parts of ice and 1 part rock salt, and allow to stand 2 hours before serving.

102 APRICOT ICE CREAM I
(Hand freezer)

¾ cup granulated sugar	2 cups heavy cream, whipped
¾ cup cold water	1½ cups canned, drained cut
¼ teaspoon salt	apricots
3 egg whites, stiffly beaten	

Make a sugar syrup with granulated sugar and water, and let it boil for 5 minutes. Carefully and very slowly pour this hot syrup over stiffly beaten egg whites to which salt has been added. Beat until cool, then fold in whipped cream, alternately with cut

[57]

apricots. Freeze in hand freezer, using 3 parts ice and one part rock salt. Pack or mold and let stand in salt and ice for at least 2 hours before serving.

Any kind of fruit, canned or fresh may be prepared in the same way, if desired.

103 APRICOT ICE CREAM II
(Hand freezer)

1 can of apricots, drained, then sieved

1 cup (more or less, according to sweetness of fruit) granulated sugar

Syrup from the can of apricots

1½ cups orange juice

¼ scant teaspoon salt

1 quart fresh cream

¼ cup lemon juice

To the syrup from the apricot can, add orange and lemon juice and salt, then stir in enough sugar to taste. Mix thoroughly; then add sieved apricots, stirred into the fresh, unwhipped heavy cream. Freeze in hand freezer, using 3 parts ice and 1 part rock salt; pack or mold and let stand 2 hours before serving.

104 APRICOT ICE CREAM III
(Hand freezer)

2 cups milk, scalded

2 whole eggs, lightly beaten

1 cup granulated sugar

½ teaspoon salt

1 teaspoon vanilla extract

½ teaspoon almond extract (scant)

2 cups of cooked dried apricots, pulp and juice

1 cup heavy cream, unwhipped

Pour over hot scalded milk the lightly beaten whole eggs, or vice versa, to which have been added sugar and salt. Stir gently but thoroughly, then cook until mixture coats a silver spoon, stirring almost constantly. Cool and add the combined vanilla and almond extracts. Combine apricot pulp and juice with heavy cream and add to cooled custard. Mix well. Freeze in hand freezer, using 3 parts ice and 1 part rock salt. Pack or mold, and let stand 2 hours before serving.

105 APRICOT ICE CREAM IV
(*Refrigerator tray*)

This delicious fresh apricot ice cream may be served with apricot sauce, if desired.

1 lb. fresh apricots	½ cup evaporated milk, chilled
1 cup boiling water	¼ cup granulated sugar
½ cup granulated sugar	Grated rind of ½ lemon
1 cup heavy cream, whipped	4 drops almond extract

Wash fresh apricots and cook with boiling water, over a very low flame for 10 minutes; then add the ½ cup granulated sugar, stirring gently until dissolved, and cook 10 minutes longer, or until fruit is soft, but not overdone. Put fruit and juice through a sieve; measure 1 cup and set aside the remaining cup to be used as a sauce, placing it in refrigerator. Now, add to the first cup the whipped cream, combined with the chilled evaporated milk, grated lemon rind and almond extract. Freeze in refrigerator tray for 1 hour; then fold or stir from bottom and sides of the tray, smooth and return to refrigerator to freeze for 3 more hours, or until firm. Serve with a side dish of the reserved cup of apricot puree, which may be sweetened to taste, if desired.

Try, after freezing for 1 hour, and just when folding and stirring to break up crystal sugar, adding 1 dozen blanched, shredded almonds, simmered for 5 minutes with equal parts of cold water and lemon juice, just enough to cover almonds. The mixture is then allowed to infuse until cold, then drained and the almonds only added to the cream mixture. The liquid may be set aside and used for either dessert or a sauce foundation, or a beverage foundation. This will add a very delicious flavor and render the cream a little crunchy.

To serve: You may scoop up balls of the ice cream, roll in coconut, or crumbled macaroons, or rice krispies, and what not, such as coarsely ground nut meats, which may be tinted, or into chocolate shots, etc.

106 BAKED APPLE ICE CREAM
(Refrigerator tray)

1 cup cold soft custard
1 cup baked apple, sieved
1 cup heavy cream, whipped

¾ cups (more or less) powdered sugar
½ teaspoon vanilla extract

Blend together soft custard, sieved baked apple and whipped cream, gently but thoroughly; then add vanilla extract and fold in enough powdered sugar (about ¾ cup) or until sweetened to taste, but not too much, lest mixture will not freeze easily. Turn mixture into refrigerator tray and freeze about 1 hour, then stir up to break crystal sugar, return to refrigerator and freeze 3 hours longer.

107 BAKED ALASKA

A solid frozen brick of ice cream is needed for this recipe. Furthermore, the ice cream should not contain water ice, it should be made of milk or cream. Here is how to operate:

Cover a bread board or an oven plank with a piece of wax or white paper. Place a layer of sponge or pound cake cut 1 inch thick on the paper, and then place the ice cream on the cake. The cake should extend about ½ generous inch beyond the ice cream all around. Cover completely with a thick coating of meringue made by beating 4 egg whites to a stiff consistency, then folding in gradually ¾ cup confectioner's sugar. This will make enough meringue for 1 quart ice cream. Remember, the meringue should be light and dry. Dust well with powdered sugar and set the whole in a very hot oven (450–475, and even 500 deg. F.) for just enough to delicately brown. Slip the ice cream, thus browned, onto a chilled platter and serve at once.

Individual baked Alaskas are made by placing slices of very solid ice cream on rounds or squares of sponge or pound cake; then topped with meringue made as indicated above, and set in very hot oven or under the flame of the broiling oven to brown quickly. Like the large ones they should be served at once.

Both large or individual baked Alaskas may be sprinkled with coarsely ground nut meats (any kind) just before setting in the oven.

Here a few words are necessary as to how to make a good meringue, which are often a puzzle to the homemaker.

108   INSTRUCTIONS ABOUT MERINGUES

Meringues are easy to make, and delicious cold and frozen desserts may be made out of them. The shell should be tender, opaque, and the interior should be almost dry and free from much of the stickiness which makes a meringue hard. If the egg whites are not beaten enough before the sugar is added, the mixture will not get stiff to keep its peaks and to shape well, even with much beating later. The meringue will be sticky and runny. Then the sugar is added gradually, a small amount at a time. Folding in the sugar may be made over gently simmering water; this will help to drive out part of the moisture naturally present in the egg white, to set a little, and also to dissolve the sugar granules.

Ice Cream Recipes

Meringues and their kindred creations, filled with whipped cream or ice cream, are a favorite dessert throughout the year. They have a great advantage as they may be prepared in advance, and be adapted to all sorts of menus without any danger of "left-overs".

Usually 8 egg whites and 1 lb. powdered sugar are used for meringue dessert. The whites are whipped very stiff and while being whipped about 1/3 of the sugar is gradually incorporated. The balance of the sugar is folded in gradually with a wooden spoon. Care must be taken not to overwork the meringue. They are baked on a wooden board, previously moistened, and baked in a slow oven (275 deg. F.) for about one hour. With a spatula remove them carefully to wire rack while hot, open side up, and when cold place them in proof box until completely dry. Thereafter, they are put back into the oven for a very short time to give them just a light yellow color.

The filling and garnish is, of course, entirely left to your own taste. Ordinarily, two shells are placed together, filled with whipped cream—they are, then, called "Meringue Chantilly", or ice cream, "Meringue Glacé", crushed berries, fruit ice, or whipped flavored gelatine, or any of the variety of creams.

Kisses are meringues baked in very small mounds, shaped either by a spoon, or pastry bag, ordinarily the size of a large walnut. They may be filled like large meringue. For large shells, which will be filled with ice cream, mousse, parfait mixture, any of the numerous cream desserts, etc., the meringue mix is shaped on the moistened board by means of pastry bag with a large plain tube, baked, cooled and filled.

109   BANANA ICE CREAM I
           (Hand freezer)

To a quart of ice cream No. 286 Vanilla Ice Cream, French
method, omitting vanilla, add the following mixture:

4 bananas, skinned, scraped, then   1 generous tablespoon lemon
   sieved   juice
                                        ¼ scant teaspoon salt

Freeze in hand freezer, using 3 parts ice and 1 part rock salt.
Pack or mold in ice and salt and let stand 2 hours before serving.

110   BANANA ICE CREAM II
              (Hand freezer)

3 large bananas, skinned, scraped   2 tablespoons powdered sugar
   then sieved   ½ cup granulated sugar
2 teaspoons lemon juice   1 cup heavy cream, whipped
   A few grains salt   ¾ cup orange juice

To the sieved bananas, add the lemon juice, salt, granulated
sugar and orange juice. Fold in the powdered sugar into the
whipped cream, and add to banana mixture. Freeze in hand
freezer, using 3 parts ice and 1 part rock salt. Pack or mold in
ice and rock salt and let stand 2 hours before serving. To serve:
With a tablespoon dipped in hot water, scoop out of the ice
cream, pieces in the shape of eggs. Pile up, operating rapidly,
pyramid-like in center of a well-chilled round platter; pour over
the pyramid-like crushed, sweetened strawberries, and garnish
with a ring of banana slices, dipped in maraschino, and decorate
with whipped cream forced through a pastry bag with a fancy
tube. You may top each rosette of whipped cream with a maraschino cherry, cut daisy-like, if desired. A fine party dessert.

[63]

111   BANANA RENNET ICE CREAM   III
(Refrigerator tray or Hand freezer)

2 renet tablets
2 tablespoons cold water
3 cups rich top milk

1 cup granulated sugar
1 cup sieved bananas
2 tablespoons lemon juice

1 cup heavy cream, whipped

Break rennet tablets into small pieces and dissolve in cold water. Heat milk, but do not allow to cook, and stir in the granulated sugar; then stir in the dissolved rennet tablets. Pour into freezing tray and let stand outside refrigerator at room temperature to become firm and set. Then chill. Add sieved banana pulp, lemon juice and the heavy cream whipped to a soft-custard-like consistency. Place freezer tray in refrigerator and freeze to a mush (about one hour); then scrape from bottom and sides, and beat until smooth. Return to refrigerator and continue freezing for 3 hours. Serve heaped up in center of a chilled platter, and garnish the base with sliced banana, dipped in lemon juice (optional).

112   BISCUIT TORTONI   I
(Refrigerator tray)

This kind of frozen dessert is not an ice cream, but rather a mousse, yet it is so popularly called and classified with ice cream that the author has deemed necessary to class it here. There exist several methods of preparing this delicious sweetmeat, which will be found below:

1 cup heavy cream, whipped
¼ cup powdered sugar
2 teaspoons sherry wine

½ cup sieved dried macaroons
Paper cups and macaroons, sieved

1 egg white, stiffly beaten

Add, or rather fold, powdered sugar gradually into the whipped cream, then fold in the stiffly beaten egg white, alternately with sieved macaroons and sherry wine. Pack in individual paper cups, sprinkle top with sieved macaroon crumbs and set in tray of refrigerator to freeze until firm. Do not stir.

113 BISCUIT TORTONI II
(Hand freezer or refrigerator)

2 cups thin cream or undiluted evaporated milk	⅛ teaspoon salt
	½ cup granulated sugar
1 cup dried macaroons, sieved	⅓ cup good sherry
2 cups heavy cream, whipped	

Combine thin cream or undiluted evaporated milk and allow to stand for 1 hour; then add salt, sugar and sherry wine (more or less according to taste), and freeze to a mush (about 1 hour) in hand freezer, using 3 parts ice and 1 part rock salt. Then add whipped cream; mold and pack in equal parts of ice and rock salt, allowing to stand 3 hours. You may use the refrigerator tray if desired. You may place the mixture in individual paper cups, top with a small pinch of sieved dried macaroons, and freeze in refrigerator for 3 hours.

114 BISCUIT TORTONI III
(Refrigerator tray)

½ cup dry macaroon crumbs, sieved	⅛ teaspoon salt
	1 cup heavy cream, whipped
¾ cup milk top	¼ teaspoon vanilla extract
¼ cup granulated sugar	¼ teaspoon almond extract

Soak macaroon crumbs with sugar, salt and milk for 1 hour. Fold in the whipped cream, vanilla and almond extract. Fill paper cases (individual) with mixture and cover, or rather sprinkle with a little sieved macaroon crumbs. Place filled paper cups in refrigerator tray to freeze for 3 hours.

115   BISCUIT TORTONI IV
(Refrigerator tray)

Using sugar syrup, egg yolks and ground almonds.

¾ cup granulated sugar	3 tablespoons warm water, and
¼ cup hot water	A few grains salt
⅛ teaspoon salt	3 tablespoons good sherry wine
5 egg yolks, beaten with	2 cups heavy cream, whipped

½ cup finely cut or coarsely ground toasted almonds

Make a sugar syrup with the sugar and hot water, and allow it to boil 5 minutes, or until mixture reaches 234 deg. F. (short thread). Remove from the fire, and pour the hot syrup over beaten egg yolk mixture, beating rapidly and constantly. Pour this mixture in top of double boiler, and set over gently bubbling water, stirring constantly until mixture is thick. Remove from hot water, cool, stir in sherry wine (more or less, according to taste), then strain mixture into whipped cream. Fill chilled paper cases; sprinkle top of each filled case with finely cut or coarsely ground toasted almonds. Place the cases in refrigerator tray, and freeze for 3 hours.

116   BISCUIT TORTONI V
(Refrigerator tray or hand freezer)

This Biscuit Tortoni is also called "Mock Biscuit Tortoni" and is not only economical, but delicious too.

½ cup brown sugar	2 egg whites, stiffly beaten
¼ cup hot water	⅛ teaspoon salt
2 tablespoons cold water	1 teaspoon vanilla extract
2 teaspoons granulated gelatine	½ cup dried macaroon crumbs,
½ teaspoon granulated gelatine	sieved, mixed with
2 teaspoons cold water	½ cup ground walnut meats

Make a sugar syrup with brown sugar and hot water, and allow it to boil to thread stage, about 5 minutes. To the hot syrup add the 2 teaspoons granulated gelatine which have been softened for 5 minutes in cold water, pouring slowly, while beating, into evaporated milk which has been whipped (see No. 8, How to Whip Evaporated Milk) with the ½ teaspoon granulated gelatine and the 2 teaspoons cold water, then combined with the stiffly beaten egg whites. Then add salt, vanilla extract, sieved macaroon crumbs and ground walnuts. Fill chilled paper cups with the mixture, and freeze in refrigerator tray for 3 long hours. You may mold mixture and freeze in hand freezer, using equal parts of ice and rock salt, if desired.

117   BISQUE VANILLA ICE CREAM
(Hand freezer or refrigerator tray)

To 1 quart of Vanilla Ice Cream made as indicated for recipe No. 286 Vanilla Ice Cream, French Method, add when mixture is still soft, that is to a mush, 1 cup ground walnut meats. Continue freezing until hard. Pack or mold in 4 parts ice to one part rock salt.

You may substitute 1 cup sieved macaroon crumbs for walnut meats if desired.

118   BLUEBERRY ICE CREAM
(Refrigerator or hand freezer)

1 pint picked, washed, fresh or canned blueberries
½ cup granulated sugar
⅛ teaspoon salt
½ cup undiluted, evaporated milk
1 cup heavy cream, whipped

Crush berries and combine with granulated sugar. Cook 5 long minutes, then strain through a fine sieve. Add salt, and allow to cool, then strain again when cold, and add evaporated milk and fold in whipped cream. Freeze in refrigerator tray, stirring twice during freezing process, once when mushy, then when beginning to solidify, for 3 hours. You may use hand freezer, using 3 parts ice and 1 part rock salt, then pack or mold in 4 parts ice and 1 part rock salt.

119   BROWN BREAD ICE CREAM
(Hand freezer)

A very popular New England ice cream for which several methods are used, as regards kind of cream flavoring to be used. As a rule, Vanilla ice cream is the one selected.

To 1 quart of your favorite vanilla ice cream (see recipe No. 285, up to No. 297) add, when mixture begins to mush, the following mixture:

Soak 1¼ cups dried, sieved brown bread crumbs in 1 quart thin cream. Let stand 15 long minutes, strain through a fine sieve, pressing a little so as to remove as much as possible of the liquid, thus making the mixture light and fluffy, and add to vanilla ice cream. Continue freezing until hard, and pack or mold in 4 parts ice and 1 part of rock salt.

120   BURNT ALMOND ICE CREAM I
(Hand freezer or refrigerator tray)

Make a Caramel Ice Cream as indicated for recipe No. 130, or 131–132 and when mixture begins to mush, add 1 cup finely chopped and toasted blanched almonds. Continue freezing until hard. Pack or mold in 4 parts ice and 1 part rock salt.

121   **BURNT ALMOND ICE CREAM   II**
(Refrigerator tray or hand freezer)

¾ cup granulated sugar   ¼ teaspoon salt
1 quart thin cream   1 teaspoon vanilla extract
½ lb. browned almonds, chopped

Combine and stir until dissolved, the sugar, thin cream, salt and vanilla extract; then stir in the browned chopped almonds which have been blanched before browning. Freeze in refrigerator tray, stirring once when mixture is mushy, for 3 hours.

122   **BURNT ALMOND ICE CREAM   III**
(Refrigerator tray or hand freezer)

Using undiluted evaporated milk, or milk top and cornstarch.

2 cups undiluted evaporated   1 tablespoon cornstarch
    milk   1 generous teaspoon vanilla ex-
¾ cup granulated sugar   tract
¼ teaspoon salt   1 cup heavy cream, whipped
¾ cup blanched, toasted, then ground almonds

Scald milk. Caramelize granulated sugar by melting it in a heavy skillet, and stirring until syrup becomes brown, and add it to scalded milk in a double boiler, stirring until mixture is thoroughly combined and sugar melted. Add salt and cornstarch which has been mixed with 1 tablespoon cold milk, and cook, stirring almost constantly, until thickened. Cool. Add vanilla extract, and freeze in refrigerator tray stirring when mixture is frozen to a mush; then add whipped cream and freeze for 3 hours.

123   BURNT WALNUT (or PECAN) BISQUE
(Hand freezer or refrigerator tray)

A fine ice cream made on the principle of French method ice cream, that is, with a custard and nut brittle flavoring.

1 cup granulated sugar   1 cup chopped, blanched walnut or pecan

Caramelize sugar by placing it in a heavy, shallow skillet or pan, stirring constantly until sugar is light brown; then while hot, add nut meats, turn into slightly buttered or olive oiled shallow pan to cool, and when cold, pound in a mortar or put through food chopper. This nut brittle is a good flavoring for many desserts, especially for custard. Then, make a custard with the following ingredients:

2 cups scalded rich milk   1 cup of the nut brittle
3 egg yolks, slightly beaten with   1 cup heavy cream, whipped
⅓ cup granulated sugar, and   with
¾ tablespoon vanilla extract   ⅛ teaspoon salt

Beat egg yolks slightly, using a fork; add sugar, salt. Mix well, but do not beat too hard. Pour hot scalded milk very slowly over the mixture, stirring constantly and rapidly. Pour into double boiler and cook, stirring constantly until mixture thickens and coats a spoon. Strain immediately, and chill; then add vanilla extract. Now add nut brittle, then stir in, very gently, the whipped cream and salt. Freeze in hand freezer, using 3 parts ice and 1 part rock salt. Pack or mold in 4 parts ice and 1 part rock salt.

124   BUTTERMILK ICE CREAM
(Hand freezer)

½ cup hot water
¾ cup granulated sugar
   Finely chopped rind of ½
   orange
2½ cups buttermilk

½ generous teaspoon grated
   lemon rind
½ cup strained pineapple juice,
   canned
⅛ teaspoon salt

Make a sugar syrup with water and sugar, and let it boil for 5 minutes. Cool slightly and add chopped orange rind, lemon rind and strained pineapple juice (canned) and salt. Freeze in hand freezer, using 3 parts ice and 1 part rock salt until mixture is to a mush. Then add buttermilk, stir well from bottom of the tray as well as sides of it, and freeze 3 long hours.

125   BUTTERSCOTCH ICE CREAM
(Hand freezer)

2 cups scalded rich milk
1 tablespoon flour
1 cup brown sugar
2 tablespoons butter
1 whole egg, slightly beaten

¼ teaspoon salt
2 teaspoons vanilla extract
1 quart undiluted evaporated
   milk, or half milk and half
   heavy cream

Cook sugar with butter in a heavy skillet or saucepan until melted and allow to boil 1 long minute. Add to scalded milk, stirring well. Beat slightly the whole egg with salt and flour, the flour added a small amount at a time, and pour milk over egg mixture, slowly, stirring constantly. Cook over boiling water, for 10 minutes, stirring constantly for 5 minutes, then occasionally for the remaining 5 minutes. Should custard have a curdled appearance, it will disappear in freezing. Cool, and when cold

[71]

add undiluted evaporated milk or half milk and heavy cream and vanilla extract. Strain through a fine sieve, and freeze in hand freezer, using 3 parts ice and 1 part rock salt. Pack or mold in 4 parts ice and 1 part rock salt.

126 BUTTERSCOTCH ICE CREAM
COUNTRY METHOD
(Refrigerator tray or hand freezer)

3 tablespoons butter	¾ cup toasted ground walnut
¾ cup rolled corn flake crumbs	meats
5 tablespoons brown sugar	1 quart vanilla ice cream

Melt butter, then sprinkle over the fine rolled corn flake crumbs, brown sugar and ground toasted walnut meats. Stir, then set in a hot oven (400 deg. F.) for 10 to 15 minutes to melt the sugar, stirring often to blend thoroughly. Cool, then crumble finely and sieve. There should be 2 cups of this mixture. Mix half of the crumb mixture to a vanilla ice cream frozen to a mush; return to refrigerator tray and sprinkle remaining cup of crumb mixture over the cream mixture evenly. Freeze for 3 hours.

127 BUTTERSCOTCH ICE CREAM
HOME METHOD
(Refrigerator tray or hand freezer)

A delicious party ice cream for 12 persons. For 6 reduce amount of ingredients to half. The two trays in the refrigerator should be used. You may use the hand freezer, if desired. In that case, the ice cream should be molded and packed in 4 parts ice and 1 part of rock salt, and let stand 2 long hours before using. A soft custard sauce, or a chocolate sauce, or crushed berries in season may be served aside, if desired.

¼ cup butter
2 cups brown sugar
4 cups milk, scalded
⅓ cup all-purpose flour
½ cup brown sugar

1 cup cold milk
¼ teaspoon salt
2 egg yolks
3 cups fresh cream
¼ teaspoon almond extract

Melt butter in a heavy skillet or pan; add the 2 cups of brown sugar, and stir, over a low flame until sugar is melted and mixture is thoroughly blended; then, add scalded milk very slowly, stirring constantly until well-blended and sugar is melted. Combine flour, the remaining ½ cup brown sugar, cold milk and salt, mix well and add to first mixture. Pour in top of double boiler and cook, over boiling water, until mixture is thick, stirring constantly; then pour mixture very slowly, while stirring rapidly, over slightly beaten egg yolks; return to boiler and cook for 2 short minutes, stirring constantly. Chill, then add un-whipped fresh cream to which has been added almond extract. Freeze in two refrigerator trays until mushy, or about one hour, then stir from bottom and sides of trays to break crystal sugars. Freeze for 3 long hours.

128 BUTTERSCOTCH PECAN ICE CREAM
(Refrigerator tray or hand freezer)

1½ cups granulated sugar
2 cups fresh milk
2½ tablespoons butter
3 egg whites, stiffly beaten
1 cup chopped pecans

3 egg yolks, slightly beaten
⅛ teaspoon salt
1 teaspoon vanilla extract
1 pint heavy cream

Caramelize half the sugar by putting it in heavy shallow pan or skillet. Melt over moderate heat, stirring constantly until melted to a light brown syrup; add the milk and when the caramel is well-dissolved, stir in the remaining sugar mixed

[73]

with butter and slightly beaten egg yolks. Cook over hot water, until mixture coats a spoon, stirring constantly. Cool, add salt, vanilla extract and the stiffly beaten egg whites mixed with whipped cream. Freeze to a mush in refrigerator tray or about 1 hour; remove from tray, stir in chopped pecans, return to tray and freeze for 3 long hours. You may use hand freezer, using 3 parts ice and 1 part rock salt, freezing until mushy, then adding the chopped pecans. Pack or mold in 4 parts of ice and 1 part of rock salt.

129   BUTTERSCOTCH PECAN ICE CREAM SANDWICH

Place a scoop of the above ice cream (No. 128) between and on top of 2 slices of plain cake and pour a butterscotch sauce over it and sprinkle with pecans, chopped coarsely.

130   CARAMEL ICE CREAM I
(Hand freezer or refrigerator tray)

⅓ cup granulated sugar
1 cup milk scalded
⅛ teaspoon salt

1 cup undiluted evaporated milk, whipped
2 egg yolks, slightly beaten
2 tablespoons granulated sugar
1 teaspoon vanilla extract

Caramelize the 1/3 cup granulated sugar in the usual way. When browned, stir in the scalded milk. Turn mixture into top of double boiler and cook over boiling water until sugar crystals are completely dissolved, or about 5 minutes, stirring occasionally. Add salt and 2 tablespoons to beaten eggs, mix well, and pour milk-caramel slowly over the egg mixture, stirring and beating alternately and constantly. Return to double boiler and cook until mixture coats a spoon, stirring constantly. Chill. Add whipped undiluted evaporated milk (see "How to Whip Evaporated Milk No. 8, under "General Information"). Pour creamy mixture in refrigerator tray and freeze until mushy, or about 1 hour. Remove from refrigerator and beat well, using a wire whisk. Return to refrigerator tray and freeze 3 hours.

131   **CARAMEL ICE CREAM II**
(Hand freezer or refrigerator tray)

2 cups scalded milk	⅛ teaspoon salt
4 egg yolks, slightly beaten	¼ cup granulated sugar
¼ cup granulated sugar, cara-	1 cup heavy cream
melized	1½ teaspoons vanilla extract

¼ cup granulated sugar, uncaramelized

Mix salt and egg yolks and ¼ cup granulated sugar (uncaramelized). To the scalded milk, add the caramelized granulated sugar and stir until thoroughly blended. Pour milk mixture over beaten egg yolk mixture, slowly and gradually, beating well, and rapidly all the while. Now cook mixture over boiling water until it coats the spoon, stirring constantly. Cool, strain, add fresh heavy cream and vanilla, and freeze in hand freezer, using 3 parts ice and 1 part of rock salt. When firm, pack or mold, using 4 parts ice and 1 part rock salt.

132   **CARAMEL ICE CREAM III**
(Hand freezer or refrigerator tray)

1 large can undiluted evapo-	1 tablespoon cornstarch
rated milk	⅛ teaspoon salt
1 cup granulated sugar	2 whole eggs, slightly beaten
⅓ cup hot water	½ teaspoon vanilla

Scald undiluted evaporated milk in top of double boiler. Chill ½ cup of scalded milk to be whipped. Caramelize 1/3 cup of the granulated sugar in the usual way, remove from heat, gradually add hot water and stir until caramel is dissolved, then add to the scalded milk. Combine remaining sugar with cornstarch and salt; add milk mixture slowly, stirring rapidly; return to double boiler and cook over boiling water for 10 minutes, stirring constantly. Now pour this gradually over slightly beaten eggs, return this mixture to double boiler, and cook, stirring constantly, until mixture coats the spoon. Cool, pour in refrigerator tray, and freeze to a mush (about 1 hour). Then, fold in undiluted, scalded evaporated milk which has been chilled, then whipped until thick and flavored with vanilla extract, into mush and freeze again for 3 hours. (See No. 8, "How to Whip Evaporated Milk" under General Information.)

To the above three recipes of Caramel Ice Cream, you may add ¾ cup broken or coarsely ground nut meats (any kind) right after cream mixture has been made to a mush, either in refrigerator tray or hand freezer, if desired.

133   CHINESE ICE CREAM
(Hand freezer only)

A delicious sugarless ice cream, which is usually served in chilled sherbet glasses. The honey to be used in this recipe should be of the strained brand.

½ lb. cashew nut meats	⅛ teaspoon salt
1 lb. strained honey	Equal amount of heavy cream,
3 egg yolks, beaten until thick	whipped, as there is of stiffly
3 egg whites stiffly beaten with	beaten egg whites

Soak cashew nut meats in warm water until soft enough to remove the outer skins, and chop coarsely. Pour over the honey, stir well, to coat every piece of cashew nut meats with honey. Then beat in the already thickly beaten egg yolks. Now, fold in the stiffly beaten and salted egg whites, alternately with the same amount of whipped cream as there is of beaten egg whites. Freeze in hand freezer, using 3 parts ice and 1 part rock salt. If after 10 minutes of churning, the cream mixture is not mushy, add ½ generous cup of cold water, stir well with a wooden spoon, and freeze until stiff. Pack in 4 parts of ice and 1 part of rock salt for 2 long hours.

134   CREAM DE VENUS ICE CREAM
(No freezing. Packing only in hand freezer, without salt)

2 cups water	½ generous teaspoon grated lemon rind
1 cup granulated sugar	
2 teaspoons ground cinnamon	6 egg yolks, slightly beaten with
1 teaspoon vanilla extract	¼ teaspoon salt
2 teaspoons aniseed	2 cups heavy cream, whipped
¼ teaspoon ground mace	

Boil sugar and water 5 minutes; remove from the fire and add combined cinnamon, vanilla extract, aniseed, mace, and grated lemon (or orange) rind. Let this infuse for 10 minutes, stirring once. Strain through a fine sieve or, still better, through a fine muslin in top of double boiler, the bottom part containing hot, but not boiling water. Then pour in, slowly, while beating briskly with a wire whisk, the slightly beaten and salted egg yolks. When all egg yolks are added, remove from hot water and continue beating, still using a wire whisk until mixture is cold. Then fold in the whipped cream and fill a chilled melon mold. Pack, do not churn, nor use rock salt or saltpeter, in cracked ice, for 3 hours.

135 CHOCOLATE ICE CREAM I
(Hand freezer or refrigerator tray)

IMPORTANT.—*When chocolate is used in cookery, it should be melted over hot water, as too high a temperature changes the flavor. Instead, it may be cut in pieces, to which a little cold water may be added and the two stirred together over a gentle fire until a smooth thick syrup results. If cocoa is used to replace chocolate in any kind of dessert requiring chocolate, it should be blended with the sugar or flour used in the recipe. When it is used as a foundation for a beverage, cold water should be added and the mixture stirred over a very gentle flame until smooth and thick. The cold milk, or whatever liquid indicated, may then be added as it is for chocolate. When the mixture begins to foam, while being heated over a gentle flame, it should be beaten with an egg beater in order to prevent a scum from forming over the top. By this method either cocoa or chocolate can be made with only one saucepan. In preparing chocolate, it is well to remember that it tends to burn easily.*

1¼ cups granulated sugar	2 cups scalded milk
1 tablespoon all-purpose flour	2 squares bitter chocolate
¼ generous teaspoon salt	2 cups heavy cream
2 whole eggs, slightly beaten	1 tablespoon vanilla extract

Combine and mix well sugar, flour and salt, then beat in the slightly beaten whole eggs. Pour the hot scalded milk over the egg mixture, slowly and gradually, stirring briskly while pouring. Cook over hot water until mixture is thickened; cool, and strain through a muslin, then add heavy, unwhipped cream, and freeze in hand freezer, using 3 parts ice and 1 part rock salt. Pack or mold using 4 parts ice and 1 part rock salt.

136   CHOCOLATE ICE CREAM II
        (Hand freezer or refrigerator tray)

Select your favorite Vanilla Ice Cream recipe from No. 285 to 297, and add 1½ squares bitter chocolate melted over hot water; add 2/3 cup hot water slowly, and gradually, stirring rapidly and constantly until mixture is smooth, and cool before adding to vanilla ice cream mixture. Freeze in hand freezer, using 3 parts ice and 1 part rock salt. Pack or mold in 4 parts ice and 1 part rock salt.

137   CHOCOLATE ICE CREAM III
        (Hand freezer or refrigerator tray)

To your favorite Vanilla Ice Cream, from which omit ¼ cup of sugar, add the following mixture, cooled, before freezing, and stirred into the vanilla ice cream mixture:

2 squares unsweetened chocolate   ¼ cup granulated sugar
                ¼ teaspoon ground cinnamon

Melt chocolate over hot water; stir in the sugar and cinnamon, and stir into the milk used for making the vanilla ice cream mixture. Cool and freeze, using 3 parts ice and 1 part rock salt. Pack or mold in 4 parts ice and 1 part rock salt.

138   CHOCOLATE ICE CREAM IV
        (Hand freezer or refrigerator tray)

1 square bitter chocolate   ½ teaspoon vanilla extract
2/3 cup sweetened condensed milk   ½ cup of heavy cream, whipped
2/3 cup hot water   to custard-like consistency with
                ⅛ teaspoon salt

[79]

Melt chocolate over hot water; add condensed milk and cook, stirring constantly for about 5 minutes until mixture thickens. Then, stir in hot water. Chill, and add vanilla extract (¼ teaspoon almond extract may be substituted for vanilla extract, if desired). Lastly fold in the heavy cream whipped to a custard-like consistency. Freeze in refrigerator tray until mushy, or about 1 hour; then remove from refrigerator and scrape mixture from bottom and sides of pan, beat until smooth. Return to refrigerator tray and continue freezing for 3 hours.

139   CHOCOLATE ICE CREAM V
(Hand freezer or refrigerator tray)

A delicious chocolate ice cream. Using tapioca, corn syrup and meringue.

2 squares bitter chocolate	¼ cup light corn syrup
2 cups cold milk	2 tablespoons granulated sugar
3 tablespoons granulated tapioca	2 egg whites, stiffly beaten
¼ teaspoon salt	1 cup heavy cream, whipped
½ cup granulated sugar	1½ teaspoons vanilla extract
¼ teaspoon almond extract	

Cook chocolate and cold milk in top of double boiler until chocolate is melted, stirring occasionally. Then beat with rotary egg beater until mixture is well-blended. Add granulated tapioca, rain-like, and salt and cook about 15 minutes until tapioca is clear, mixture thickened, stirring almost constantly. Combine the ½ cup granulated sugar and add to milk-chocolate-tapioca mixture, stirring until thoroughly blended and sugar dissolved. Now, strain through a very fine sieve by stirring, but not rubbing, then chill. Add the 2 tablespoons of granulated sugar to stiffly beaten egg whites, then fold into creamy mixture, lastly fold in heavy cream, whipped custard-like consistency with vanilla and almond extract. Freeze in refrigerator tray, without stirring for 4 hours. You may pack in mold in 4 parts ice and 1 part rock salt, if desired, and let stand for 3½ hours.

This chocolate ice cream should be melting (mellow) and soft. For effect you may unmold over an ice block made as indicated for No. 24, under "General Information."

140 CHOCOLATE BREADCRUMB ICE CREAM
(Refrigerator tray or hand freezer)

To ice cream recipe No. 139 above, omit tapioca and add 1½ cups sieved bread crumbs. Do not strain. Freeze as indicated. Or, make as follows:

1½ cups sieved bread crumbs	¾ cup granulated sugar
1 cup undiluted evaporated milk	¼ teaspoon salt
1 cup water, hot	¾ teaspoon vanilla extract
¼ cup cocoa	1 cup heavy cream, whipped thick

Scald milk with crumbs; add hot water, in which cocoa and sugar and salt, mixed together, have been added, and beat until mixture is smooth. Chill, add vanilla extract and thickly whipped heavy cream. Place in refrigerator tray and freeze for 30 minutes. Remove, scrape and stir from bottom and sides, then beat well. Return to refrigerator tray and freeze for 3½ hours.

Macaroon or cake crumbs may be substituted for bread crumbs, if desired.

141   CHOCOLATE MARSHMALLOW
ICE CREAM
(Refrigerator tray)

2 squares bitter chocolate, grated then melted over hot water	4 tablespoons granulated sugar
1 cup fresh scalded milk	1 cup undiluted evaporated milk
16 marshmallows, cut small	1 tablespoon lemon juice
¼ scant teaspoon salt	½ teaspoon ground cinnamon

To the chocolate melted over hot water, add scalded milk, slowly and gradually, stirring constantly, until mixture is thoroughly blended. Add marshmallows, cut small with scissors, dipped in flour, salt and sugar, and place over hot water, heating slowly, while stirring constantly, until marshmallows are dissolved and sugar melted, then chill. When cold, fold in the whipped undiluted evaporated milk to which has been added lemon juice and ground cinnamon. Freeze in refrigerator tray without stirring for 3½ hours. To serve: With a tablespoon dipped in hot water, rapidly cut eggs into the frozen ice cream, and arrange, crown-like on a well-chilled platter. Fill center of the ring with Raspberry whipped cream made as follows:

1¼ cups raspberries	1 cup powdered sugar	1 egg white

Put all the above ingredients in a mixing bowl, and beat with a wire whisk until stiff enough to hold its shape, or about 25 minutes. Pile lightly or force through a pastry bag with a large fancy tube, in center of the ice cream ring. You may dust the whip with shredded blanched almonds, or crumbled dry macaroons, if desired.

142   CHOCOLATE MOCHA ICE CREAM
(*Refrigerator tray*)

*An ice cream to delight mothers, young and not so young.
The food, including the dessert needn't be expensive—but it must
be unusual. Try this:*

2 squares bitter chocolate, melted over hot water
1 can sweetened condensed milk
1 cup very strong coffee
½ teaspoon vanilla extract

¼ teaspoon salt
1 can undiluted evaporated milk whipped custard-like consistency
½ teaspoon ground cinnamon

Into the melted bitter chocolate, stir in the can of sweetened
condensed milk, until mixture is blended, and cook, over boiling water, until mixture thickens, stirring constantly. Combine
whipped custard-like evaporated milk, strong coffee, vanilla extract and ground cinnamon. Cool. When cold, freeze in refrigerator tray, for 1 long hour, or when to a mush. Remove from refrigerator and scrape bottom and sides of tray, then beat until
mixture is smooth. Return to refrigerator tray and freeze again
another hour; scrape again and beat until smooth, then freeze
for 2 hours longer.

143   CHOCOLATE SPICE ICE CREAM
(*Mexican recipe. Hand freezer*)

1 square bitter chocolate melted over hot water
2 cups fresh milk, scalded
1 stick cinnamon, 1 inch long
2 tablespoons all-purpose flour
2 tablespoons cold water
¼ scant teaspoon ground ginger

2 egg yolks slightly beaten
⅛ teaspoon salt
1 scant teaspoon vanilla extract, combined with
3 drops almond extract
1 cup heavy cream, whipped to custard-like consistency

¾ cup granulated sugar

[83]

Stir into the melted chocolate, slowly, while stirring constantly, the scalded milk, adding the cinnamon stick and ground ginger. Mix the flour and cold water to a smooth paste, and add slowly to the chocolate mixture, stirring rapidly and constantly, over a gentle flame, until mixture is thickened, or about 15 minutes. Then, add combined sugar and egg yolks and cook two minutes, stirring constantly. Strain mixture through a fine sieve, and beat it thoroughly with rotary egg beater. When cold, add heavy cream, whipped to a custard-like consistency with salt and flavoring extracts. Freeze in hand freezer, using 3 parts ice and 1 part of rock salt. Pack or mold in 4 parts ice and 1 part rock salt.

144   CHOCOLATE TAPIOCA ICE CREAM
(Refrigerator tray)

1½ squares bitter chocolate melted over hot water	1½ tablespoons quick-cooking tapioca
1 cup boiling water	½ scant teaspoon salt
1 can undiluted evaporated milk scalded	¾ cup granulated sugar
	1 teaspoon vanilla extract

1 cup heavy cream, whipped stiff

To the hot melted chocolate, add water very slowly, stirring constantly, and cook over direct low flame until mixture thickens, stirring constantly. Remove from the fire and stir in the hot scalded, undiluted evaporated milk. Add tapioca, salt and sugar and cook until tapioca is clear, stirring frequently. Cool, add vanilla extract, then thickly beaten heavy cream. Freeze in refrigerator tray for ¾ hour, remove, scrape bottom and sides, then beat until smooth. Return to refrigerator tray and freeze without scraping or beating for 3 hours.

145 ### COCOMALT ICE CREAM
(Refrigerator tray)

1 teaspoon granulated gelatine	1/3 cup cocomalt
1/4 cup cold water	1 teaspoon vanilla extract
1/4 cup boiling water	1 cup heavy cream, whipped
2/3 cup undiluted condensed milk	thick

1/2 cup ground nut meats (any kind)

Sprinkle granulated gelatine over cold water and let stand for 5 minutes, then pour over the boiling water. To the condensed, sweetened milk add vanilla extract and cocomalt and beat to a custard-like consistency, then add whipped thick heavy cream alternately with the ground nut meats. Mix well, but gently. Freeze in refrigerator tray for 1 hour, remove, scrape bottom and sides, then beat until smooth; return to refrigerator and freeze for 3 hours.

146 ### COCONUT STRAWBERRY SUNDAE

The amount of ingredients are according to how many persons there are to be served. The ingredients are:

Vanilla ice cream—Sweetened crushed strawberries—Moist, sweetened coconut.

Over each portion, pour 1 or 2 tablespoons of crushed sweetened strawberries, then sprinkle moist, sweetened coconut over.

147 ### COFFEE CHARLOTTE ICE CREAM
(Refrigerator tray or hand freezer)

In the following recipe no freezing, either in refrigerator tray or the hand freezer is required. Only packing in 3 parts ice and 1 part of rock salt is necessary.

Cream together 1 lb. butter and ½ lb. powdered sugar, until almost white, then gradually add 4 egg yolks, unbeaten and one at a time, continuing creaming until thoroughly blended, smooth and creamy; then add, almost drop by drop ½ cup of extra strong coffee liquid, and continue creaming constantly. Line a melon mold with lady fingers placed close together, or a straight charlotte mold, if desired, spoon creamy mixture into it very carefully and evenly; sprinkle over ½ cup of chopped, assorted candied fruits. Adjust cover, rub edge with butter to prevent salted water from penetrating into the mold, and pack into hand freezer, using 3 parts ice and 1 part rock salt, for 4 hours. When ready to serve, unmold over an ice block (optional) which may be colored according to fancy, and decorate the base of the dessert with a ribbon of whipped cream, unflavored and unsweetened, forced through a pastry bag with tube. The above recipe is rather a mousse than an ice cream.

148   COFFEE CARAMEL PORCUPINE
(Hand freezer)

A fine dessert for children's party . . . and grown-ups too. It's more a parfait than an ice cream, yet it is very unusual and delicious.

1 cup of rich milk, scalded	1 scant teaspoon vanilla extract
½ cup granulated sugar, caramelized	1 cup blanched almonds
	½ cup granulated sugar, and
2 tablespoons freshly ground coffee	⅛ generous teaspoon salt
	1 cup undiluted evaporated
3 egg yolks beaten with	milk, or thin cream
¼ cup shredded angelica	

Scald milk with freshly ground coffee, then add the caramelized sugar, allow this to infuse for 10 minutes, strain over top of double boiler, and add the egg yolk mixture. Stir well until blended, then cook, over boiling water, until mixture thickens, stirring constantly. Remove from the water and add the undiluted evaporated milk or thin cream. Cool, then strain and add vanilla extract. Freeze in hand freezer, using 3 parts ice and 1 part rock salt until solid. Pack in solidly in empty, chilled 16 oz. milk cans, filling the cans to overflowing. Adjust cover (empty cans with a cover may be used preferably to milk cans), pack, using equal parts ice and rock salt, and let stand for 2 long hours before unmolding. Quickly roll in half cup of the blanched chopped almonds; stick the remaining almonds which have been shredded interspersed with small sticks of shredded angelica.

149 COFFEE ICE CREAM I
(Hand freezer)

Like chocolate ice cream, there are several versions or formulas to make coffee ice cream, at home.

To 1 quart of your favorite vanilla ice cream (see recipes No. 285 or 297) scald 1/3 of the milk with 1/3 cup of freshly ground coffee, and strain through a fine sieve or cloth, before adding anything else. Freeze as directed. This method applies to Vanilla Ice Cream, Philadelphia Method, Vanilla Ice Cream, French Method, as well as Vanilla Ice Cream, Home Method.

150 COFFEE ICE CREAM II
(Hand freezer)

In this recipe extra strong coffee liquid is used, yet it is still the custard method.

1 cup milk (cold)	1 cup granulated sugar
¼ cup extra strong coffee liquid	3 cups undiluted evaporated
3 egg yolks, slightly beaten	milk or thin cream
⅛ teaspoon salt	

Scald cold milk with coffee, and add half the sugar. Combine slightly beaten egg yolks with the remaining ½ cup granulated sugar and slowly add to scalded milk-coffee mixture, stirring rapidly until mixture is thoroughly blended. Cook over hot water until mixture thickens, stirring almost constantly. Remove from hot water, cool slightly, then add 1 cup of the undiluted evaporated milk or thin cream, and allow to stand for half an hour, to mellow and cool. Then strain through double cheesecloth; add remaining milk or thin cream and freeze in hand freezer, using 3 parts ice and 1 part rock salt. Pack or mold in 4 parts ice and 1 part rock salt and let stand 2 hours before serving.

151   COFFEE ICE CREAM III
(Refrigerator tray)
Using granulated gelatine, no cream, and grape nuts cereal.

1 teaspoon granulated gelatine	½ cup grape nuts cereals
1 cup extra strong cold coffee liquid	1 cup undiluted evaporated milk, whipped to custard-like consistency
½ cup granulated sugar	

½ teaspoon vanilla extract

Soak, or rather spinkle gelatine over cold coffee, and allow to stand 5 minutes, then heat, stirring constantly until gelatine is dissolved and coffee is up to the boiling point; then add granulated sugar and cook, over a low flame for 5 short minutes, stirring frequently. Strain through a double cheesecloth. Chill. Combine slightly whipped undiluted evaporated milk and grape nuts, and add to chilled coffee mixture; then stir in the vanilla extract. Freeze in refrigerator tray for 1 hour, or until mixture is mushy, then scrape bottom and sides, and beat until smooth. Return to refrigerator tray, and freeze for 3 hours.

152 ## COFFEE ICE CREAM IV
(Refrigerator tray)

1 can sweetened condensed milk
1 cup very strong coffee liquid
⅛ teaspoon salt

1 teaspoon vanilla extract
1 cup heavy cream, whipped stiff
1 egg white stiffly beaten

Combine ingredients in order metioned, and stir well. Freeze in refrigerator tray until mushy, or about 1 short hour; then, scrape bottom and sides, and beat mixture until smooth. Return to refrigerator and freeze until firm, or about 3 hours.

153 ## COFFEE ICE CREAM V
(Hand freezer)

This really delicious ice cream which used to be the favorite ice cream at the court of Austria when the father of the author was Esquire of Cuisine and under whom the author learned this beautiful art of preparing food, is made from whole coffee beans which are scalded with light cream—undiluted evaporated milk may be used, if desired. During the scalding, the mixture is hermetically covered, so as to infuse gradually without any chance of losing the delicate flavor of the coffee. The mixture is then cooled, and used to prepare the ice cream. The result is an almost snow white ice cream.

1 cup of green coffee beans, roasted in the usual way in a heavy skillet, or
1 cup of already roasted coffee beans heated in a moderate oven to enhance the flavor

4 cups undiluted evaporated milk or light cream
½ cup granulated sugar
4 drops vanilla extract
¼ teaspoon salt

[89]

Let us assume you use the already roasted coffee beans. Heat coffee beans in spider or heavy skillet, over a gentle flame or a moderate oven (350 deg. F.). Add the undiluted evaporated milk and very gently bring to the scalding point. Remove from the flame, stir in granulated sugar, cover hermetically as follows: spread a clean kitchen towel over the skillet or spider and adjust the cover fittingly so that there is no chance for the coffee flavor to escape. Allow to stand until cold; then strain through double cheesecloth or fine muslin, add salt and vanilla extract, and freeze in hand freezer, using 3 parts ice and 1 part rock salt until hard. Then pack or mold in 4 parts ice and 1 part rock salt.

154   COFFEE ICE CREAM VI
(Hand freezer)

Like the preceding recipe, this method requires whole coffee beans. This ice cream is made on a basis of custard-like mixture. The results are smoothness, lightness and richness. Undiluted evaporated milk or light cream may be used, if desired. A more elaborate ice cream dish, which is optional, of course, and which used to be the favorite frozen dessert of the Archduchess Stephanie of Austria, may be made by spooning the frozen hard mixture (operating when just ready to serve, and rapidly at that) with a soup spoon dipped in hot water, shaping egg-like, and placing these ice cream eggs, mound-like, onto a chilled serving platter, then pouring over a Cold Dulcet Cream made as indicated below, and covering the entire surface with a meringue forced through a pastry bag, which has been sweetened and prepared as indicated for recipe No. 107, Baked Alaska. Sweeten and flavor the meringue with a few drops of either your favorite flavoring extract, cordial or liqueur, and delicately tint with a few drops of vegetable coloring, the color being according to the occasion, forced through a pastry bag with a tube. This frozen dessert may seem complicated and elaborate, yet it is as simple and in the same principle as Baked Alaska Ice Cream and may easily be made at home.

This royal treat, with an indefinable flavor and a tempting eye appeal, was served for the first time at a dinner at Heilbrunnen, near Salzburg, Austria, August 28, 1882, by the author's father, then Esquire of Cuisine of Their AA. LL. II, and RR., Archduc Rodolph and Archduchess Stephanie of Austria, in honor of the Emperor of Germany, Whilhelm I, the Grand Duc and Grand Duchess Constantin, and Prince Bismarck of Germany. Since then, the writer has often served it while chef in private families in America, and the hostess always in quest of delicious novelties, may try it at home without any difficulty.

1 cup roasted coffee beans	6 egg yolks, unbeaten
⅔ cup powdered sugar	¼ teaspoon salt
1 quart undiluted evaporated milk or light cream, scalded	¼ teaspoon vanilla extract

Spread whole coffee beans in bottom of a slightly buttered heavy skillet, then sprinkle over the coffee beans ½ of the powdered sugar. Place over a gentle flame and stir constantly until powdered sugar is caramelized and beans are entirely coated. Then, very slowly, pour the scalded undiluted evaporated milk or light cream, stirring constantly, but do not allow to boil. Pour mixture into a mixing bowl, cover with a dry clean towel, then with a lid, hermetically. Allow this to infuse for 15 minutes, the bowl placed over cracked ice, and when cold, strain through double cheesecloth or fine muslin; add unbeaten egg yolks, one at a time, alternately with remaining powdered sugar, salt and vanilla extract, beating well, but gently after each addition. Strain again, still through double cheesecloth or muslin. Chill, then freeze in hand freezer, using 3 parts ice and 1 part rock salt, until firm. Pack for 2 long hours in 4 parts ice and 1 part of rock salt.

154A DULCET CREAM

If you wish to make the fancy frozen party dessert as described above, proceed as follows:

Over the spooned ice cream described above, pour the following cream:

2 dozen blanched almonds, pounded or ground

¼ cup undiluted evaporated milk or thin cream, scalded

½ cup granulated sugar

5 egg yolks, beaten until thick with

¼ teaspoon salt, and

2 or three tablespoons good brandy

1 quart heavy cream

Add pounded or ground blanched almonds to the scalded milk or thin cream, then slowly and gradually, beat in the already thickly beaten egg yolks with salt, alternately with brandy which has been sweetened with sugar. Lastly stir in the heavy cream. Place over boiling water (double boiler) and stir, but do not allow mixture to boil, until mixture thickens. Cool before spreading over the heaped up ice cream, then, when the ice cream is entirely covered with a coat of this delicious cream, called "Dulcet Cream," an Italian recipe, cover with a meringue made as indicated for recipe No. 107, and set in a very hot oven (450 to 500 deg. F.) until delicately browned. Serve at once. Of course, you may tint the meringue according to occasion. You may also use any other kind of your favorite flavoring, either liqueur, or extract.

155   COFFEE ICE CREAM   VII
(RUM PRALINE)
(Use either hand freezer or refrigerator tray)

Here is a clever and delicious French method to brighten up your favorite coffee ice cream recipe. The mixture to be added, called "Rum Praline," special for ice cream and all its derivatives, bombes, ices, mousses, parfaits or sherbets, has the great advantage in that it keeps for months when packed into an airtight container and kept in a cool dry place. It is to be used with numerous cold desserts, such as custards, whips, creams, fillings, and the like. Of course, it should be made in advance and be on hand when wanted for use. It is made as follows:

4½ ozs. blanched coarsely ground almonds	Enough cold milk to make a soft paste, not too soft
4½ ozs. or equal amount of powdered sugar	1 generous tablespoon good rum 5 drops orange extract
	½ cup heavy cream, whipped stiff

Combine and blend well coarsely ground almonds and sugar. Gradually add enough milk so as to make a spreading paste, adding milk almost drop by drop. Spread, using a spatula, over a pie tin or a baking sheet, which has been very lightly olive oiled, and toast under the flame of the broiling oven or in a moderate oven (350 deg. F.) until dry, crisp and breakable. Break into small pieces, then grind coarsely. When ready to use, add the whipped stiff heavy cream into which has been folded the combined rum and orange extract.

Now, how to add this delicious mixture:

If hand freezer is used, freeze your coffee ice cream mixture to a mush, that is not too hard; add the Rum Praline, and continue freezing until ice cream is firm. Pack or mold in 4 parts of ice and 1 part of rock salt.

[93]

If refrigerator tray is used, freeze coffee ice cream mixture to a mush; remove from the tray; scrape bottom and sides, then beat in the Praline mixture. Return to refrigerator tray, and freeze for 3 hours.

IMPORTANT.—*It sometimes happens that homemakers have difficulties in freezing ice cream or any other kind of frozen desserts into which rum has been mixed. If rum is whipped with the cream, the mixture will freeze without any trouble. If fruits, fresh, canned or preserved are used, they should be crushed and drained or sieved, then drained before being added to mixture to be frozen. The moisture in large pieces of fruit, either berries or other kind of fruit, causes large crystals of ice to form in the frozen mixture, thus often preventing a smooth, creamy product.*

Another very important point which the homemaker should know, is that when canned or preserved fruits are substituted for fresh fruit in an ice cream recipe, and in fact in every frozen dessert, the sugar content should and must be lowered, according to sweetness of the substituted fruit, sometimes slightly, sometimes as much as to half its content, so the freezing point and the desired texture may be obtained.

Lastly when fruit juice is to be used in any kind of frozen dessert, it should be measured and substituted for a like amount of the indicated liquid in the recipe, no matter the kind of fruit.

156   COFFEE ICE CREAM ICEBERG VIII
(Serve 1)

For each scooping of coffee ice cream, use 1 cup of cold milk, 2 tablespoons of chocolate syrup and a few grains of cinnamon (optional). Add milk slowly to chocolate syrup, stirring constantly. Beat or shake well. Pour into tall parfait or coupe glass, which should be chilled, and add a scoop of your favorite coffee ice cream. A fine beverage and a dessert at the same time which is very much liked by children . . . and grown ups . . . too.

157   **CONCORD GRAPE ICE CREAM**
(Hand freezer or refrigerator tray)

6 lbs. concord grapes	1½ cups granulated sugar
1 pint heavy cream	⅛ teaspoon salt

Pick and wash grapes. Stem. Place in a saucepan, and heat very slowly, over the lowest flame possible, pressing very gently with a wooden spoon to separate the pulp from the skins and seeds. Add sugar and allow to simmer gently for 10 minutes. Put through a sieve and cool slightly, then strain through a double cheesecloth. Cool, then stir in the heavy cream which has been whipped stiffly. You may use refrigerator tray, but mixture should be scraped from bottom and sides, beaten, then returned to refrigerator tray and frozen for 3 long hours.

158   **CORNFLAKE ICE CREAM**
(Refrigerator tray)

1 cup fresh milk	1 egg yolk, slightly beaten
½ cup granulated sugar	⅛ teaspoon salt
1 tablespoon cornstarch	2 cups corn flakes cereal
½ teaspoon vanilla extract, combined with	2 cups heavy cream, whipped custard-like
¼ teaspoon almond extract	

Combine sugar and cornstarch and mix well. Stir in the milk, a small amount at a time, and cook over hot water until mixture is thickened, stirring constantly. Remove from hot water, cool slightly, then stir in slightly beaten egg. Return to hot water and cook for 2 short minutes, stirring constantly. Strain through double cheesecloth. Stir in the heavy cream, whipped to custard-like consistency, alternately with corn flakes and flavoring ex-

[95]

tracts. Freeze in refrigerator tray until mushy. Remove from refrigerator, scrape bottom and sides, then beat smooth. Return to refrigerator tray and freeze for 3 hours.

159 CRANBERRY SUNDAE
(Serve 1)

For each serving, place 1 generous scoop of your favorite Vanilla ice cream recipe, and top with a generous tablespoon of cranberry sauce. Chilled coupe or sherbet glasses are here indicated.

160 DATE AND GINGER SYRUP ICE CREAM
(Hand freezer or refrigerator tray)

3 whole eggs, slightly beaten with
¼ teaspoon salt
2 cups fresh milk, scalded
½ cup granulated sugar

1 cup heavy cream, whipped stiff
2 teaspoons vanilla extract
⅔ cup dates, washed, sponged, then chopped coarsely

⅓ cup syrup from jar of preserved ginger

Beat whole eggs slightly adding the salt. Gradually pour over them the hot scalded milk, stirring rapidly and constantly, lest texture curdle. Place in double boiler and cook, over boiling water, until mixture thickens, stirring constantly. Cool, strain through a fine sieve and add stiffly beaten heavy cream to which has been added the vanilla extract. Freeze to a mush. If using hand freezer, when mixture is mushy, stir in very gently the dates and ginger syrup, and freeze until stiff, using 3 parts ice and 1 part rock salt, then pack in 4 parts ice and 1 part rock salt. If using refrigerator tray, when mixture is frozen to a mush, remove from refrigerator tray, scrape bottom and sides, then beat in the dates and ginger syrup. Return to refrigerator tray and freeze for 3 hours.

161   ECONOMY ICE CREAM
             (Refrigerator tray)

⅔ cup sweetened condensed   1 teaspoon vanilla extract
   milk   ½ teaspoon ground ginger
½ cup warm water   1 cup heavy cream

Blend sweetened condensed milk, warm water, vanilla and ginger thoroughly. Cool, then chill. Meanwhile whip heavy cream to custard-like consistency and fold into chilled creamy mixture. Freeze in refrigerator tray until mushy. Remove from refrigerator. Scrape creamy mixture from sides and bottom of tray; then beat until smooth; return to refrigerator and freeze for 3 hours.

162   EGGNOG ICE CREAM
             (Refrigerator tray)

6 egg yolks, beaten until thick   6 egg whites, stiffly beaten
½ cup granulated sugar   ¼ teaspoon salt
4 tablespoons (more or less)   1 cup heavy cream whipped stiff
   sherry   Nutmeg

Beat egg yolks until thick, then add sugar gradually and continue beating until sugar is thoroughly blended. Set in refrigerator while beating egg whites until stiff with the salt. Then fold egg yolk mixture with stiffly beaten egg whites, adding gradually the sherry wine (rum or brandy may be substituted, if desired). Lastly fold in the heavy cream beaten stiff. Freeze in refrigerator tray, without scraping or stirring, for 4 hours. When ready to serve, sprinkle over each serving a small pinch of ground nutmeg, or still better a grating from a whole nutmeg.

163   EXCELSIOR ICE CREAM
(No freezing—molding and packing in hand freezer)

Very appropriate for a birthday, wedding, or anniversary dinner party.

2 cups chopped assorted candied or crystallized fruit, combined ¼ cup together and in equal parts of kirsch and maraschino
1 cup heavy cream, whipped
1 pint vanilla ice cream

Soak chopped, mixed assorted candied or crystallized fruit in the combined kirsch and maraschino liqueurs for 30 minutes. (Fruit may be prunes, apricots, pineapple, cherries, pears, and so forth.) Drain; then mix with whipped cream (unsweetened and unflavored). Line a chilled melon mold, having a close fitting cover, with part of the vanilla ice cream, either made at home or purchased, reserving a small amount to cover the fruit. Fill center of the thus lined melon mold with fruit mixture; cover with the reserved ice cream; place a buttered paper over; adjust melon mold cover and pack in 4 parts ice and 1 part rock salt for 2 long hours.

You may unmold over an ice block made as indicated for No. 24, under "General Information," if desired.

164   FIG ICE CREAM
(Hand freezer)

5 egg yolks, slightly beaten
1 cup granulated sugar
1½ cups undiluted evaporated milk
1½ cups warm water
¾ teaspoon salt
1 lb. dried figs, ground
1 tablespoon vanilla extract
5 egg whites, stiffly beaten
1½ cups heavy cream, whipped stiff

To the combined undiluted evaporated milk and warm water, add the slightly beaten egg yolks, pouring very slowly, while beating constantly to prevent curdling. Then stir in the sugar until melted. Cook over hot water, until mixture thickens, stirring constantly. Then add the salt, and stir in the ground dried figs and vanilla extract. Lastly fold in the stiffly beaten egg whites, alternately with the stiffly beaten heavy cream. Freeze in hand freezer, using 3 parts ice and 1 part rock salt, until stiff. Pack or mold in 4 parts ice and 1 part rock salt, for 2 hours.

165   FIG AND GINGER ICE CREAM
        (Hand freezer or refrigerator tray)

Proceed as indicated for recipe No. 160, Date and Ginger Syrup Ice Cream, substituting figs for dates. Freeze, pack or mold as directed.

166   FLAMING ICE CREAM SAUCE
        (Serve 1)

½ brandied peach, sliced
½ brandied apricot, sliced
4 brandied pitted cherries
¼ teaspoon curacao liqueur
 Sugar to taste

1½ teaspoons brandy
1 small round of sponge cake
 cut the size of a biscuit
1 scoop vanilla ice cream

Heat the combined brandied fruits in a small frying pan. Add curacao, then sprinkle with sugar. Stir gently, but do not allow to boil, simply heat. Then pour brandy over mixture and touch it with a match. Place round of sponge cake, or any other kind of cake, cut the size of a biscuit, using a biscuit cutter, on dessert plate; top with ice cream and pour the fruit over it. Serve at once. This may be prepared right on the table, if desired. Variations to the above may be made by using any kind of canned or fresh fruit.

167   GELATINE CUSTARD ICE CREAM
(Hand freezer or refrigerator tray)

The addition of granulated gelatine to a frozen dessert adds body and consistency and helps to prevent the formation of icy crystals, as well as to improve the texture of the mixture.

1 tablespoon granulated gelatine   1 scant cup granulated sugar
1 quart fresh milk   ¼ teaspoon salt
2 egg yolks, slightly beaten   1 teaspoon vanilla extract
2 egg whites stiffly beaten

Sprinkle granulated gelatine over ¼ cup of cold milk. Make a custard of the milk, egg yolks, slightly beaten, sugar and salt in the usual way. Strain while still hot, then add soaked gelatine and stir until dissolved. Cool. Add flavoring extract, and freeze in refrigerator tray until mushy. Remove from refrigerator. Fold in stiffly beaten egg whites. Do not scrape. Return to refrigerator tray and freeze for 3 hours.

168   GERMAN CHOCOLATE ICE CREAM

To your favorite chocolate ice cream, add, when mixture is not too hard, that is, mushy, 2 cups of dry zweiback broken in very small pieces, and continue freezing until mixture is hard.

169   GERMAN GINGER ICE CREAM
         (Hand freezer or refrigerator tray)

½ cup granulated sugar   1 cup heavy cream, scalded
1 tablespoon all-purpose flour   1 egg yolk, slightly beaten
¼ scant teaspoon salt   ⅓ cup preserved ginger, chopped
1 cup fresh milk, scalded   ¾ teaspoon vanilla extract
              1 cup heavy cream, whipped stiff

Combine then sift sugar, flour and salt; then stir in combined scalded fresh milk and heavy cream. Pour mixture in top of double boiler and cook, stirring constantly, until mixture is smooth, thick and creamy. To the slightly beaten egg yolk, add 2 or 3 tablespoons of the hot mixture, stirring rapidly and constantly until blended, then stir in remaining creamy mixture. Strain, then add while hot the chopped preserved ginger. Cool, and add vanilla extract. Lastly fold in the stiffly beaten heavy cream. Freeze in hand refrigerator, using 3 parts ice and 1 part rock salt, until hard and firm. Pack or mold in equal parts of ice and rock salt for 2 hours.

You may freeze in refrigerator tray as follows: Add the custard-like whipped heavy cream to the frozen mixture which has been frozen to a mush, scraped on bottom and sides, then whipped with the custard-like consistency whipped cream. Freeze in refrigerator tray for 3 long hours.

170   GINGER ICE CREAM
         (Short method—hand freezer)

To your favorite vanilla ice cream recipe, when frozen to a mush, add ½ scant cup of preserved chopped ginger and 2 tablespoons ginger syrup. Then freeze until firm. Pack or mold in 4 parts ice and 1 part rock salt.

171   GINGER SHERRY ICE CREAM
(Short method—hand freezer)

To your favorite vanilla ice cream recipe, add ¼ cup preserved chopped ginger, 3 tablespoons of sherry wine, and omit
vanilla extract. These ingredients should be added when creamy
mixture is mushy. Then freeze until firm. Pack or mold in 4
parts ice and 1 part rock salt.

172   GRAPEJUICE ICE CREAM I
(Refrigerator tray)

*For the following recipe you may use either red or white
grapejuice, but a little more sugar should be added to the white
grapejuice because it is less sweet.*

1¼ cups grapejuice	2 cups heavy cream
⅓ cup granulated sugar	2 teaspoons lime juice
½ teaspoon ground ginger	

Combine and mix well, but do not beat grapejuice, granulated
sugar and heavy cream. Add then lime juice and ground ginger.
Freeze in refrigerator tray until mushy. Remove from refrigerator, scrape bottom and sides, then beat until smooth. Return to
refrigerator and freeze for 3 long hours.

173   GRAPEJUICE ICE CREAM II
(Refrigerator tray)

*An economical ice cream in which sweetened condensed milk
is used.*

⅔ cup sweetened condensed milk	⅛ teaspoon salt
½ cup grapejuice	1 cup heavy cream, whipped to custard-like consistency

Combine and blend thoroughly sweetened condensed milk, grapejuice, salt, lemon extract. Chill. When well-chilled, add whipped cream, folding it gently. Freeze in refrigerator tray to a mush. Remove from refrigerator, scrape bottom and sides and beat until smooth. Return to refrigerator and freeze for 3 hours.

174 GREENGAGE ICE CREAM

Proceed as indicated for recipe No. 104, Apricot Ice Cream III, substituting fresh greengage for apricots. Freeze, pack or mold and serve as directed.

175 HALLOWEEN

Good food, more than anything else, adds to the rapture of the occasion for always the food itself is the best uniter that any party can produce for any group of guests from six to seventy.

176 HALLOWEEN ICE CREAM CLOWN
(Serve 1)

For children's Halloween party.
Put a scoop of ice cream in an ice cream cone, invert on round cooky, features from gumdrops and make a ruff with whipped cream put on through pastry bag and tube.

177 HALLOWEEN WITCH'S CAPS
(Serve 1)

For children's Halloween party.
Cover ordinary ice cream cones with chocolate icing, made from confectioner's sugar. Allow to stand until hardened. When ready to serve, fill the cone with chocolate ice cream. Invert on a chocolate cooky and serve a not-too-rich piece of cake with it.

178   ICE CREAM CROQUETES

Ice cream (home made)   —Coconut, browned

Shape any kind of your favorite ice cream into croquette
shapes. Roll until coated in toasted coconut. Serve with Hot
Chocolate Fudge Sauce, made as follows:

2 squares bitter chocolate   1 cup granulated sugar
1 tablespoon butter   ⅛ teaspoon salt
⅓ cup milk   2 tablespoons corn syrup
          ½ teaspoon vanilla extract

Melt chocolate and butter; stir in milk gradually. Add sugar,
salt and corn syrup. Boil 5 long minutes or until mixture reaches
the very soft ball stage (236 deg. F.).

179   ICE CREAM ÉCLAIRS

*This is a very nice suggestion for making full use of the pos-
sibilities of dainty frozen desserts, such as tartlets and patties,
puffs and éclairs, to dress up your meals. They are pleasing to
the eye and tempting to the appetite and have a certain air of
elegance that lends a festive note to the table. For example, is
there anything more inviting for luncheon or even dinner, formal
or informal, than a frozen éclair, or a tender patty shell (individual) filled with a little of your favorite jam, or a fruit puree
topped with a scoop of ice cream?*
*Éclair shells as well as puff shells are made on the same basic
principles. They may be large or just tiny little mouthfuls.*

1 cup water   1 cup all-purpose flour
¼ teaspoon salt   4 unbeaten eggs
½ cup butter   ½ teaspoon vanilla extract
          Ice cream (any kind)

Place water and butter in a large, heavy saucepan, and heat to boiling point. When boiling vigorously, add the flour all at once and beat hard and fast. A smooth ball will be formed, which will leave the sides of the pan clean. Turn this ball into a large mixing bowl. Add unbeaten eggs, one at a time, beating each egg well after adding it and before adding another one. Continue until all eggs are incorporated and the mixture is shiny, stiff and appetizing. Shape on a baking sheet or wrap in waxed paper and place in refrigerator for overnight. To shape, use pastry bag or a spoon. The pat of dough should be about 3 inches across for large puffs or 1 tablespoon across for small puffs. Eclairs are made from strips about 4 inches long by 1 inch wide. They may be forced through a pastry bag or molded with a spoon. Now, when ready to use, bake in a very hot oven (450 deg. F.) for 15 minutes, then reduce to moderate oven (350 deg. F.) and continue baking for 20 minutes.

If very small puffs or éclairs are desired, cut down the baking time to half, or according to size. This will yield 12 large puffs or éclairs, large size, or 24 puffs or éclairs, small size. The small ones are usually served for cocktail parties. Remember, they may be filled with almost any kind of cold mixture, such as cream, custard, whipped cream flavored and sweetened to taste, or any kind of ice cream, at the moment of serving. They may be iced or frosted with a thin butter icing in white or chocolate or mocha. The baking sheet should not be buttered or greased.

To serve, make a slit in one side, insert the selected ice cream or other filling, ice or frost according to taste or fancy. On chocolate icing, it is suggested a sprinkling of finely chopped pistachio nuts; on the white icing, a sprinkling of finely chopped candied peel, or candied or crystallized fruit; leave the mocha plain.

Meringues are made, as regards to filling, in the very same way. You may fill them with any kind of your favorite ice cream. For more information as how to make meringues, or kisses, see recipe No. 108, Instruction About Making Meringues.

180   LEMON ICE CREAM
          (Refrigerator tray)

Very economical and easy to make.

Grated rind and juice of 3 lemons   1 can sweetened condensed milk
Grated rind and juice of 1 orange   2 cups water
⅛ teaspoon salt   2 tablespoons cornstarch

Strain the juice of the 3 lemons and the juice of the orange into the sweetened condensed milk, poured in top of double boiler, and stir, off the fire, until mixture is blended. Add 1 cup hot water to which has been added the salt, and stir the cornstarch into the remaining cup of cold water. Combine with the milk mixture and cook over hot water until mixture is thickened, stirring constantly. Cool. Add the lemon and orange rinds. Stir well and freeze in refrigerator tray, until mushy. Remove from refrigerator and scrape bottom and sides, then beat until smooth. Return to refrigerator tray and freeze for 3 hours.

181   LEMON FLOWER ICE CREAM
          (Hand freezer)

A really surprisingly delicious ice cream, the creation of which is attributed to the famous French writer Alexandre Dumas, who not only confined his talent to many interesting books, known the world over, but also to a culinary book, the authoritative "Grand Dictionnaire de Cuisine" (The Great Culinary Dictionary) published in Paris in 1873.

This ice cream was served very often, at his Chateau de Belle-

vue, near Paris, France, where all the illustrious writers of his time used to meet.

Any kind of flower may be substituted for lemon flowers if desired. It is very easy to make, the basis being a plain custard.

1 pint fresh heavy cream, un-beaten	½ generous cup granulated sugar
¼ scant teaspoon salt	2 oz. ground lemon flowers (from drugstore)

8 egg yolks, slightly beaten

Scald heavy cream with the salt. Gradually and slowly, almost drop by drop pour this hot cream over the slightly beaten egg yolks, beating rapidly and constantly from the bottom of the mixing bowl, adding with the last amount of scalded cream the ground lemon flowers. Cook, over boiling water, until mixture is of a soft custard-like consistency, stirring constantly. Strain through a double cheesecloth, cool, and when cold, freeze in hand freezer, using 3 parts ice and 1 part rock salt. Pack or mold in 4 parts ice and 1 part rock salt.

182   MACAROON ICE CREAM I
(Hand freezer)

1 cup macaroon crumbs	1 teaspoon almond extract
½ cup confectioner's sugar	1 quart cream (heavy)

¼ scant teaspoon salt

Combine all the above ingredients. Stir well, and freeze in hand freezer, using 3 parts ice and 1 part rock salt, until firm. Pack or mold in 4 parts ice and 1 part rock salt.

183   MACAROON ICE CREAM II
            (*French method. Hand freezer*)

1 pint fresh heavy cream, scalded	5 whole eggs, slightly beaten
½ cup granulated sugar	½ cup macaroon crumbs
¼ teaspoon salt	¼ scant teaspoon vanilla extract
	1 tablespoon kirsch liqueur

Scald the cream, then stir in the granulated sugar and salt, until sugar is entirely dissolved. Slowly, almost drop by drop, pour hot cream over slightly beaten whole eggs, stirring rapidly and constantly. Cook this mixture over boiling water, stirring constantly, until mixture thickens. Strain through double cheesecloth, cool, then add macaroon crumbs, vanilla extract and kirsch liqueur. Freeze in hand freezer, using 3 parts ice and 1 part rock salt, until firm. Pack or mold in 4 parts ice and 1 part rock salt.

184   MACAROON MAPLE ICE CREAM III
    (*Using hand freezer or simply packing in ice and salt*)

4 egg yolks, beaten thickly with	1 pint heavy cream, whipped
½ cup maple syrup, heated	¼ teaspoon vanilla extract
⅛ teaspoon salt	1 cup macaroon crumbs

Beat egg yolks until thick, then beat again very rapidly while pouring almost drop by drop the heated, but not boiled, maple syrup. Turn mixture into top of double boiler, and cook, stirring constantly, until mixture thickens. Remove from fire, cool slightly, add macaroon crumbs, stirring well, then cool. Lastly fold in the thickly whipped cream to which has been added the vanilla extract. Freeze in hand freezer, using 3 parts ice and 1 part rock salt, until firm, or pack in hand freezer pail, using 4 parts ice and 1 part salt, for 3 hours.

185 MAPLE PEANUT BUTTER ICE CREAM
(Refrigerator tray)

Typical of the intriguing table delights that may be evolved with the aid of modern refrigerators, are these delicious recipes made out of maple, and peanut butter, so well relished by children.

¼ cup peanut butter   1½ cups heavy cream, beaten to
½ cup maple syrup   a soft custard-like consistency
                    ⅛ teaspoon salt

Combine all the above ingredients and beat lightly until mixture is smooth and all the ingredients are blended. Freeze in refrigerator tray until mushy; remove from refrigerator, scrape sides and bottom and beat until smooth. Return to refrigerator tray and freeze for 3 hours.

186 MAPLE WALNUT ICE CREAM I
(Refrigerator tray)

1 cup maple syrup   3 egg whites, stiffly beaten
3 egg yolks, slightly beaten, with   1 cup heavy cream, beaten to a
¼ teaspoon salt   custard-like consistency
1 teaspoon vanilla extract   ½ cup chopped, skinned walnuts

Place maple syrup in upper part of double boiler, and heat, but do not boil, over hot water. Then, stir in the slightly beaten egg yolks until well-blended. Cook, stirring constantly, over hot water, until mixture thickens. Remove from water, and add vanilla extract. Chill. When cold, fold in the stiffly beaten egg whites, alternately with the heavy cream, which has been beaten to a custard-like consistency. Freeze in refrigerator tray, to a

[109]

mushy consistency, or until a layer is frozen 1 inch from sides of tray; remove from refrigerator and scrape and stir from bottom and sides of tray. Then beat until smooth, incorporating at the same time the chopped, skinned walnut meats. Return to refrigerator and freeze for 3 hours.

187 MAPLE WALNUT ICE CREAM II
(Hand freezer)

1½ cups maple syrup	½ scant teaspoon vanilla extract
2 whole eggs, slightly beaten with	1 pint heavy cream, beaten custard-like consistency
⅛ teaspoon salt	½ cup chopped, skinned walnuts

Place syrup in upper part of double boiler and scald over hot water, but do not boil. Gradually pour slightly beaten whole eggs, stirring rapidly and constantly until thoroughly blended; remove from hot water and continue beating until cold; then add vanilla extract and heavy cream which has been beaten to custard-like consistency. Freeze in hand freezer, using 3 parts ice and 1 part rock salt, until mushy, then add chopped, skinned walnut meats, and continue freezing until mixture is stiff. Pack or mold in 4 parts ice and 1 part rock salt.

188 MAPLE SUNDAE

Serve maple ice cream, or vanilla, or coffee ice cream with maple syrup cooked down until thick, to which chopped nut meats (any kind) have been added. Strew over a few broken pieces of nut meats and top with a rosette of whipped cream forced through a pastry bag with a tube.

189   MARASCHINO ICE CREAM I
           (Hand freezer)

To a quart of your favorite Vanilla Ice Cream recipe, add, when brought to a mush, the juice of 1 large orange and 2 scant tablespoons of maraschino liqueur. Continue freezing until mixture is hard. Pack or mold in 4 parts ice and 1 part rock salt for 2 hours.

190   MARASCHINO ICE CREAM II
       (Using hand freezer, or simply packing when molded)

This really fine French ice cream recipe is the basic foundation of almost all the large tribe of liqueur-flavored ice creams. For a formal or informal dinner party, they have no equal. They may be colored, according to fancy or occasion, using vegetable coloring, in orange, water green, vegetable green, sky blue, champagne, lie de vin, etc. For effect, and when molded, they may be served on a colored ice, made as indicated for recipe No. 24, under General Information. The following recipe will easily serve 12 persons. For 6 reduce amount of ingredients accordingly.

As may be seen, it is simple and very easy to make. It may be frozen in hand freezer, or simply frozen in ice and salt.

12 oz. granulated sugar   ½ teaspoon salt
10 egg yolks, slightly beaten   1 quart milk, scalded
              ½ cup maraschino liqueur

Add granulated sugar to beaten egg yolks to which has been added the salt, and beat until foamy. Then very slowly, while beating rapidly and constantly, pour hot milk over sugar-egg mixture. Strain through double cheese cloth, then cook over hot

[111]

water, until mixture thickens, stirring constantly from bottom and sides of the pan. Strain again through double cheesecloth, cool and chill. Just before filling the chilled can of hand freezer, add ½ of the maraschino liqueur, and freeze to a mush, using 3 parts ice and 1 part rock salt. Add, then, the remaining ¼ cup of maraschino liqueur, and continue freezing until solid. Pack or rather mold, using 4 parts ice and 1 part rock salt for 2 long hours.

191   MARRON GLACÉ ICE CREAM I
       (Home method, using hand freezer)

Prepare marrons (chestnuts) as follows:
Shell chestnuts, using about 1 lb., by cutting a ½-inch slit or gash on the flat side. Put chestnuts in a heavy pan; add ½ teaspoon of oil or butter to each cup of chestnuts. Shake over the fire for 5 minutes, then set in a moderate oven (350 deg. F.) for 5 minutes longer. Remove from oven and remove the shells and skins, while still hot, using a sharp knife. Place shelled, skinned chestnuts in a pan, cover with boiling, salted water, and cook gently for 15 to 20 minutes, or steam for 45 minutes. Rice, that is, put through ricer while hot.

5 egg yolks, slightly beaten with	¼ cup pineapple syrup
1½ cups granulated sugar, and	2 cups undiluted evaporated milk
½ teaspoon salt	1½ cups boiled chestnuts, riced
3 cups milk, scalded	

Pour hot scalded milk over sugar-egg mixture very slowly, stirring rapidly and constantly. Cook over hot water, until mixture thickens, stirring constantly. Strain through double cheesecloth. Cool. Add undiluted evaporated milk, alternately with pineapple syrup and riced cooled chestnuts. Freeze in hand freezer, using 3 parts ice and 1 part rock salt, until firm and solid. Pack or mold in 4 parts ice and 1 part rock salt for 2 hours.

You may use the same amount of chestnuts, prepared as follows, Shell chestnuts as indicated above, blanch with enough water to cover, then allow to simmer until nearly tender, or about 35 minutes. Drain and place in a thin sugar syrup made by boiling 1 cup sugar with 2¼ cups water for ten minutes, which may be flavored with 1 teaspoon vanilla extract, maraschino, etc., for each quart of water. In this case use ½ teaspoon. Simmer chestnuts in syrup for 1 hour, lift chestnuts, drain and cool. Then put through ricer. If using this method, omit the pineapple syrup.

Prepared in this way, the chestnuts are then called marrons, in French. They may be preserved, by boiling down the syrup until quite thick, and pouring it boiling over prepared chestnuts, which have been placed in sterilized jars to overflowing, then sealing while hot.

192   MARRON GLACÉ ICE CREAM II
(French method. Hand freezer)

Why custards usually whey or separate is because they are cooked at too high a temperature. Soft custards may curdle when they are cooked for too long a time or are not stirred constantly. Milk that is a little sour may cause curdling of a custard, too. The best way to prevent wheying, separating or curdling is to regulate the temperature and time of cooking of all custards by cooking them over or surrounding them with water slightly below the boiling point (205 up to 210 deg. F.) by removing them from the heat when they are done, and by being sure that milk used in making them is entirely sweet. If a soft custard begins to separate, it should be removed immediately from the heat. The pan containing it may be set in a pan of cold

[113]

*water and the custard may be beaten vigorously to redistribute
the particles of egg and milk solids, using an egg beater, a wire
whisk or a wooden spoon.*

6 egg yolks, slightly beaten	1 teaspoon vanilla extract
½ cup granulated sugar	5 ozs. riced cooked chestnuts
¼ generous teaspoon salt	¼ cup hot water

3 drops almond extract
4 cups evaporated milk, scalded

To the slightly beaten egg yolks, add sugar and salt, then
slowly pour scalded undiluted evaporated milk, stirring rapidly
and constantly. Turn mixture in a double boiler, and cook, stirring constantly, until mixture thickens, and a coating is formed
on the spoon. Strain immediately through double cheese cloth,
then add rice, cooked chestnuts, as indicated for the recipe No.
191 and stirred with the hot water. Mix well and chill. When
cold, add combined flavoring extracts, and freeze in hand freezer,
using 3 parts ice and 1 part rock salt, until firm. Pack or mold
in 4 parts ice and 1 part rock salt for 2 hours.

*Almost any kind of nut meats which have been reduced to a
pulp, using the same amount as chestnuts, may be used instead
of chestnuts if desired. The nuts should be toasted, cooled,
pounded or ground, and mixed with ¼ cup hot water.*

193 MARSHMALLOW PINEAPPLE ICE CREAM
(Refrigerator tray)

18 marshmallows, quartered	⅛ teaspoon salt
¾ cup undiluted evaporated milk	⅓ cup orange juice
	Grated rind of ½ small lemon
½ cup drained, canned pineapple	

1 cup heavy cream, whipped stiffly

Place quartered marshmallows in double boiler, add undiluted evaporated milk and melt over hot water, stirring and cooking until mixture is slightly thickened. Add well-drained crushed pineapple, salt, orange juice and grated lemon rind. Remove from the fire, cool slightly, then fold in the stiffly beaten heavy cream. Chill. Freeze in refrigerator tray, without stirring, for 4 hours.

194 MARSHMALLOW PISTACHIO ICE CREAM
(Refrigerator tray)

Very appropriate for a dessert party. It may be colored, according to occasion: in green, for Saint Patrick's Day; in red, for Saint Valentine's Day; in pink, for Mother's Day, and so on, according to fancy, using vegetable coloring until the desired hue is attained. The contrast of the green pistachio nut against another tender color is very effective.

1 cup rich milk	⅛ teaspoon salt
30 marshmallows, quartered	¼ teaspoon each vanilla and almond extracts, combined
A few drops vegetable coloring	
1 cup heavy cream, whipped stiff	

Scald rich milk (undiluted, evaporated milk may be used), add quartered marshmallows, and heat óver hot water, but do not boil, stirring constantly, until mixture has slightly thickened and marshmallow melted. Remove from hot water, and continue stirring, always in the same direction, until light. Add selected vegetable coloring (see No. 11 "How to Tint Whipped Cream"). Cool, fold stiffly beaten heavy cream, and freeze without stirring, in refrigerator tray for 3 long hours.

195 MARSHMALLOW ICE CREAM SUNDAE

Use either vanilla or chocolate ice cream, or a combination of both. Serve with Fudge Sauce made as follows:

In the top of double boiler cook together until smooth ½ cup hot, undiluted, evaporated milk, or if richness is desired, use heavy cream, and ½ lb. marshmallows, cut into small pieces, using a floured pair of scissors; then add ¼ lb. of bitter or sweet, grated chocolate. You may sprinkle each serving with a little nut meats, chopped fine, if desired.

196 MINT ICE CREAM
(Refrigerator tray)

1 cup fresh milk, scalded	1 egg yolk
¼ cup granulated sugar	1 teaspoon granulated gelatine
1 tablespoon all-purpose flour	2 tablespoons cold water
¼ teaspoon salt	1½ cups heavy cream, whipped
1 teaspoon peppermint flavoring	stiff
extract	Green vegetable coloring

Stir half of the sugar into hot scalded milk. Add salt and flour which has been stirred in a little water, and cook over hot water for 15 minutes, stirring almost constantly. Beat egg yolk with remaining ¼ cup sugar, and very slowly pour the milk mixture over it, stirring rapidly and constantly for 2 long minutes, or until mixture coats the spoon. Add gelatine which has been soaked in cold water for 5 minutes, and stir until entirely dissolved. Cool slightly, add green vegetable coloring. Chill; fold stiffly beaten heavy cream into creamy mixture, then add the peppermint extract (not oil of peppermint). Freeze in refrigerator tray until mushy, then scrape bottom and sides, and beat until smooth. Return to refrigerator tray, freeze again until a little stiff, or about 30 minutes, and repeat the scraping and stirring; then, freeze for 3 hours.

197   MOCHA FUDGE SUNDAE

Use vanilla ice cream, and serve with a Fudge Sauce, made as indicated for recipe No. 195, Marshmallow Ice Cream Sundae, adding 1 generous tablespoon of coffee syrup to the mixture when well-blended. Pour over each serving, and decorate with small rosette of whipped cream, forced through a pastry bag with a small fancy tube.

198   MOCHA ICE CREAM
(Hand freezer)

To a preparation of Vanilla Ice Cream, selecting your favorite recipe, substitute extra strong coffee for milk. Freeze as indicated.

199   MOCK FRENCH ICE CREAM
(Hand freezer)

To a preparation of Vanilla Ice Cream, made as indicated for recipe No. 286 Vanilla Ice Cream, French Method, substitute for 2 egg yolks 1 tablespoon of cornstarch mixed smooth with an equal quantity of cold milk, add to the milk while scalding it, freeze as directed.

200   MYLORD'S VANILLA ICE CREAM

Unmold your favorite Vanilla Ice Cream onto a chilled large platter, and decorate as follows: Surround the base with drained maraschino cherries which have been soaked in 2 tablespoons of kirsch for 15 minutes, interspersed with canned pineapple. sticks, also well drained, and decorate with small dots of unflavored, unsweetened whipped cream, forced through a pastry bag with a small fancy tube.

201 ## NEAPOLITAN ICE CREAM I
(Hand freezer)

A sort of Tutti-Frutti ice cream which is very appropriate for special parties. The flavor is a mingling of caramel nuts and candied fruits. A very rich ice cream.

1 quart thin cream, heated	½ cup chopped pecans
½ cup granulated sugar, caramel-ized	¼ cup chopped candied cherries
2 egg yolks, slightly beaten	¼ cup chopped candied pine-apple
	¼ teaspoon salt

To the heated cream (not boiled, nor scalded) add caramelized sugar, and stir until thoroughly dissolved; then slowly pour in the slightly beaten egg yolks, stirring rapidly until mixture is well-blended. Then stir in salt. Cool, and freeze in hand freezer using 3 parts ice and 1 part rock salt until mushy. Add pecans and candied fruit, stir, and continue freezing until firm and solid. Pack or mold using 4 parts ice and 1 part rock salt for 2½ hours.

202 ## NEAPOLITAN ICE CREAM II
(Hand freezer)

This method is rather complicated, although easy to make. It is a mixture of vanilla, strawberry, and pistachio ice cream, arranged in layers and molded together.

203   **NEAPOLITAN ICE CREAM III**
(Hand freezer)

This method consists of putting 2 kinds of ice cream, either vanilla and strawberry ice cream or chocolate and vanilla ice cream and an ice in layers in a brick mold, then packing in hand pail freezer, using 4 parts ice and 1 part rock salt, for 3 hours.

204   **NOUGAT ICE CREAM I**
(Hand freezer)

In distinguished homes and in rendez-vous of gourmets and connoisseurs this really delicious ice cream is often served.

Nougat, a French candy, is a very favorite and exceedingly attractive sweetmeat, and may be made easily at home.

3 cups rich milk, scalded	5 egg whites, stiffly beaten
1 cup granulated sugar	¼ cup each: blanched almonds,
5 egg yolks, slightly beaten, with	hazelnuts, pistachios and walnuts finely chopped
¾ teaspoon salt	1 teaspoon almond extract
1½ cups heavy cream, whipped stiff	1¾ teaspoons vanilla extract

Make a custard with the 4 first ingredients, operating as indicated for recipe No. 192, Marron Glacé Ice Cream II. Strain while hot through double cheesecloth, then cool. When cold, fold in the stiffly whipped cream, alternately with stiffly beaten egg whites combined with chopped nuts and flavoring. Freeze in hand freezer, using 3 parts ice and 1 part rock salt until firm and solid. Pack, or mold in 4 parts ice and 1 part rock salt.

This delicious ice cream deserves to be unmolded onto a colored ice block made as indicated for recipe No. 24.

205   NOUGAT ICE CREAM II
(Hand freezer)

An economical method of preparing Nougat Ice Cream, which of course has not the fineness, nor the delicacy of the above, is as follows:

To your favorite Vanilla Ice Cream recipe preparation, add when ready to freeze ½ cup of nougat candy (see below) coarsely chopped, equal parts of finely chopped pecan nut meats, ¼ cup toasted, then coarsely chopped hazelnut, and ¼ cup of roasted, chopped peanuts. Then add 3 or 4 drops of vegetable coloring, and freeze in hand freezer, using 3 parts ice and 1 part rock salt, until solid. Pack or mold in 4 parts ice and 1 part rock salt.

To make French Nougat, proceed as follows: (Short way)

1 cup confectioner's sugar   ¼ lb. blanched, chopped almonds

Melt confectioner's sugar in a skillet or heavy pan, stirring constantly. Add blanched almonds which have been chopped very fine, but not ground; stir and pour mixture on slightly oiled marble slab. Fold mixture as it spreads with a large spatula, keeping it constantly in motion. Now, divide mixture into 4 equal parts, and as soon as cool enough to handle, shape in long rolls about 1/3 inch in diameter, keeping the rolls in constant motion until almost cold. When cold, snap in pieces. This is done by holding roll over the sharp edge of a broad-bladed knife and snapping.

The second method is as follows:

1½ cups fine granulated sugar	¼ cup strained honey
1½ cups corn syrup	¼ cup each: pistachio, almonds,
½ cup cold water	hazelnut and walnut, chopped
¼ cup chopped candied cherries	2 egg whites, stiffly beaten

Cook sugar, corn syrup, and water to 300 deg. F., or until a little dropped into cold water immediately becomes brittle. To the stiffly beaten egg whites, add and beat in the strained honey, and when syrup is at the desired point, pour it over the egg white-honey mixture, a small amount at a time, but in a continuous stream, beating hard and rapidly until mixture is quite thick. Then add nut meats which have been combined with the chopped candied cherries. Now turn mixture onto an oiled marble slab, or a large chilled platter, also oiled, keeping in shape with bars until thoroughly firm, which will take several hours. Then cut into oblong pieces, wrap in waxed paper, or use for and as indicated in recipe.

You may color according to fancy, either pale pink, pale or deep green, or both combinations. The vegetable coloring should be added to the hot syrup just before pouring it over egg white-honey mixture.

For a special afternoon occasion, nougat ice cream filled meringues are very appropriate.

206   ORANGE FLOWER ICE CREAM
(Hand freezer)

ORANGE FLOWER ICE CREAM, which is in great favor in Paris today:

Take 1 quart of orange blossoms, from which keep only the petals or flower-leaves. Cover the blossoms, layer by layer with powdered sugar, and allow to stand thus for 1 hour, to mellow, to ripen, and absorb as much sugar as possible, which will mingle with the perfume of the blossoms. Place the orange blossoms in a deep large porcelain vase or container. Then, pour over them 2 quarts of rapidly boiling water and the juice of 2 medium-sized lemons. Cover and let infuse for 2 long hours. Strain through 2 cheese cloths, and use this water to make the ice cream.

It may seem tedious, but how great will be the reward. You may use orange water flower, purchased in any drugstore, if desired, but the fineness will not be the same.

For the rest of the ingredients use your favorite Vanilla Ice Cream recipe, omitting the milk and vanilla, and using the water instead. To freeze, use hand freezer, with 3 parts ice and 1 part rock salt. To pack or mold, use 4 parts ice and 1 part rock salt. Of course you will have to reduce the amount of sugar according to sweetness of orange blossom water, which should be tested before using.

207   ORANGE ICE CREAM I
                (Refrigerator tray)

An economical ice cream in which sugar is substituted by sweetened condensed milk and sugar contained in orange juice.

⅔ cup sweetened condensed milk
½ cup orange juice
2 teaspoons grated orange rind

⅛ teaspoon salt
3 drops orange extract
1 cup heavy cream, whipped to a custard-like consistency

Combine sweetened condensed milk, orange juice and grated orange rind, salt and orange extract. Mix well and chill. Fold in the heavy cream, whipped to a custard-like consistency and freeze in refrigerator tray until mushy (about 40 minutes), remove from refrigerator, scrape bottom and sides, then beat until smooth. Return to refrigerator and freeze for 2½ hours.

208 ORANGE ICE CREAM II
(Hand freezer)

1 cup undiluted evaporated
  milk
1 cup heavy cream
¼ teaspoon salt

2 cups orange juice
⅓ cup (more or less) granulated
  sugar

Combine milk and heavy cream, add slowly to orange juice, stirring constantly, stir in salt and sugar, adding more or less sugar, according to sweetness of orange juice. Chill, then freeze in hand freezer, using 3 parts ice and 1 part rock salt, until firm. Pack or mold in 4 parts ice and 1 part rock salt. A fine result if served with a side dish of crushed berries (any kind) sweetened to taste.

209 ORANGE ICE CREAM III
(Hand freezer)

½ cup boiling water
  Grated rind of 3 large oranges
1½ cups granulated sugar
¼ teaspoon salt
½ cup cold water

1 tablespoon granulated gelatine
3 whole eggs, slightly beaten
2 cups heavy cream, whipped to
  a custard-like consistency
½ cup finely chopped peanuts

2 cups orange juice, mixed with 1 tablespoon lemon juice

Boil grated orange rind and boiling water for 1 minute. Remove from the fire and stir in ½ cup of the sugar and salt. Strain and add cold water. Pour this slowly over the whole eggs, slightly beaten, with the remaining sugar, while stirring constantly. Cook over boiling water, stirring constantly, until mixture thickens. Then, stir in the granulated gelatine which has been softened in a little cold water until dissolved. Then stir in the orange juice mixture. Cool. Add whipped cream and chopped

[123]

peanuts, and freeze in hand freezer, using 3 parts ice and 1 part rock salt, until firm. Pack or mold in 4 parts ice and 1 part rock salt.

210 ORANGE ICE CREAM IV
(Hand freezer)

1½ cups granulated sugar
1½ cups orange juice
2 tablespoons lemon juice
¼ scant teaspoon salt
5 egg yolks, slightly beaten

1½ tablespoons granulated gelatine
2 tablespoons boiling water
1 pint heavy cream, whipped stiff

Combine sugar, orange juice, lemon juice and salt; pour over slightly beaten egg yolks, stirring constantly. Turn mixture in top of double boiler and cook, over hot water until mixture thickens, stirring constantly. Then stir in granulated gelatine, which has been dissolved in boiling water. Strain through double cheesecloth. Chill. Freeze to a mush, using 3 parts ice and 1 part rock salt. Add stiffly beaten heavy cream and freeze until firm. Pack or mold in 4 parts ice and 1 part rock salt for 2 hours.

211 ORANGE ICE CREAM V
(Hand freezer)

A smooth, velvety ice cream, the basis of which is a custard, combined with an orange-sugar-syrup. The shredded candied orange peel should be added only when the mixture has been frozen to a mush.

1 cup cold water
2 cups granulated sugar
2 cups orange juice
1 cup undiluted evaporated milk, scalded
¼ teaspoon salt

2 egg yolks, slightly beaten
1 cup heavy cream, whipped stiff
¼ cup chopped candied orange peel

Stir sugar in cold water until dissolved. Bring to the boiling point, then allow to boil for 5 minutes and add orange juice. Set aside while making the custard. To the scalded undiluted evaporated milk, add slowly the slightly beaten egg yolks with the salt, stirring rapidly and constantly to prevent curdling. Cook custard over hot water, until it begins to thicken, then combine with sugar syrup. Strain through double cheese cloth. Cool, then stir in the stiffly beaten heavy cream. Freeze in hand freezer, using 3 parts ice and 1 part rock salt, until mushy. Add finely chopped candied orange peel and continue freezing until firm and solid. Pack or mold in 4 parts ice and 1 part rock salt for 1 hour.

For effect, you may use the kind of oranges, often found on our market, which are red and called "sanguine."

212 ORANGE ICE CREAM VI
(Refrigerator tray)

⅔ cup sweetened condensed milk

¼ cup strong tea, cold

¼ cup orange juice

⅛ teaspoon salt

1 tablespoon sherry wine

1 cup heavy cream, whipped to a custard-like consistency

Combine milk, tea, orange juice, salt and sherry wine (if sherry extract is used, use same amount as real sherry wine). Blend well and chill. Stir in, very gently, the heavy cream, whipped to a custard-like consistency, and freeze in refrigerator tray until mushy; remove from refrigerator, scrape bottom and sides and beat until smooth. Return to refrigerator and freeze for 3 hours.

213   PEACH GLACÉ MARIANNE

You may use fresh peaches when in season, if desired.

12 halves canned peaches   Ginger syrup
6 rounds of stale cake   Ice cream
       Shredded toasted almonds

Place 2 halves of fresh or well-drained canned peaches, hollow side up, on each side of a round of stale cake (sponge or any other kind of cake). Pour 1 teaspoon of ginger syrup into the hollow of each half. Place a scoop of your favorite ice cream between each peach and on top of the round of cake, and pour over 1 or two tablespoons of drained crushed pineapple.

For a variation, you may serve crushed fresh strawberries, or raspberries, sweetened to taste, instead of crushed pineapple.

214   PEACH ICE CREAM I
(Hand freezer)

¾ cup fresh peach pulp   1½ cups undiluted evaporated
¾ cup granulated sugar   milk, whipped to custard-like
    Juice of ½ lemon   consistency

Put fresh peach through ricer, collecting juice and pulp. There should be ¾ cup. Add sugar, stir, then stir in the lemon juice. Freeze in hand freezer, using 3 parts ice and 1 part rock salt, until mushy; then add whipped milk, and freeze until firm. Pack or mold in 4 parts ice and 1 part rock salt.

215   PEACH ICE CREAM II
(Refrigerator tray)

Very economical method.

½ cup peach jam
½ cup undiluted evaporated
    milk
⅛ teaspoon salt

3 or 4 drops almond extract
¾ cup heavy cream, whipped to
    a custard-like consistency

Add evaporated milk to peach jam and stir until blended, add salt and almond extract, then fold in the heavy cream whipped to a custard-like consistency. Freeze in refrigerator tray until mushy; remove from refrigerator, scrape bottom and sides, then beat until smooth. Return to refrigerator and freeze for 3½ hours.

216   PEACH ICE CREAM III
(Hand freezer or refrigerator tray)

2 cups ripe peach pulp
¼ cup granulated sugar
1⅓ cups (1 can) sweetened con-
    densed milk

¼ teaspoon salt
1 cup undiluted evaporated
    milk
1 cup cold water

1 tablespoon lemon juice
2 tablespoons ground fresh peach kernels

Sprinkle granulated sugar over fresh peach pulp, and let stand for 10 minutes until sugar is dissolved. Combine sweetened condensed milk, salt and undiluted evaporated milk and water; stir in peach pulp mixture, lemon juice and ground peach kernels. Freeze in hand freezer, using 3 parts ice and 1 part rock salt, until firm and solid. Pack or mold in 4 parts ice and 1 part rock salt for 2 hours.

217 **PEACH ICE CREAM IV**
(Hand freezer or refrigerator tray)

As a rule the average peaches (fresh) require about ¼ cup sugar for every 2 cups of pulp when sweetened condensed milk is used.

⅔ cup sweetened condensed milk
½ cup cold water
⅛ teaspoon salt

1 generous cup fresh peach pulp
¼ cup granulated sugar
1 cup heavy cream, whipped to a custard-like consistency

Combine all the above ingredients, which have been chilled, and freeze in refrigerator tray until mushy. Remove from refrigerator and scrape bottom and sides, then beat until smooth. Return to tray and continue freezing for 3 long hours.

218 **PEACH ICE CREAM V**
(Refrigerator tray)

1½ cups fresh peach pulp
⅓ (more or less) granulated sugar
⅛ teaspoon salt

1 tablespoon lemon juice
1 cup heavy cream, whipped to a custard-like consistency

1¾ cups undiluted evaporated milk
2 tablespoons blanched ground almonds

Sprinkle granulated sugar over peach pulp and allow to stand 5 minutes, then add salt and lemon juice, stir and let stand 5 minutes longer. Combine, very gently, heavy cream which has been whipped to a custard-like consistency, with undiluted evaporated milk, and add to peach pulp mixture with ground blanched almonds. Freeze in refrigerator tray until mushy. Remove from refrigerator and scrape bottom and sides, then beat until smooth. Return to refrigerator and freeze for 3 hours.

219 PEACH ICE CREAM VI
(Hand freezer)

3 cups crushed fresh peach
¼ teaspoon salt
1¾ cups granulated sugar
¼ teaspoon almond extract
1 quart heavy cream, un-whipped
1½ tablespoons lemon juice

To the crushed peach pulp, add salt and sprinkle over sugar and lemon juice combined with almond extract. Let stand 10 minutes, stirring two or three times. Chill. Add unwhipped heavy cream and freeze in hand freezer, using 3 parts ice and 1 part rock salt. Pack or mold in 4 parts ice and 1 part rock salt for 2 hours, to mellow and ripen.

220 PEACH ICE CREAM VII
(Hand freezer)

4 egg whites, stiffly beaten with
¼ teaspoon salt
3 cups undiluted evaporated milk
1 cup canned, sieved peach and juice
½ tablespoon lemon juice
¼ cup peanut brittle (optional)

Combine stiffly beaten egg whites, undiluted evaporated milk and salt very gently, taking your time. Freeze in hand freezer, using equal parts salt and ice, until mushy. Add canned, sieved peach pulp and juice to which has been added lemon juice, (here you may add nut brittle if desired) and continue freezing until firm and solid. Pack or mold in 4 parts ice and 1 part rock salt.

221 PEACH ICE CREAM VIII
(Refrigerator tray)

Another method of making ice cream with canned peaches which is greatly used on the Pacific Coast is made as follows:

1 large can of peaches, drained, and sliced then sieved	½ teaspoon vanilla extract
½ cup granulated sugar	½ teaspoon almond extract
½ tablespoon granulated gelatine	¼ teaspoon salt
	Coloring (vegetable) optional

1 cup heavy cream, whipped stiff

To ¼ cup of sieved canned peaches, add gelatine and let soak for 5 minutes. To the remaining sieved peaches, add sugar and bring to a boil. Add the gelatine-peach mixture and stir until dissolved. Cool, then freeze in refrigerator tray until mushy. Remove from refrigerator, scrape bottom and sides, and beat until smooth. Then add combined flavoring extracts, salt, 1 drop of red vegetable coloring (optional) and fold in stiffly whipped heavy cream. Return to refrigerator and freeze for 3 hours.

Crushed raspberries or strawberries, sweetened to taste and served aside, add to deliciousness of this fine, economical ice cream. Or to serve, you may spoon the ice cream in center of a jelly ring, as follows:

222 PEACH ICE CREAM IN JELLY RING IX

While ice cream is freezing, prepare the following:

¼ teaspoon granulated gelatine	2 egg whites, stiffly beaten
1 tablespoon cold water	1 teaspoon vanilla extract
¼ cup boiling water	Peach ice cream, made as
⅔ cup cream (heavy)	above

¼ cup granulated sugar

Soak gelatine in cold water and dissolve in boiling water; then stir in sugar until thoroughly dissolved. Stir in the heavy cream, and when beginning to stiffen, pour very, very slowly over the stiffly beaten egg whites, beating vigorously all the while until mixture is stiff and holds its peaks, then beat in vanilla extract. Line a chilled ring with the peach ice cream, and fill center with whipped mixture. Pack in 4 parts ice and 1 part rock salt for at least 4 hours, or pack in refrigerator tray, if desired.

A very fine party dessert for which you may use any other kind of ice cream.

223 PEACH MELBA
(Home method)

For each serving take a round of sponge cake; place on it a scoop of Vanilla Ice Cream and top with a preserved or canned peach. Pour over a tablespoon or two of Melba sauce, garnish with small rosettes of whipped cream, forced through a pastry bag with a fancy tube.

MELBA SAUCE I.—

1 cup canned or fresh raspberries   ¼ cup granulated sugar

Rub berries through a sieve to remove the seeds; add sugar and cook to a heavy syrup, stirring frequently to prevent scorching.

MELBA SAUCE II.—

1 cup of pulp and juice of fresh raspberries, rubbed through a sieve to remove the seeds	⅛ teaspoon salt ½ tablespoon arrowroot or corn-starch
1 small glass jar currant jelly	1 tablespoon cold water
½ cup granulated sugar	¼ teaspoon lemon juice

Combine currant jelly, sugar and pulp and juice of berries. Place over direct flame and bring to boiling point (210 deg. F.). Add salt, arrowroot or cornstarch, and cook, stirring constantly, until mixture thickens and becomes clear. Strain through double cheesecloth. Cool.

Pears may be prepared in this delicious way.

224   **PEACH SUNDAE**
(Serve 6)

1 cup granulated sugar	6 canned or fresh peaches
½ cup cold water	⅛ teaspoon almond extract
	Peach ice cream

Combine sugar and water in a large skillet, and off the fire, and stir until sugar is dissolved. Boil 5 minutes, add sliced peaches (if fresh peaches are used, peel before slicing, discarding the stones) to hot syrup and allow to simmer for 6 to 8 minutes, occasionally stirring very carefully to prevent scorching. Remove peaches with a skimmer to individual or large platter. Now boil down syrup in the skillet until thick, add flavoring (more or less, according to taste), and pour over the peaches. Chill. Serve over peach ice cream.

If a piquancy is desired, you may add to the syrup, before boiling down, ¼ teaspoon ground ginger.

225   **PEANUT BRITTLE ICE CREAM**

Grind 1 cup (when ground) peanut brittle, sift, and add to your favorite Vanilla ice cream recipe.

226 PEANUT ICE CREAM
(Hand freezer)

4 whole eggs, slightly beaten with	¼ teaspoon salt
	1 pint unwhipped heavy cream
1 cup granulated sugar	¾ teaspoon vanilla extract
2 cups fresh milk, scalded	¼ scant teaspoon almond extract
1 cup peanut butter	

Break whole eggs in top of double boiler, and beat slightly with sugar and salt. Gradually add hot scalded milk, stirring rapidly and constantly. Cook over hot water, until mixture begins to thicken. Remove from hot water, stir in unwhipped heavy cream; strain through a double cheesecloth. Cool. Add flavoring extracts which have been combined and peanut butter. Freeze in hand freezer, using 3 parts ice and 1 part rock salt, until firm. Pack or mold, using 4 parts ice and 1 part rock salt, for 2 hours. *You may use roasted, ground peanuts instead of peanut butter if desired. They should be sifted.*

227 PEPPERMINT ICE CREAM I

Substitute mint flavoring (not oil of peppermint) for vanilla to your favorite Vanilla Ice Cream recipe, and color to the desired hue, using green vegetable coloring. Freeze and pack as directed.

Hollowed-out melon shells (cantaloupe, honey-dew or watermelon) make perfect ice cream dishes. They may also be used for mousses, parfaits or sherbets. Pineapple shells are pretty and appealing, too.

228 PEPPERMINT ICE CREAM II
(Hand freezer)

1 cup undiluted evaporated milk   1 pint heavy cream, whipped
1 pound peppermint candy   stiff
¼ teaspoon salt

Pour undiluted evaporated milk over peppermint candy. Let stand overnight in refrigerator. Next day pour mixture through double cheesecloth to remove undissolved particles of candy; fold in the heavy cream which has been whipped stiff with the salt, and freeze in hand freezer, using 3 parts ice and 1 part rock salt, until firm. Mold in melon mold. Pack 2 hours in 4 parts ice and 1 part rock salt.

The mixture should be velvety, smooth, and light to melt in the mouth.

PHILADELPHIA ICE CREAM

The so-called Philadelphia ice cream usually does not contain anything else but light cream, 1 cup of sugar for each quart of cream, desired flavoring, and a few grains salt. Philadelphia ice cream may be frozen either in the refrigerator tray, or by hand freezer, following the usual directions pertaining to each method, and using 3 parts ice to 1 part rock salt, if hand freezer method is applied.

VARIATIONS:

229

Vanilla ice cream: use 1½ generous teaspoons of vanilla extract.

230

Chocolate ice cream: to a vanilla ice cream, add 2 squares grated chocolate.

231

Pecan ice cream: to a recipe of vanilla ice cream, add 1 cup finely chopped or coarsely ground pecan meats.

232

Pistachio ice cream: to a vanilla ice cream recipe, flavored with almond extract (1 scant teaspoon), instead of vanilla, add 1 cup finely chopped or coarsely ground pistachio nut meats, and color to the desired hue, with a few drops green vegetable coloring.

233

Strawberry ice cream: to a vanilla ice cream recipe, add 2 cups strawberry pulp, sieved and sweetened to taste.

234

Raspberry ice cream: proceed as directed for strawberry ice cream, substituting raspberry pulp for strawberry.

235

Peach ice cream: to a vanilla ice cream recipe, substitute ½ generous teaspoon almond extract for vanilla, add 1 tablespoon lemon juice and 1½ cups fresh peach pulp.

236   PINEAPPLE ICE CREAM
(Hand freezer)

2 cups crushed canned pineapple   ½ cup granulated sugar
   (juice and pulp)   ⅛ teaspoon salt
     2½ cans undiluted evaporated milk, or thin cream

Combine pineapple and undiluted evaporated milk, stir and allow to stand 30 minutes. Strain, through double cheese cloth, add sugar and freeze in hand freezer, using 3 parts ice and 1 part rock salt until solid. Pack or mold in 4 parts ice and 1 part rock salt for 1 hour.

237   PINEAPPLE ICE CREAM SUNDAE

Pour over either pineapple or vanilla ice cream, the following sauce:

6 tablespoons granulated sugar   ⅛ teaspoon salt
1½ cups crushed pineapple and   ⅔ cup nut meats
   juice

Combine sugar and pineapple in top of double boiler and cook, over direct fire for 3 long minutes, stirring constantly. Remove from the fire, and allow to cool, but do not chill. Pour 1 or two tablespoons of this over each serving and sprinkle with nut meats.

238   PINEAPPLE SURPRISE

This delicious dessert is the creation of Chef Hunziker, formerly Executive Chef of the S/S Leviathan. Very appropriate for an intimate party.

[136]

Scoop out a fresh pineapple. Chop the pulp and mix with fresh small strawberries (wild strawberries, if available) which have been soaked in port wine for 15 minutes. Garnish the pineapple shell as follows: A layer of pineapple-strawberry mixture, then a layer of vanilla ice cream or a vanilla mousse No. 355, then a sprinkling of maraschino liqueur, or rum or brandy, or any of your favorite liqueur, using for each sprinkling a teaspoon of the chosen liqueur. Repeat until pineapple shell is full. Chill for several hours with the lid on the pineapple shell, before serving.

239   PINEAPPLE ICE CREAM SUZETTE

To your favorite vanilla ice cream, add, when cream mixture has been frozen to a mush, the following:—Cut 3 slices of canned pineapple into small cubes; sprinkle with 2 tablespoons of maraschino liqueur, the juice of a small orange and 1 teaspoon of ground almonds. Add to mushy mixture, and continue freezing until solid. Pack or mold in 4 parts ice and 1 part rock salt for 2 long hours.

240   PINEAPPLE ICE CREAM TARTLETS

Fill baked individual tartlet shells with a scoop of pineapple ice cream, cover with 1 tablespoon of canned, drained crushed pineapple, and cover the entire surface with a meringue made of 2 egg whites and 4 tablespoons of sugar, and brown quickly in a very hot oven (450 deg. F.). Serve immediately.

241 PISTACHIO ICE CREAM I
(Hand freezer)

If you follow the directions exactly, you will have a pistachio
ice cream which will be mellow, and light.

1 cup blanched ground pistachio   ¾ cup granulated sugar
   nuts   1 quart heavy cream
1 generous teaspoon heavy cream   1 tablespoon spinach juice, or a
1 scant teaspoon grated lemon   few drops of green vegetable
   rind   coloring
8 egg yolks, slightly beaten

Grind the pistachio nut meats three times, combine with the
teaspoon of cream, more or less, and grated rind of lemon. Mix
to a paste, adding more cream if necessary, so as to obtain a soft,
yet solid paste. Place this paste in a large saucepan, or still better
in top of a double boiler, and pour all at once, the slightly
beaten egg yolks with the sugar. The flame should be low, the
water in bottom of double boiler up to boiling point. Stir con-
tinually, while cooking until mixture is thoroughly blended, then,
gradually pour in the unbeaten heavy cream, stirring constantly.
Bring to the boiling point, and cook until mixture coats the
spoon. Remove from hot water and strain through double
cheesecloth. Cool, add either spinach juice or vegetable coloring
to the desired hue, and freeze in hand freezer, using 3 parts ice
and 1 part rock salt, until solid. Pack or mold in 4 parts ice and
1 part rock salt. *This is the French method of making Pistachio
ice cream. In it you have the full flavor of the nuts, plus the entire nutrient power, plus delicateness, fineness and mellowness.*

242   PISTACHIO ICE CREAM II
(Short method)

To your favorite vanilla ice cream recipe, omit vanilla, add 1 teaspoon almond extract, ¼ cup ground pistachio nuts and a few drops of vegetable coloring. Freeze as directed.

243   PISTACHIO ICE CREAM BISQUE III

When the creamy mixture of your favorite pistachio ice cream recipe has been brought to a mush, add ½ cup each of ground macaroons, sieved, chopped, or rather ground, almonds and peanuts. Freeze as indicated until solid, and pack or mold in 4 parts ice and 1 part rock salt.

244   PISTACHIO FRUIT ICE CREAM IV
(Hand freezer)

Expensive, yes!, but how delicious. The basis of this frozen dessert is a custard which should be cooked just to the point of soft custard, over simmering water.

5 egg yolks, slightly beaten with	½ teaspoon grated lemon rind
½ teaspoon salt, and	1½ cups chestnut purée (recipe No. 192)
1½ cups granulated sugar	
3 cups undiluted evaporated milk or fresh milk, scalded	½ teaspoon almond extract
	1 teaspoon vanilla extract
2 cups heavy cream, unwhipped	¾ cup mixed in equal parts of finely chopped candied or crystallized fruit

To the slightly beaten egg yolk mixture, add, very slowly, the scalded evaporated milk or fresh milk, stirring gently, but thoroughly and constantly. Cook over simmering water, not boiling, until mixture begins to coat the spoon. Strain immediately through double cheesecloth, then cool. Add combined almond extract, vanilla and grated lemon rind, and mix well. Add then, the finely chopped, not ground, candied or crystallized fruit, alternately with the unwhipped heavy cream, which has been colored to the desired hue with green vegetable coloring or spinach juice. Freeze in hand freezer, using 3 parts ice and 1 part rock salt until solid. Pack or mold in 4 parts ice and 1 part rock salt for 2 hours.

245 PRALINE ICE CREAM I
(French method. Short cut)

To your favorite Vanilla Ice Cream recipe, add, when mushy, 1 cup ground, sifted stale macaroons and 2 generous tablespoons of Nougat, made as indicated for recipe No. 205, using either method, and freeze until solid. Pack or mold in 4 parts ice and 1 part rock salt for 2 hours to mellow.

246 PRALINE ICE CREAM II
(Hand freezer)

1 quart thin cream or undiluted evaporated milk	¾ cup granulated sugar, caramelized
¼ teaspoon salt	1 cup blanched, roasted ground almonds
1 teaspoon vanilla extract	
¼ teaspoon almond extract	

Combine thin cream, or undiluted evaporated milk, salt, vanilla and almond extract, and mix well. Caramelize granulated sugar in the usual way and pour over the combined milk mixture, slowly, while stirring constantly. Freeze in hand freezer, using 3 parts ice and 1 part rock salt until mushy; then add blanched, roasted ground almonds, and freeze until solid. Pack or mold in 4 parts ice and 1 part rock salt for 2 hours.

247   PRALINE ICE CREAM III
(Hand freezer)

To your favorite Vanilla Ice Cream recipe, add 1 cup of Praline Powder, made as indicated for recipe No. 14, "General Information", using pecan nut meats for equal amount of sugar. Freeze as directed. To make an ice cream Praline Sundae, sprinkle each serving with a little Praline Powder, or combine Praline Powder with whipped cream and force through a pastry bag, forming fancy designs.

248   PRUNE ALMOND ICE CREAM I
(Refrigerator tray)

1 cup prune pulp and juice, scalded	¼ cup granulated sugar
¼ cup granulated sugar	1 teaspoon granulated gelatine
1 tablespoon all-purpose flour	2 tablespoons cold water
⅛ teaspoon salt	1½ cups heavy cream, whipped
1 egg yolk, beaten with	½ cup blanched ground almonds

2 tablespoons lemon juice

To the scalded pulp and prune juice, add ¼ cup granulated sugar combined with flour and salt, a small amount at a time, stirring briskly and constantly until smooth. Then, cook over boiling water for 15 minutes, stirring almost constantly. Cool a little, and slowly pour over beaten egg and second ¼ cup of granulated sugar. Return to hot water and cook 3 minutes, or until mixture coats the spoon, stirring constantly. Add immediately the gelatine soaked with cold water, and stir until dissolved. Chill. Lastly add the stiffly beaten heavy cream, alternately with ground almonds and lemon juice. Freeze in refrigerator tray, until beginning to become mushy, remove from refrigerator and scrape bottom and sides, then beat until smooth. Return to refrigerator and freeze again until mushy, and repeat scraping and beating, then freeze for 3 hours.

249   ## PRUNE ICE CREAM II
(Hand freezer)

A richer prune ice cream:

1 cup of washed, picked prunes	1¼ cups heavy cream, whipped stiff
1½ cups hot water	
1 cup granulated sugar	¼ scant teaspoon salt
4 tablespoons lemon juice	½ cup ground peanuts

Wash and pick the prunes, and soak in hot water for 30 minutes. Cook in the same water until prunes are soft. Remove stones and put fruit pulp through ricer. Combine prune pulp, sugar, lemon juice, salt and mix well. Then fold in the stiffly beaten heavy cream. Freeze in hand freezer to a mush, using 3 parts ice and 1 part rock salt; add ground peanuts, which have been roasted before being ground, and continue freezing until solid. Pack or mold in 4 parts ice and 1 part rock salt.

250   ## PRUNE ICE CREAM III
(Hand freezer or refrigerator tray)

Another rich prune ice cream:

Prepare enough whole prunes as indicated for recipe No. 249, Prune Ice Cream II, so as to have 2 cups pulp. Remove the pit, and put prunes through food chopper using a fine blade. Then continue as follows:

1 cup undiluted evaporated milk	1 tablespoon cold water
2 cups prune pulp	4 eggs, slightly beaten
½ cup granulated sugar	½ teaspoon vanilla extract
1 teaspoon granulated gelatine	¼ teaspoon almond extract
¼ teaspoon salt	1 cup heavy cream

Scald milk, stir in sugar, then add soaked granulated gelatine. Stir until gelatine is dissolved, then pour hot mixture over slightly beaten eggs, stirring briskly, until mixture begins to coat the spoon. Strain through double cheesecloth. Chill. Then add all the remaining ingredients. Freeze in hand freezer, using 3 parts ice and 1 part rock salt, until solid. Pack or mold in 4 parts ice and 1 part rock salt for 2 hours.

You may freeze in refrigerator tray, scraping once, when creamy mixture is mushy, then freeze for 3 hours.

251 PUMPKIN ICE CREAM COUNTRY STYLE I
(Hand freezer)

8 egg yolks, slightly beaten	½ teaspoon each of ground cinnamon, nutmeg and ginger
1 cup cooked pumpkin, sieved	
1 cup granulated sugar	4 cups undiluted evaporated milk
¼ teaspoon salt	

To the slightly beaten egg yolks, add the cooked, cooled, sieved pumpkin, sugar and spices and blend thoroughly. Cook over hot water, stirring constantly, until mixture coats the spoon. Cool. Strain through a fine sieve, then freeze in hand freezer, using 3 parts ice and 1 part rock salt, until solid. Pack or mold in 4 parts ice and 1 part rock salt.

252   PUMPKIN ICE CREAM II
(Hand freezer)

In the following recipe the fine flavor of the pumpkin is much
enhanced by the addition of ground nutmeg.

1 egg yolk stiffly beaten
1 can of pumpkin
½ cup cold milk
¾ cup granulated sugar
¼ teaspoon ground cinnamon
⅛ teaspoon salt

1 egg white, stiffly beaten
1 tablespoon powdered sugar
1 cup heavy cream, whipped to
a custard-like consistency
1 teaspoon vanilla extract
⅛ teaspoon ground clove

Into the pumpkin pulp, placed in a large mixing bowl, stir in
the slightly beaten egg yolk which has been stirred into the milk,
combined with vanilla extract, cinnamon, cloves and salt. Blend
well. Then stir in the granulated sugar until dissolved, and add
the stiffly beaten egg white, into which has been folded,
meringue-like, the tablespoon powdered sugar. Lastly stir in the
heavy cream, which has been whipped to a custard-like consistency. Freeze in hand freezer, using 3 parts ice and 1 part rock
salt, until solid. Pack or mold in 4 parts ice and 1 part rock salt
for 2 long hours.

253   PUMPKIN CARAMEL ICE CREAM
(Hand freezer)

1 quart thin cream, scalded, or
3 can undiluted evaporated
milk, also scalded
1¼ cups brown sugar, caramelized
1 teaspoon ground cinnamon
½ teaspoon ground nutmeg

½ teaspoon ground ginger
½ teaspoon ground cloves
¼ teaspoon salt
½ teaspoon vanilla extract
2 whole eggs, slightly beaten
1 can (2 cups) pumpkin

Stir in the scalded thin cream or undiluted evaporated milk, the caramelized brown sugar combined with spices, salt and vanilla extract. Blend well. Gradually pour slightly beaten eggs over milk mixture, stirring briskly and constantly. Place over hot water and let simmer, stirring constantly, until mixture slightly coats the spoon. Strain, add pumpkin and chill. Freeze in hand freezer, using 3 parts ice and 1 part rock salt, until solid. Pack or mold in 4 parts ice and 1 part salt for 2 long hours.

If for a special occasion, such as Thanksgiving, or Labor Day, you may pack, or rather mold in individual molds, if desired. You may, when creamy mixture is mushy, add 1 cup of nut meats, then continue freezing until solid.

254   QUINCE ICE CREAM
(Hand freezer)

2 cups fresh milk, scalded	¼ teaspoon salt
1 tablespoon all-purpose flour	1 tablespoon vanilla extract
1 cup granulated sugar	2 cups undiluted evaporated
2 egg yolks, slightly beaten	milk
2 cups quince pulp and juice	

Pour slowly scalded milk over slightly beaten egg yolks which have been beaten with combined flour, sugar and salt. Cook over hot water for 10 minutes, or until mixture has a curdled appearance, which will disappear in freezing. Cool, add vanilla, undiluted milk and quince, and blend thoroughly. Then chill. Freeze in hand freezer, using 3 parts ice and 1 part rock salt until solid and firm. Pack or mold in 4 parts ice and 1 part rock salt for 2 long hours.

You may, when creamy mixture is mushy, add ½ cup coarsely chopped nut meats, if desired, and continue freezing until mixture is solid. Pack or mold as indicated.

255   RAISIN CHOCOLATE ICE CREAM
(Refrigerator tray)

1¼ cups milk scalded
⅓ cup granulated sugar
1 tablespoon cornstarch
2 squares bitter chocolate, grated
2 egg whites, stiffly beaten

¼ cup cold milk
2 egg yolks, unbeaten
1 teaspoon vanilla extract
1 cup seedless raisins
1 cup heavy cream, whipped to a custard consistency

⅛ teaspoon salt

Combine sugar, cornstarch, grated chocolate and moisten with cold milk; then add unbeaten egg yolks, one at a time, beating well after each addition. Combine this mixture with scalded milk, stirring constantly, over hot water, until mixture is smooth and slightly coats the spoon. Remove from the hot water and cool a little, then stir in the vanilla extract. Strain. Chill. Boil seedless raisins for 5 minutes, or until plump, in enough water to cover; drain and chill. Then add them to the chilled custard, alternately with the heavy cream which has been whipped to a custard-like consistency. Pour in refrigerator tray, and freeze, stirring every 30 minutes during the first hour. Then remove from the refrigerator and scrape again, then beat until smooth. Return to refrigerator and freeze for 3 hours.

256   RAISIN NUT ICE CREAM
(Short cut. Hand freezer)

Put 1 cup washed, sponged seedless raisins through food chopper, alternately with 1 cup nut meats (any kind), and add to your favorite Vanilla Ice Cream recipe before freezing. The recipe should be a hand freezer one, as in the refrigerator, the mixture would require too much scraping.

257   RASPBERRY ICE CREAM I
            (Hand freezer)

The pressed juice of raspberries, red currants or blackberries makes a cooling and refreshing beverage or "shrub" when added to some effervescent water. Aside from making delicious desserts, raspberries are very popular for ice cream.

Their chemical composition is approximately that of straw-berries.

2 quarts fresh raspberries
2 cups granulated sugar
¼ scant teaspoon salt

3 pints thin cream, or equal amount of undiluted evaporated milk (3 cups)

Wash, hull and coarsely crush the raspberries, sprinkle with sugar and salt, and allow to stand for 2 hours in a warm place. Then mash again, strain. Freeze chilled thin cream or undiluted evaporated milk to a soft mush, then gradually add raspberry juice and continue freezing, using 4 parts ice and 2 parts rock salt, until firm and solid. Pack or mold in 3 parts ice and 2 parts rock salt for 2 hours to mellow.

258   RASPBERRY ICE CREAM II
             (Hand freezer)

This method results in a smooth, light and velvety ice cream. The amount of sugar depends on the acidity of the fruit.

1 quart fresh raspberries
1 cup granulated sugar
1½ cups heavy cream

4 egg whites, stiffly beaten
¼ teaspoon salt
4 or 5 drops almond extract
1½ cups undiluted evaporated milk

[147]

Wash, pick over, hull, and mush the raspberries. Sprinkle with granulated sugar, cover and allow to stand 3 hours in a warm place; then squeeze through a double thickness of cheesecloth. Combine heavy cream, undiluted evaporated milk, stiffly beaten egg whites and salt, and freeze to a mush; then add strained fruit juice and continue freezing, using 3 parts ice and 1 part rock salt until solid. Pack or mold, using 4 parts ice and 1 part rock salt for 2 hours.

You may, when creamy mixture is frozen to a mush, add with the fruit juice ½ cup of blanched, coarsely chopped almonds.

259   RASPBERRY ICE CREAM III
(Hand freezer or refrigerator tray)

A calamity which has proven to be a blessing in disguise is sour milk or cream. They have a magical way with almost any kind of foods, meats, fish, vegetables, breads and desserts, hot, cold or frozen ones, turning them into perfectly delectable creations.

1 pint box fresh raspberries	2 cups heavy sour cream,
½ cup cold water	whipped stiff
½ cup granulated sugar	⅛ teaspoon salt
½ teaspoon grated lemon rind	

Wash, pick over, hull, coarsely mush raspberries and combine with cold water and sugar in a saucepan. Cook for 5 minutes. Strain immediately through double cheesecloth. Chill, stir in salt and lemon rind, then fold in heavy sour cream whipped stiff. Freeze in refrigerator tray until mushy. Remove, scrape bottom and beat until smooth. Return to refrigerator tray and freeze 3 hours.

You may use half raspberries and half strawberries if desired. You may, also, add ¼ cup ground roasted peanuts, after mixture has been scraped and beaten.

260 ## RASPBERRY ICE CREAM IV
(Hand freezer)

Did you ever try to mold ice cream—any kind of ice cream—in a flower bouquet, a fruit cluster, or in the shape of a fish, a hen on a nest, etc.? This looks like professional caterer's art. These molds are cheap and are found in most first class home furnishing stores, hardware stores and department stores.

½ cup granulated sugar (more or less, according to acidity of fruit)

3 cups washed, picked over, hulled fresh raspberries

1⅓ cups (1 can) sweetened condensed milk

1 cup undiluted evaporated milk or thin cream

1 teaspoon lemon juice

1½ cups cold water and ¼ teaspoon salt

Sprinkle sugar over coarsely crushed fruit and allow to stand for 2 hours, stirring occasionally. Combine sweetened condensed milk, undiluted evaporated milk or thin cream, water and salt. Chill. Add unstrained fruit mixture, and freeze in hand freezer, using 3 parts ice and 1 part rock salt, until solid. Pack or mold in 4 parts ice and 1 part rock salt for 2 hours.

IMPORTANT.—*All the different methods of making Strawberry ice cream may be applied for raspberries.*

261 ## RASPBERRY ICE CREAM V
(Refrigerator tray)

1¼ cups undiluted evaporated milk scalded, then chilled and whipped to a custard-like consistency

½ cup granulated sugar, caramelized

1 package lemon flavored gelatine

2 egg yolks, slightly beaten

1 cup heavy cream, whipped to a custard-like consistency

2 egg whites, stiffly beaten

¼ teaspoon salt

1 cup crushed fresh raspberries

6 slices canned pineapple, drained

2 cups boiling water

Dissolve lemon-flavored gelatine in boiling water in which caramelized sugar has been added and well-blended; then pour gelatine mixture over slightly beaten egg yolks, slowly, while stirring briskly. To this add whipped evaporated milk (custard-like consistency), alternately with combined whipped heavy cream to custard-like consistency, and stiffly beaten egg whites, to which salt has been added. Lastly fold in unstrained crushed raspberries. Freeze in refrigerator tray until mushy, then remove, scrape bottom and sides, then beat until smooth. Return to refrigerator tray and freeze for 3 hours. Serve each scooping over chilled pineapple slices.

262 RED CURRANT AND RASPBERRY
ICE CREAM
(Hand freezer)

2 lbs. red currants, stemmed
1 pint box raspberries
1 cup granulated sugar

1 pint heavy cream, whipped stiff
¼ teaspon salt

½ teaspoon vanilla extract

Stem red currants, wash, drain. Wash, pick over, hull raspberries and combine both fruit, then crush coarsely. Sprinkle sugar over the fruit and let stand 1 hour; then turn mixture into an enamel saucepan, cover and cook over a very low flame for 10 minutes, stirring occasionally to prevent scorching. Remove from the fire and squeeze through double cheesecloth. To this add the following sugar syrup:

½ cup granulated sugar   ¼ cup cold water

Stir sugar into cold water until dissolved; bring to boiling point, then boil 5 minutes. Remove and stir into fruit mixture and strain again through double cheese cloth. Chill, then fold in the heavy cream, whipped stiff with salt and vanilla extract, and freeze in hand freezer, using 3 parts ice and 1 part rock salt until solid. Pack or mold in 4 parts ice and 1 part rock salt for 2 hours to mellow.

263 ROSE ICE CREAM
(Hand freezer)

4 cups light cream or evaporated milk
3 cups heavy cream, unwhipped
1 cup fresh milk
1 cup granulated sugar

1¾ teaspoons rose extract
¼ generous teaspoon salt
1 or two drops red vegetable coloring

Mix all the ingredients thoroughly and freeze in hand freezer, using 3 parts ice and 1 part rock salt. Pack or mold in 4 parts ice and 1 part rock salt for 2 hours to ripen and mellow.

264 SAINT HELENA ICE CREAM

A very tempting way to serve two kinds of ice cream.

On each individual plate, place 1 tablespoon of vanilla ice cream and 1 tablespoon of raspberry ice cream, scooped with a spoon dipped in hot water, and the ice cream scooped in egg-like shape. Decorate with small rosettes of whipped cream forced through a pastry bag with a small fancy tube, and separate the two ice creams with fancy chocolate or vanilla wafers.

265 SALLY'S ICE CREAM DELIGHTS
(Refrigerator tray)

Line the bottom and sides of freezing tray with lady fingers, or vanilla or chocolate wafers; then cover with a recipe of your favorite refrigerator raspberry ice cream or strawberry ice cream, which does not require scraping or stirring. Repeat until tray is full, finishing with a layer of lady fingers or wafers, and allow to freeze for 3 hours. When ready to serve, unmold, or rather invert tray over a serving platter, and garnish with designs of colored whipped cream, forced through a pastry bag with small fancy tube.

Almost any kind of ice cream may be prepared this way.

266   SHERRY WINE ICE CREAM
(Refrigerator tray)

A very appropriate Saint Patrick's Day frozen dessert. The milk and water should be brought to simmering point (it should not boil), then poured over slightly beaten egg yolks. The sherry wine may be sweet or dry. Any other kind of sweet white dessert wine may be substituted if desired. If recipe is used for any other occasion or festive party, the color scheme may be changed, but the hue should be a tender one if the effect is desired. The lady fingers should be placed in the freezing tray after the scraping and beating of the mush mixture has been done and before returning mixture into the tray. For more effect the frozen mass may be unmolded over a block of ice made as indicated for recipe No. 24.

½ cup boiling water
⅔ cup sweetened condensed milk
2 egg yolks, slightly beaten
⅛ teaspoon salt

2 egg whites, stiffly beaten
1 cup heavy cream, whipped stiff
Vegetable coloring (2 drops)
Lady fingers, split open

¼ cup good sherry wine

To the boiling water just removed from the fire, add the sweetened condensed milk, and blend thoroughly. Immediately pour over slightly beaten egg yolks, beating briskly and rapidly to prevent curdling. Cool. When cold, add sherry wine and salt; then add combined stiffly beaten egg whites and stiffly whipped heavy cream which has been colored to the desired hue with coloring. Freeze in refrigerator tray until mushy. Remove from refrigerator, scrape bottom and sides, then beat for 2 minutes or until smooth. Now line bottom and sides of tray with split open lady fingers, round side down, cutting fingers in two for the sides. Pour—you should operate rapidly—a layer of the creamy mushy mixture over lady fingers, smoothing evenly; repeat until tray is full, seeing to it that top, which will become the bottom, is of lady fingers, round side up. Freeze 3 long hours.

267   SNOW ICE CREAM
(Hand freezer or refrigerator tray)

1 cup heavy cream	⅛ teaspoon salt
2 cups rich milk, or undiluted evaporated milk	¾ teaspoon vanilla extract
	½ teaspoon lemon extract
1 cup powdered sugar	3 egg whites, stiffly beaten

Combine heavy cream, rich milk or evaporated milk, powdered sugar, salt and flavoring extracts; stir and chill. Freeze in hand freezer, using 3 parts ice and 1 part salt, to a mush. Then, add stiffly beaten egg whites and finish freezing to a solid mass. Pack or mold in 4 parts ice and 1 part rock salt for 2 hours. The above recipe may be frozen in refrigerator tray. If so, when mixture is mushy, scrape bottom and sides then beat for 2 minutes or until smooth, add then stiffly beaten egg whites and freeze for 3 hours.

268   SPANISH MANDARINES (TANGERINE)

A delicious way to serve ice cream.

Arrange on individual chilled plates (dessert plates) 4 teaspoons of vanilla ice cream, scooped with a teaspoon which has been dipped into hot water, and shaping cream into small bird's eggs. Top each small egg with a section of tangerine which has been dipped into maraschino liqueur, and decorate with whipped cream forced through a pastry bag with a small fancy tube.

269 SPUMONE ICE CREAM
(Hand freezer or refrigerator tray)

1½ cups fresh milk, scalded
⅔ cup granulated sugar
2 tablespoons cornstarch
⅛ teaspoon salt
½ cup fresh cold milk
3 egg yolks slightly beaten with

1 egg white
2 egg whites, stiffly beaten with a little of the sugar
1 teaspoon vanilla extract
1 cup heavy cream, whipped to a custard-like consistency
⅓ cup cocoa

Stir in the hot scalded milk the sugar, reserving 2 tablespoons. Combine and blend cornstarch, salt and ½ cup of milk, add to the scalded milk and cook, stirring constantly, until mixture coats the spoon. Add then the slightly beaten egg yolks and egg white, slowly and gradually, stirring briskly and constantly. Return to hot water and continue cooking for 5 short minutes. Remove from hot water, cool then chill. When thoroughly chilled, add stiffly beaten egg whites combined with heavy cream, which has been whipped to a custard-like consistency with the vanilla extract. Freeze in refrigerator tray until mushy; remove from refrigerator, scrape bottom and sides, then beat in the cocoa. Return to tray and freeze for 3 hours.

270   STRAWBERRY (Fresh) CHARLOTTE

*A very tempting dessert, and easy to make during the straw-
berry season.*

Lady fingers	1 pint fresh strawberries
1 pint vanilla ice cream	2 tablespoons kirsch liqueur
1 cup heavy cream, whipped stiff	

Have ready the fresh strawberries which have been washed,
picked over, hulled and chilled. Combine vanilla ice cream and
whipped heavy cream, then mix with the prepared strawberries
which have been soaked in kirsch for 10 minutes. Line a charlotte mold with lady fingers, and fill up with the mixture. Chill
for 2 hours. When ready to serve, decorate with whipped cream
flavored with a little raspberry juice and part of the kirsch used
for soaking the berries.

271   STRAWBERRY ICE CREAM I
                (Hand freezer)

IMPORTANT.—*All the different methods of making ice cream
with raspberries may be applied to strawberries, substituting
strawberries for raspberries.*

3 cups thin cream or undiluted evaporated milk	Syrup from canned strawberries
	Sugar as necessary
1/8 teaspoon salt	Red vegetable coloring

Flavor thin cream or evaporated milk with enough syrup to
make it sweet according to taste, adding more sugar if necessary.
Add salt and a few drops of red vegetable coloring and freeze
in hand freezer, using 5 parts ice and 2 parts rock salt until
solid. Pack or mold in 4 parts ice and 1 part rock salt.

[155]

272   STRAWBERRY ICE CREAM II
(Refrigerator tray)

1 pint fresh ripe strawberries washed, picked over, and hulled
½ cup granulated sugar
3 tablespoons quick-cooking tapioca

¼ teaspoon salt
6 tablespoons light corn syrup
2 tablespoons powdered sugar
2 egg whites, stiffly beaten
1 cup heavy cream, whipped stiff

2 cups fresh milk, scalded

Sprinkle granulated sugar over prepared berries and crush well. Let stand for 30 minutes. Add quick-cooking tapioca to hot scalded milk in double boiler and cook, over boiling water, for 5 minutes, stirring frequently. Strain while hot through double cheesecloth, over corn syrup and salt, stirring gently, but not rubbing. Chill. To the stiffly beaten egg whites, add powdered sugar and beat until egg whites are stiff and sugar thoroughly blended, and add to chilled creamy mixture. Freeze in refrigerator tray until mushy; remove from refrigerator and scrape bottom and sides, then beat until smooth. Then add whipped stiff cream which has been folded into the strawberry pulp and juice, and freeze 3 hours.

273   STRAWBERRY ICE CREAM III
(Refrigerator tray)

1 cup sweetened condensed milk
½ cup cold water

1½ cups crushed strawberries
1 cup heavy cream, whipped stiff

⅛ teaspoon salt

Combine and mix sweetened condensed milk and water thoroughly. Add crushed fresh ripe strawberries, which have been washed, picked over, hulled. Stir in gently but thoroughly the heavy cream whipped stiff with the salt, and freeze in refrigerator tray until mushy; remove from refrigerator, scrape bottom and sides, beat 2 minutes, or until smooth, and return to refrigerator tray to freeze for 3 hours. You may add ½ teaspoon vanilla extract to the whipped cream before stirring in the whipped heavy cream, if desired.

274   STRAWBERRY ICE CREAM   IV
        (Hand freezer or refrigerator tray)

A strawberry ice cream which has just the piquancy that is deserves and fit to be served in the form of flowers. The thing to do is to freeze slowly in the usual way until almost completely frozen (hard mush), then fill fruit and flower molds and freeze an hour longer, if refrigerator tray is used, and if hand freezer is used, pack in 4 parts ice and 1 part rock salt for 1 hour.

2 cups fresh ripe strawberries, washed, picked over, hulled, crushed, then sieved through a coarse strainer to remove the seeds.
¼ scant teaspoon salt

2 teaspoons lemon juice
½ cup granulated sugar
¾ cup orange juice
1 pint heavy cream, mixed with
2 tablespoons confectioner's sugar

To the strawberry pulp and juice, add salt, lemon juice, granulated sugar and orange juice. Let stand 30 minutes to ripen, stirring frequently, with the vessel in a warm place. Then add unwhipped heavy cream into which has been stirred the confectioner's sugar. Chill. Freeze in hand freezer, using 3 parts ice and 1 part rock salt, and turning slowly until mixture is solid. Pack or mold as indicated above.

275 STRAWBERRY DUCHESS

For success you must operate rapidly.

Into a cocktail glass, pile, pressing very gently, small fresh ripe strawberries. Unmold onto chilled dessert plates. Sprinkle with a little kirsch liqueur after sprinkling them with a little powdered sugar. Have ready your favorite vanilla ice cream recipe, and with a round tablespoon dipped in hot water scoop small eggs through the ice cream. Arrange two or three eggs, according to size, around the strawberries, and sprinkle over a small pinch of spun sugar made as indicated for recipe No. 15. (optional).

276 STRAWBERRY ICE CREAM GLACÉ
(Hand freezer)

For this delicious ice cream, I advise to serve a side dish of sponge cake.

1 pint rich milk	1 teaspoon vanilla extract
1 cup heavy cream	¼ scant teaspoon salt
1 cup powdered sugar	3 egg whites, stiffly beaten
1 cup crushed, sieved fresh strawberry pulp and juice	

Combine cold milk, cream, powdered sugar, salt and vanilla extract, which have been chilled, and beat to a custard-like consistency. Freeze in hand freezer until mushy, using 3 parts ice and 1 part rock salt. Then add stiffly beaten egg whites into which have been stirred the strawberry pulp and juice. Then freeze until solid and pack or mold in 4 parts ice and 1 part rock salt.

Any kind of fruit pulp may be prepared in this method, using the same amount of fruit pulp as indicated for the above recipe, either fresh, canned or cooked cooled dried fruit.

The ice cream may be served between two meringue shells, or baked puffs, or between two wafers, sandwich-like.

277 SUMMER GLORY

A very attractive, delicious, refreshing fresh fruit and ice cream dessert.

Place in a dessert glass dish layers of assorted fresh fruits, such as cherries, currants, black, red or whites, greengages, prunes, apples, pears, pineapple and so on, cut into small cubes for the large fruit. Sprinkle the whole with sugar according to taste; sprinkle then with ¼ cup of maraschino liqueur, or simply the maraschino juice from a bottle of maraschino cherries, and chill thoroughly. When ready to serve, arrange small eggs of your favorite ice cream, made by dipping a spoon into hot water and scooping into a brick of ice cream. Decorate with whipped cream forced through a pastry bag. Serve at once.

278 SUSIE'S PARTY ICE CREAM

6 pieces sponge cake
1 quart strawberry ice cream
  Spun sugar No. 15, pink
  colored

6 brandied peaches
1 cup crushed sweetened strawberries, not too liquid

Place 1 layer of sponge cake, the size of a large biscuit, on a chilled platter. Top with a scoop of strawberry ice cream; quickly flatten the ice cream with the bowl of a soup spoon, and place over this a brandied peach. Pour over 1 or two tablespoons of sweetened crushed fresh strawberries, not too liquid, and cover the entire dessert with a sprinkling of pink spun sugar, made as indicated for recipe No. 15.

279   TEA ICE CREAM
                          (Hand freezer)

2 cups milk, scalded	4 egg yolks, slightly beaten with
3 tablespoons of your favorite	¼ teaspoon salt
good tea	Grated rind of 1 orange
1½ cups granulated sugar	2 cups heavy cream, unwhipped

To the hot scalded milk add the tea and allow to infuse, covered for 5 long minutes. Then, stir in the sugar until dissolved and strain through a double cheesecloth. Return to double boiler, and slowly, very slowly, while beating and stirring briskly, pour the slightly beaten egg yolks. Cook, over simmering water, stirring constantly, until mixture begins to coat the spoon. Strain again; add grated orange rind and unwhipped heavy cream, and freeze in hand freezer, using 3 parts ice and 1 part rock salt until solid. Mold in 4 parts ice and 1 part rock salt.

280   TUTTI FRUTTI ICE CREAM   I
            (Hand freezer or refrigerator tray)

Tutti frutti, meaning all kinds of fruits, in Italian, may be made in different methods.

1 cup orange pulp, cut into small pieces	1 teaspoon granulated gelatine
	1 tablespoon cold water
¼ cup drained maraschino cherries cut into small pieces	¾ cup undiluted evaporated milk, whipped as indicated for recipe No. 8
2 bananas, peeled then mashed	
½ cup drained crushed pineapple	¼ cup blanched chopped finely almonds
2 tablespoons lemon juice	
¾ cup granulated sugar	

Combine all the fruit with sugar. Stir well and add gelatine which has been softened in cold water and dissolved over hot water. Fold in the whipped undiluted evaporated milk (whipped stiff) and freeze in hand freezer, using 3 parts ice and 1 part rock salt until mushy, then add chopped almonds, and freeze until solid. Pack or mold in 4 parts ice and 1 part rock salt. If using refrigerator tray, freeze to a mush, remove from refrigerator, scrape bottom and sides, then beat in the chopped almonds until smooth. Return to refrigerator and freeze for 3½ hours.

281   TUTTI FRUTTI ICE CREAM II
         (Hand freezer or refrigerator tray)

1 quart heavy cream, scalded
½ cup granulated sugar, caramelized
3 egg yolks, slightly beaten
¼ teaspoon salt
¼ cup dates, chopped fine
¼ cup well-drained green maraschino cherries, chopped fine
¼ cup dried figs, chopped fine
1 tablespoon dried apricot, uncooked, and chopped fine
½ cup roasted coarsely ground peanuts
¼ cup well-drained red maraschino cherries, chopped fine

Pour hot scalded cream over caramelized sugar, stirring while pouring to dissolve the sugar. Then, pour this, very slowly, over slightly beaten egg yolks, which have been beaten with the salt. Set over simmering water, stirring constantly until mixture coats the spoon. Remove from hot water and strain through double cheesecloth. Chill, and freeze in hand freezer, using 3 parts ice and 1 part rock salt, until mushy; then add combined fruit and ground peanuts, and freeze until solid. Pack or mold in 4 parts ice and 1 part rock salt.

If freezing is done in refrigerator, freeze as indicated above, that is, until mushy. Remove from refrigerator, scrape bottom and sides then beat in the mixed fruit and nuts. Freeze for 3½ hours.

282   TUTTI FRUTTI ICE CREAM III

To your favorite vanille ice cream recipe, either frozen in
hand freezer or refrigerator tray, add, when mixture is mushy,
1½ cups of assorted candied or crystallized fruit, chopped very
fine, and continue freezing as directed until solid.

283   TUTTI FRUTTI ICE CREAM IV
(Hand freezer or refrigerator tray)

2 cups fresh milk, scalded
1 tablespoon cornstarch
1 cup granulated sugar
¼ scant teaspoon salt
4 egg yolks, slightly beaten

1 teaspoon orange extract
1 full cup assorted candied or
crystallized or preserved figs,
raisins and maraschino cherries
and syrup in equal parts

1 cup heavy cream, whipped stiff

Combine cornstarch, sugar, salt and slightly beaten egg yolks
and blend thoroughly; then pour over the hot scalded fresh milk,
slowly and gradually, while stirring briskly and constantly. Place
over simmering water and cook, stirring constantly, until mixture coats the spoon. Strain through double cheesecloth, and
chill. When chilled, add the combined fruits and syrup, orange
extract and fold in the stiffly whipped heavy cream. Freeze in
refrigerator tray until mushy; then remove from tray, scrape
bottom and sides, beat two minutes; return to tray, freeze again to
a more solid mush, then scrape again from bottom and sides,
beat 1 long minute, and return to refrigerator tray for 3½ hours.

284 VANILLA COCONUT ICE CREAM
(Refrigerator tray)

When it comes to pleasing children . . . and grown-ups, too,
serve them coconut.

½ cup cold water
⅔ cup sweetened condensed milk
½ cup shredded coconut, finely
    chopped and slightly toasted

1½ teaspoons vanilla extract
1 cup heavy cream, whipped to
    custard-like consistency
⅛ teaspoon salt

Combine cold water, sweetened condensed milk, finely chopped, toasted coconut and vanilla extract. Blend well. Chill, then fold in the heavy cream, whipped to a custard-like consistency and also well chilled. Freeze in refrigerator tray until mushy; remove from tray and scrape creamy, half frozen mixture from bottom and sides of tray, then beat until smooth. Smooth out and return to refrigerator. Freeze for 3 hours.

285 VANILLA ICE CREAM I
(American method. Hand freezer or refrigerator tray)

2 cups scalded milk
1 tablespoon flour
1 cup granulated sugar
2 egg yolks, slightly beaten

¼ teaspoon salt
1½ teaspoons vanilla extract
1 quart thin cream, or undi-
    luted evaporated milk

Combine flour, sugar and salt, and add to slightly beaten egg yolks; then slowly, while stirring briskly and constantly, pour scalded milk over egg mixture. Turn this into top of double boiler, and cook over hot water 10 minutes, stirring constantly, until custard coats the spoon. Strain through double cheese-cloth while hot; cool, chill, and freeze in hand freezer, using

[163]

3 parts ice and 1 part rock salt, until solid. Pack or mold in 4 parts ice and 1 part rock salt.

NOTE.—*Notice the difference, a slight one, between the American method and the French method for making vanilla ice cream. In the American method as in the French method, the foundation basis is a custard. The first uses flour, the second uses more egg yolks. The freezing is absolutely the same, and both may be made in the refrigerator tray; the only extra work being the scraping of the creamy mixture when in a mushy state. While American and French methods require a custard foundation, the Philadelphia method (see recipe No. 229) does not. The ingredients are combined, then frozen.*

286   VANILLA ICE CREAM II
(French method. Hand freezer or refrigerator tray)

2 cups rich milk, scalded
4 egg yolks, slightly beaten
½ cup granulated sugar

1 cup heavy cream, unwhipped
1 generous teaspoon vanilla extract

⅛ generous teaspoon salt

Combine sugar and salt, and add slightly beaten egg yolks, beating gently until sugar is dissolved and mixture is thoroughly blended. Pour rich scalded milk over, slowly, while stirring briskly and constantly. Turn creamy custard into top of double boiler and cook, over simmering water, stirring constantly, until mixture coats the spoon. Strain through double cheesecloth, cool, then chill. Add unwhipped heavy cream and vanilla, and freeze in hand freezer, using 3 parts ice and 1 part rock salt, until solid. Pack or mold in 4 parts ice and 1 part rock salt. For refrigerator tray, see note in previous recipe.

287   VANILLA ICE CREAM III
              (Refrigerator tray. No stirring)

In the following recipe, quick-cooking tapioca is used. The amount of sugar is reduced by the use of corn syrup. This method is widely used in the Middle West. The result is a richer and more nourishing product requiring longer freezing, as it is more starchy.

2 cups milk, scalded	¼ teaspoon salt
2½ generous tablespoons of quick-cooking tapioca	2 egg whites, stiffly beaten
⅓ cup granulated sugar	2 tablespoons powdered sugar
2½ tablespoons light corn syrup	1 cup heavy cream, whipped stiff

                1¾ teaspoons vanilla extract

Drop, rain-like the quick-cooking tapioca into the hot scalded milk, placed in top of double boiler, and cook, over boiling water for 10 minutes, stirring occasionally. Strain while hot through a cheesecloth placed over a colander; then add combined sugar, salt and light corn syrup, a small amount at a time, stirring gently until well blended and sugar is dissolved. Chill. Add stiffly beaten egg whites, to which have been added the powdered sugar. Lastly fold in the heavy cream, whipped stiff with vanilla extract. Freeze in refrigerator tray, without stirring, for 4 hours.

288   VANILLA ICE CREAM IV
                  (Refrigerator tray)

The following method is very easy, economical and delicious. Thin cream, sugar and vanilla extract. That's all!

5 cups thin cream, or	1 cup granulated sugar
4 cups undiluted evaporated milk and 1 cup heavy cream	⅛ teaspoon salt
	2 teaspoons vanilla extract

Put thin cream or undiluted evaporated milk and heavy cream in top of double boiler, stir in the sugar and salt, and scald until a thin scum forms on top of the cream. Do not remove this scum. Remove the cream from the hot water, cool and chill 3 hours. When ready to freeze, add vanilla extract and freeze in refrigerator tray until mushy; remove from refrigerator, scrape bottom and sides, beat 2 minutes or until smooth; return to refrigerator and freeze 3 long hours.

289   VANILLA ICE CREAM V
(Refrigerator tray)

1 cup sweetened condensed milk   ⅛ teaspoon salt
¾ cup cold water (iced)   1 cup heavy cream, whipped stiff
1½ generous teaspoons vanilla extract

Combine chilled sweetened condensed milk, water (iced), vanilla and salt and stir to blend thoroughly. Fold in the heavy cream, whipped stiffly, and freeze in refrigerator tray until mushy. Remove from refrigerator, scrape bottom and sides, then beat 2 minutes or until smooth, and return to tray to freeze 3½ hours.

290   VANILLA ICE CREAM VI
(Refrigerator tray)

2 cups fresh milk, scalded   ¼ scant teaspoon salt
⅔ cup granulated sugar   1½ cups heavy cream
3 whole eggs, beaten with   2 teaspoons vanilla extract

To the hot scalded milk, add sugar, whole eggs and salt which have been combined and slightly beaten, until sugar is dissolved, very slowly while stirring briskly and constantly, lest mixture curdle. Strain through double cheesecloth, cool and chill. Then add unwhipped heavy cream (you may use the same amount of thin cream, if a not too rich ice cream is desired) and vanilla extract. Freeze in refrigerator tray until mushy; remove from refrigerator, scrape bottom and sides, then beat 2 minutes or until smooth. Return to tray and freeze for 3 hours.

291   VANILLA ICE CREAM CARMELITA

A very appealing and tempting frozen dessert made out of pears, apricot marmalade, currant jelly and vanilla ice cream, which is very easy to prepare. The following recipe is for one serving.

Pare as many fresh pears as required. Cook them in a sugar syrup made of equal parts of granulated sugar and water, cooked 5 long minutes over direct flame. When cool, cut each pear crosswise, right in center; empty, or rather carefully scoop the inside, so as to obtain a shell; fill with apricot marmalade, mixed with a little candied or crystallized fruit; adjust the top; place the pear on a chilled dessert plate; pour over 1 tablespoon of slightly melted currant jelly, and surround with small eggs (about 3 or 4) of your favorite vanilla ice cream, scooped with a teaspoon dipped in hot water, then into the ice cream. Sprinkle with a dusting of finely chopped pistachio nut meats. Serve at once.

292   VANILLA ICE CREAM CARMEN

Another of these fancy desserts which may be made with ice cream, for a formal or informal dinner. The indicated ice cream may be changed according to taste and facilities.

Have ready, or purchase 1 pint each vanilla and strawberry ice cream. With a tablespoon dipped in hot water, scoop out ice cream, egg-shape alternately in the two different flavored ice creams. Arrange crown-like on a large, round, chilled platter. Then place in center, 2 cups of canned pineapple and fresh figs, cubed small and in equal parts, which have been soaked in your favorite liqueur, either kirsch, maraschino, curacao, and so forth, for 15 minutes, stirring occasionally so as to flavor all the fruit. Decorate with fancy designs of whipped cream, unflavored and unsweetened, forced through a pastry bag with fancy tube. Serve immediately. For success you must operate very rapidly. Try.

293   VANILLA ICE CREAM JEANETTE

To your favorite Vanilla ice cream recipe, either frozen in hand freezer or refrigerator tray, add, when mushy, ¼ cup of Praline Powder, made as indicated for recipe No. 14. When solid, mold in 4 parts ice and 1 part rock salt for 1 long hour. When ready to serve, unmold and rapidly cover entirely the molded ice cream with whipped cream, which has been flavored and sweetened to taste, forced through a pastry bag, and dot here and there with crystallized or.candied violets.

A side dish of soft custard sauce may be served with this delicious dessert.

294   VANILLA ICE CREAM MARINETTE

Whip stiff 2 cups of heavy cream with 1 generous tablespoon of powdered sugar, or confectioner's sugar and flavor with ½ teaspoon of vanilla extract. Have ready ½ quart of your favorite vanilla ice cream recipe (or purchase it). With a tablespoon dipped in hot water scoop out ice cream, egg-shaped. Arrange these in center of a round, chilled serving platter, then place around the ice cream eggs, 6 meringues made as indicated for recipe No. 108. Decorate with whipped cream forced through a pastry bag with a fancy tube.

295   VANILLA ICE CREAM PIE

For those of you homemakers who cannot make up your mind
what to serve for a birthday party, here is a suggestion:

Have ready or purchase 1 quart of vanilla ice cream—your
favorite recipe. Spread it quickly, about 2-inches thick in the bottom of a shallow mold, having a tight-fitting lid or cover, about
the size of an ordinary 8 or 9 inch pie plate. Now, operating
rapidly, press a meat plate into the cream in such a way as to
form and shape an indentation in the centre similar to a baked
pie shell. Seal on the lid or cover with a piece of cloth, or muslin,
dipped in melted butter and as an additional precaution, spread
some butter over the cloth. Pack in 4 parts ice and 1 part rock
salt for 2 hours. When ready to serve, unmold, or rather turn
over the ice cream shell to serving platter, lifting out the plate.
Fill the shell with sweetened raspberries or strawberries. Rapidly
brush the berries with a small jar of melted currant jelly. Serve
immediately, decorated with whipped cream, sweetened and
flavored to taste, forced through a pastry bag with a small fancy
tube. Tempting? . . . I should say!

Of course you may use almost any kind of fruit, fresh and
canned, as well as any kind of ice cream. If you have individual
molds, use them also for this real surprise dessert.

296   VANILLA ICE CREAM PLOMBIERE
(Hand freezer)

Have ready your favorite vanilla ice cream recipe, frozen in
a hand freezer. When ready to mold, sprinkle a layer of assorted
candied or crystallized fruits, cubed small, then a layer of ice
cream. Repeat until mold is full. Adjust lid, seal with butter and
pack in 4 parts ice and 1 part rock salt for 2 hours.

297 VANILLA ICE CREAM BALLS

When ready to serve your favorite ice cream recipe, scoop out, using an ice cream scooper, portion balls. Quickly roll in shredded coconut, which may be toasted and colored, and serve with a side dish of chocolate sauce, or fruit sauce.

Then we have infinite varieties of sundaes for parties, home luncheons or dinners, which are usually served with a sauce, a syrup, to which may be added chopped nut meats. These ice cream sundaes are very economical, as 1 quart may stretch enough to serve 8 persons.

SECTION VII

Mousse Recipes

>>> >>> >>> >>> >>> >>> >>> >>> >>> >>> >>> <<< <<< <<< <<< <<< <<< <<< <<< <<< <<< <<<

298   WHAT IS A MOUSSE?

Mousse, means "MOSS" in French and so-called because of its spongy consistency. The original basic foundation is sweetened and flavored whipped heavy cream. To this may be added sieved cooked or raw fruit, and flavoring or flavorings. A little gelatine may be added as a stabilizer. These delicate desserts are the simplest to freeze in the automatic refrigerator because of their richness. Here, too, the sweet cordials and sweet dessert wines may be used either alone or in conjunction with flavoring extracts. The mixture should be well combined, then poured into the trays, and stirred or not, according to directions, only once after the mixture has been frozen to a mush, operating as for ice cream.

Mousses are seldom served in chilled glasses. They may be packed in large or individual molds or frilled or scalloped paper cups. Or, the refrigerator tray may be lined with home made or purchased ice cream, the center filled with whipped cream, or undiluted evaporated milk, sweetened and flavored to taste, or combined with chopped candied or crystallized fruit, or any kind of nut meats. The tray is then unmolded on a chilled platter, or on an ice block (Recipe No. 24) and served at once, after being allowed to freeze 2 to 3 hours.

Packed in large or individual plain or fancy molds, mousses afford attractive desserts for formal or informal functions. All these are· left to the imagination of the homemaker, according to her budget, or the occasion.

299   **APRICOT MOUSSE I**
(Refrigerator tray)

1 cup heavy cream, whipped stiff	¼ cup granulated sugar
2 egg whites, stiffly beaten	½ scant teaspoon salt
1 can canned apricot, drained	½ teaspoon almond extract
then sieved	2 tablespoons ground almonds

Combine gently, stiffly beaten egg whites and heavy cream, whipped stiff. Combine sieved apricot pulp (no juice), sugar, salt and flavoring extract and blanched ground almonds; then add to combined egg whites and heavy cream. Blend well, but gently. Turn mixture into refrigerator tray and freeze 4 hours without stirring. You may substitute apple sauce, or apricot marmalade for canned apricots if desired. You may also use fresh apricot pulp.

300   **APRICOT MOUSSE II**
(Refrigerator tray)

Using fresh apricot pulp, well-drained, and granulated gelatine. This mixture requires to be stirred every twenty minutes during the first hour of freezing. Cooked, dried, sieved apricot pulp may be used.

1 pint heavy cream, whipped stiff	¼ teaspoon salt
1 teaspoon granulated gelatine	1¼ cups apricot pulp
3 tablespoons of apricot juice or	¼ teaspoon almond extract
syrup, according to kind used	2 tablespoons ground peanuts

¼ cup granulated sugar

If using fresh apricots, sieve, with skin on, after washing the fruit. If using dried apricots, soak overnight and cook with sugar until tender, then sieve or put through food chopper. Dissolve gelatine in 3 tablespoons of apricot syrup, and soften over hot water. Combine apricot pulp, gelatine, salt, almond extract and ground peanuts and blend well. Then fold in the stiffly whipped heavy cream. Turn creamy mixture into refrigerator tray, and freeze until beginning to be mushy. Remove from refrigerator and scrape bottom and sides, then beat for 2 minutes. Return to refrigerator and freeze again for 20 minutes, then repeat the scraping and beating. Return to refrigerator and freeze for 3 long hours. You may mold and pack as indicated for recipe No. 298.

301   AVOCADO MOUSSE
              (Refrigerator tray)

1 cup sieved avocado pulp	2 generous tablespoons granu-
1½ tablespoons lemon juice	lated sugar
1 teaspoon lime juice	¼ scant teaspoon salt
1 cup heavy cream, whipped stiff	

Into the sieved pulp stir in the combined lemon and lime juice, sugar and salt, fold in the stiffly whipped heavy cream, and freeze in refrigerator tray until mixture is mushy. Scrape bottom and sides, then beat for 2 short minutes, or until smooth. Return to refrigerator and freeze for 3 long hours.

302   BANANA APRICOT MOUSSE
              (Refrigerator tray)

Either cooked dried apricots or canned apricots may be used. Two large or three medium-sized bananas will make approximately one cup of pulp.

[173]

1 cup mashed banana
¾ cup sieved apricot pulp
⅓ cup granulated sugar
¼ scant teaspoon salt

2 teaspoons lime juice
2 tablespoons lemon juice
⅓ cup apricot juice
1 cup heavy cream, whipped stiff

Combine apricot and banana pulp and sieve, adding all the remaining ingredients, but the stiffly whipped heavy cream. Blend well. Chill. Fold in stiffly beaten heavy cream, and freeze in refrigerator tray, without stirring, for 3½ hours.

VARIATIONS.—The following variations may be made with banana, using the same amount of indicated ingredients, substituting for apricot the following fruit pulp: (a) Banana-avocado; (b) banana-blueberry; (c) banana-cantaloupe; (d) banana-cranberry; (e) banana-date; (f) banana-fig; (g) banana-honeydew; (h) banana-peach; (i) banana-pear; (j) banana-pineapple (using canned pineapple); (k) banana-prune; (l) banana-quince; (m) banana-rhubarb; (n) banana-raspberry; (o) banana-strawberry; (p) banana-watermelon.

303 BANANA MOUSSE I
(Refrigerator tray)

A very smooth and light mousse appropriate for a dinner party.

1 cup banana pulp
2 tablespoons lemon juice
⅓ cup granulated sugar
1 egg white, stiffly beaten

2 tablespoons powdered sugar
⅛ teaspoon salt
Candied fruit (assorted) to garnish

1 cup heavy cream, whipped stiff

Combine banana pulp, lemon juice, sugar and ⅛ teaspoon salt, then sieve again. Chill. When well chilled beat in the stiffly beaten egg white; then fold in the heavy cream which has been whipped stiff, and stir in the finely chopped candied, assorted fruit, using about ¼ generous cup. Freeze, without stirring, packed in a mold placed in tray of refrigerator for 4 hours. No stirring required.

304   **BANANA MOUSSE II**
(Refrigerator tray)

In the following recipe, sliced bananas are used; they should be sliced very thin, and just when ready to use, lest they turn dark. The added vanilla extract enhances the flavor of the fruit. No stirring is required. The creamy mixture may be placed into the refrigerator tray, or molded in a large or 6 small individual fancy molds or paper cases, and frozen in the tray of the refrigerator.

2 cups heavy cream, whipped stiff	1 cup sliped ripe bananas
½ cup powdered sugar	2 egg whites, stiffly beaten
	⅛ generous teaspoon salt

1¼ teaspoons vanilla extract

Into the stiffly whipped heavy cream, fold in the sugar and continue beating until mixture is stiff. Very gently fold in the thinly sliced bananas, alternately with the stiffly beaten egg whites beaten with the vanilla and salt. Spread creamy mixture into refrigerator tray, and freeze 4 long hours. You may mold, after mixture has been frozen, and let stand 1 hour longer, if desired.

305 BANANA MARSHMALLOW MOUSSE
(Hand freezer or refrigerator tray)

4 medium-sized ripe bananas
¾ cup granulated sugar
Juice of ½ lemon

¼ scant teaspoon salt
1½ cups heavy cream, whipped
stiff

½ lb. toasted marshmallows

Sieve bananas with granulated sugar and lemon juice. Re-sieve twice to ensure smoothness and blending; then fold in the whipped heavy cream to which has been added the salt. *If using hand freezer:* Fill a mold to overflowing; spread buttered paper over the top of the creamy mixture and over this adjust the lid. Spread butter all over the seams, and pack in 3 parts ice and 1 part rock salt. Do not churn. Let stand 3 hours, repacking once after 2 hours of packing. *If using refrigerator tray,* operate as for hand freezer pail. Place sealed mold in tray of refrigerator and freeze 4 hours without repacking. Unmold on to chilled serving platter, and decorate the mousse with toasted marshmallows, and candied fruit, cut into small fancy pieces, if desired.

306 BLUE PLUM MOUSSE
(Refrigerator tray)

2 cups blue plums, sieved
¼ cup (more or less) granulated
sugar
½ teaspoon granulated gelatine

¼ scant cup cold water
1 cup heavy cream, whipped
stiff
⅛ generous teaspoon salt

Dissolve granulated gelatine (you may use lemon-flavored, or lime-flavored gelatine, if desired) in cold water. Heat blue plum over hot water, but do not boil, and add and stir in gelatine. Cool. When mixture begins to congeal, fold in the heavy cream which has been whipped stiff with salt. Freeze in refrigerator tray, for 4 hours, scraping bottom and sides, then beating mixture for 2 short minutes, every half hour for the first hour.

307   BRANDY MOUSSE
(Refrigerator tray)

1 cup heavy cream, whipped stiff
⅓ scant cup powdered sugar

⅛ generous teaspoon salt
1 tablespoon good brandy
2 egg whites, stiffly beaten

Fold into the stiffly whipped heavy cream, the powdered sugar and salt, then gently fold in the stiffly beaten egg whites, to which has been added the brandy. Freeze in refrigerator tray, scraping once when mixture begins to mush, or about 20 minutes, then continue freezing for 4 hours.

Rum, Madeira wine, or any other liqueur, according to taste, may be substituted for the brandy.

308   BURNT ALMOND MOUSSE
(Refrigerator tray or hand freezer)

Any other kind of nut meats may be substituted for almonds, if desired. In the following recipe undiluted evaporated milk, whipped stiff is suggested. The creamy preparation may be packed in hand freezer, using equal parts of ice and rock salt. But do not churn.

½ cup granulated sugar, caramelized
½ cup boiling water
1 teaspoon granulated gelatine

1 tablespoon cold water
1½ cups undiluted evaporated milk whipped (see recipe No. 8)
1 teaspoon vanilla extract

¼ cup blanched, roasted almonds

[177]

Place sugar into a heavy skillet, over a gentle flame and cook, stirring constantly until sugar is golden brown and melted. Then add boiling water, and let simmer until mixture is thoroughly blended, stirring occasionally. To this, add gelatine, softened in the cold water, alternately with ½ cup of the cold milk. Cool until mixture is thickened, and fold in the remaining cup of undiluted evaporated milk, whipped stiff, and the vanilla extract. Freeze in refrigerator tray or in mold, using hand freezer pail, until mixture is mushy; then add almonds, beat and scrape at the same time for 2 minutes, then continue freezing for 3½ hours.

309   **CHANTILLY MOUSSE I**
(Refrigerator tray)

This mousse requires no stirring at all, and if meringues—small or broken ones—are not on hand, they may be purchased for a few cents, or you may substitute crumbled macaroons, if desired.

1 cup heavy cream, whipped stiff	½ teaspoon vanilla extract
¼ cup powdered sugar	1 egg white, stiffly beaten
⅛ teaspoon salt	1 cup, broken small, macaroons or meringues

To the stiffly whipped heavy cream, add powdered sugar and salt and whip again to blend sugar and salt thoroughly. Fold in stiffly beaten egg white, to which has been added the vanilla extract, alternately with the broken meringues (see meringues, recipe No. 108) or broken macaroons. Mold either in large or individual molds, plain or fancy, and set in refrigerator tray for 3 hours.

310 CHANTILLY MOUSSE II
(Refrigerator tray. No stirring)

¼ cup cold water
½ cup granulated sugar
3 egg whites, stiffly beaten with
¼ teaspoon salt
¼ teaspoon granulated gelatine

1 teaspoon cold water
¾ cup heavy cream, whipped stiff
½ generous teaspoon vanilla extract

1 cup broken meringue

Make a sugar syrup with water and granulated sugar, stir until sugar is dissolved, bring to a boil, and let boil for 5 minutes without stirring. Very slowly pour hot syrup, while beating briskly and rapidly, over stiffly beaten egg whites. Place in pan of ice water and beat until mixture is cold and light. Soften granulated gelatine in 1 teaspoon of cold water, and dissolve over hot water, then strain into syrup-egg mixture, stirring rapidly. Now fold in the stiffly whipped heavy cream, to which has been added the salt and vanilla extract, alternately with the broken meringues. Mold, and freeze in refrigerator tray for 3 hours.

311 CHERRY MOUSSE I
(Refrigerator tray or hand freezer)

You may use the hand freezer pail if desired, using equal parts ice and rock salt, stirring once after 30 minutes of packing, but do not churn.

1 No. 2 can red pitted cherries
2 teaspoons granulated gelatine
2 tablespoons cold water

½ cup granulated sugar
1 tablespoon lemon juice
⅛ teaspoon salt

1 cup heavy cream, whipped to a custard-like consistency

Reserve a few whole cherries to garnish the mousse when unmolded. Rub the remaining cherries through a coarse sieve.

Heat cherry pulp and juice to the boiling point; add gelatine which has been softened in cold water. Stir, then add sugar and lemon juice, and chill. When well-chilled, stir in the whipped cream, and freeze in refrigerator tray until mushy, then scrape bottom and sides, then beat for 2 minutes. Return to refrigerator and continue freezing for 3 hours. A fine mousse for Valentine's Day.

312   CHERRY MOUSSE II
        (Refrigerator tray or hand freezer)

This is an imposing looking frozen dessert, and if the directions are followed there will be many an "encore". It consists of alternate layers of whipped cream, delicately flavored with praline powder flavoring (recipe No. 14), combined with the popular maraschino flavor, and a mixture of grated sweet chocolate, combined with chopped maraschino cherries, placed between the whipped cream layers. No stirring required. The molded mixture may be packed in hand freezer pail, using 3 parts ice and 1 part rock salt, and frozen, without stirring, for 3 hours.

1 cup heavy cream, whipped stiff
¼ cup praline powder (recipe No. 9)
¼ cup maraschino syrup from the maraschino cherries bottle
⅛ teaspoon salt
2 teaspoons sweet chocolate, grated
6 green maraschino cherries chopped fine
2 teaspoons ground blanched almonds

Fold into the whipped cream, a small amount at a time, the praline powder flavoring made as indicated for recipe No. 14, alternately with the strained maraschino syrup from the bottle of maraschino cherries with the salt. Combine grated sweet chocolate, chopped fine green maraschino cherries, which have been gently squeezed through a dry cloth, and the blanched ground almonds. Mix well. Now pour a layer of the whipped cream mixture in a melon mold, which has been rinsed in cold water. Over the cream sprinkle ½ of the chocolate-cherries-almond mixture; again a layer of the cream mixture, still again the remaining chocolate mixture, and top with the remaining whipped cream mixture. Adjust over the cream a buttered paper, put on the lid, spread butter around the seam, and freeze in refrigerator tray for 3 hours. If freezing is made in a hand freezer, follow the directions given at the beginning of this recipe.

Should this fine dessert be made for a special occasion, and the hostess desire effect combined with goodness, unmold the mousse in a *Strawberry Nest,* made as follows:

4 egg whites, stiffly beaten	1 cup heavy cream, whipped stiff
½ cup powdered sugar	½ cup crushed fresh strawberries
3 tablespoons powdered sugar	

Fold into the stiffly beaten egg whites the powdered sugar (½ cup only) to which has been mixed ⅛ teaspoon salt, continuing beating until egg whites hold their peaks. Force this uncooked meringue through a pastry bag with a large fancy tube into a ring, large enough to hold the unmolded mousse, on to a baking sheet, and bake in a slow oven (275 deg. F.) until delicately browned, or about 25 to 30 minutes. Cool, and unmold the mousse mold in the center of the meringue ring. When ready to serve, only then, pour over the crushed strawberries (raspberries may be used, if desired) with the 3 tablespoons of powdered sugar. You may omit the strawberries and serve simply the unmolded mousse into the meringue ring. Very effective, but not expensive.

313 CHESTNUT MOUSSE
(Hand freezer or refrigerator tray)

1 cup heavy cream, whipped stiff	1 egg white, stiffly beaten
¼ cup powdered sugar	¾ teaspoon vanilla extract
⅛ teaspoon salt	½ cup chestnuts

To the stiffly whipped heavy cream, add sugar, vanilla and salt, continuing whipping until well blended; then fold in stiffly beaten egg white, alternately with marrons (chestnuts) prepared as indicated for recipe No. 191. Freeze, without stirring in refrigerator tray after molding the mixture, for 3 hours.

You may, when ready to mold, add ¼ cup chopped red or green maraschino cherries, squeezed through a dry cloth, if desired.

314 CHOCOLATE MOUSSE I
(Hand freezer or refrigerator tray)

2 squares bitter chocolate, melted over hot water	2 generous teaspoons granulated gelatine, soaked in
½ cup powdered sugar	3 tablespoons cold water
1 cup scalded fresh milk	¾ cup granulated sugar
¼ teaspoon salt	1 teaspoon vanilla extract
2 cups heavy cream, whipped stiff	

To the melted chocolate, add powdered sugar and stir until well blended, then, gradually pour over the hot scalded milk, stirring constantly. Place over a gentle flame and allow to come to the boiling point. Do not allow to boil. Remove from the fire and stir in the soaked gelatine, alternately with the granulated sugar and vanilla extract. Strain through a single cheesecloth or a fine strainer. Chill until mixture begins to thicken, then beat, using rotary egg beater until mixture is light. Lastly fold in the stiffly whipped cream with the salt. Mold, and freeze in refrigerator tray for 3 hours.

315 CHOCOLATE MOUSSE II
(Refrigerator tray)

The following is a very economical chocolate mousse.

1 can undiluted evaporated milk, ⅛ teaspoon salt
whipped ½ cup rich chocolate sauce

Make a chocolate sauce as follows:

2 squares bitter chocolate, grated ⅛ teaspoon salt
6 tablespoons water 3 tablespoons butter
½ cup granulated sugar ¼ teaspoon vanilla extract

Add grated chocolate to water (hot or cold) and cook over direct flame, stirring constantly until blended. Add sugar and salt and cook over low flame until sugar is dissolved and mixture slightly thickened, stirring constantly. Remove from the flame, add butter and vanilla and stir well. This will make 1 standard cup. Store the remaining unused half cup which may come very handy, in an air-tight jar and keep in refrigerator until wanted. May be served hot or cold. Have the undiluted evaporated milk thoroughly chilled and whip as indicated for recipe No. 8. Fold in the salt and chocolate sauce, mold and freeze in refrigerator tray for 3 hours.

For the chocolate sauce, you may use ½ cup cocoa, instead of chocolate, if desired.

316 CHOCOLATE MOUSSE III
(Refrigerator tray)

A very rich, nourishing as well as smooth mousse.

2 cups heavy cream, whipped stiff

¼ teaspoon salt

¾ generous cup chocolate syrup made as for recipe No. 315, Chocolate Mousse II

1 whole fresh egg, slightly beaten

To the heavy cream whipped with the salt, add the slightly beaten whole fresh egg, and beat until well-blended. Add, folding gently, but thoroughly, the chocolate syrup, and mold or freeze in refrigerator tray for 3 hours.

317 CHOCOLATE MOUSSE PRALINE IV
(Refrigerator tray)

½ cup (generous) chocolate syrup

2 cups heavy cream, whipped stiff

⅛ generous teaspoon salt

1 teaspoon vanilla extract

¼ teaspoon almond extract

2 tablespoons Praline Powder Flavoring (No. 14.)

Prepare, or have ready ½ cup of chocolate syrup, made as indicated for recipe No. 315, Chocolate Mousse II. Fold in the stiffly whipped heavy cream, salt, combined extracts, and Praline Powder Flavoring. Fill individual paper cases with the creamy mixture, and set in refrigerator tray for 2½ hours. You may, after filling the paper cases, sprinkle over a dusting of very finely chopped pistachio nut meats.

318 COCOMALT MOUSSE
(Refrigerator tray)

Very appropriate for children's party, this healthy mixture may be served in paper (individual) cases, molded, or right from the freezing tray. It is very easy to make and exceptionally delicious.

2 cups heavy cream, whipped stiff or you may use ¾ cup undiluted evaporated milk, whipped (No. 8.)

1 egg, slightly beaten
¼ teaspoon salt
¼ teaspoon vanilla extract
4 tablespoons powdered sugar

6 tablespoons cocomalt

Whip heavy cream or undiluted evaporated milk to a custard-like consistency; add slightly beaten whole egg, and continue whipping, adding salt and vanilla extract, until stiff. Then fold in the combined powdered sugar and cocomalt. Freeze in refrigerator tray for 4 hours.

319 COFFEE MOUSSE I
(Refrigerator tray or hand freezer)

As may be seen when looking at the index of this book, coffee lends itself to many a delicious frozen dessert. The following, in fact, any of the recipes in this book, may be frozen in individual paper cups. Shallow cups the right size should be chosen because the mixture will freeze more rapidly than in larger ones. Fit cups into freezing tray and pour in the mixture, filling to the rim. The dessert need not be removed from the cases before serving. Attractive decorations to surround the cup may be made from crepe paper. The following recipe is a French method:

½ tablespoon granulated gelatine
2 tablespoons cold water
1 cup very strong black coffee
1 teaspoon vanilla extract
¼ teaspoon salt

4 egg yolks and
1 egg white, beaten together
3 tablespoons good brandy
2 cups heavy cream, whipped stiff

1 cup granulated sugar

Soak gelatine in cold water. Stir in very hot coffee to which has been added the sugar, and which has been boiled for 5 minutes or to a syrupy consistency. Pour over slightly beaten egg yolks and egg white, beaten together while hot, stirring briskly and constantly from bottom of saucepan to prevent curdling. Strain through double cheesecloth. Cool. Add vanilla and good brandy, then fold in the stiffly beaten heavy cream with the salt. Pour into mold or individual paper cases. If desired, and when using a large mold, you may pack in hand freezer pail, using equal parts ice and rock salt and allow to stand 2½ to 3 hours. If using refrigerator tray, freeze, if in paper cases, for 2½ hours, if large mold, freeze for 4 hours.

320 COFFEE MOUSSE II
(Refrigerator tray or hand freezer)

½ tablespoon granulated gela-tine
2 tablespoons cold water
1½ cups very strong black coffee
1 scant cup granulated sugar
3 whole eggs, slightly beaten

1 teaspoon vanilla extract
2 tablespoons sherry flavoring or good sherry wine
¼ teaspoon salt
1½ cups undiluted evaporated milk

Soak gelatine in cold water. Cook coffee and sugar together until syrupy; then pour over slightly beaten eggs. Cook in double boiler 5 minutes, stirring often; add soaked gelatine; strain through double cheesecloth and cool. When cold, add vanilla extract and selected sherry (flavoring or real sherry wine), and lastly fold in the whipped evaporated milk with the salt. Freeze as indicated above (No. 319).

321 **COFFEE MOUSSE III**
(Refrigerator tray or hand freezer)

1 cup very strong black coffee
¾ cup granulated sugar
2 teaspoons granulated gelatine
2 tablespoons cold water
3 teaspoons hot water

¼ teaspoon salt
1 teaspoon vanilla extract
2 cups heavy cream, whipped
stiff

2 tablespoons good rum (optional)

Stir in sugar into hot black coffee. Boil 5 short minutes, add soaked gelatine, dissolved in hot water, stir, strain through double cheesecloth; cool until mixture thickens, then beat until light, adding while beating the vanilla extract and salt. Lastly fold in the heavy cream, whipped stiff, then the rum (optional). Freeze as indicated for recipe No. 315.

322 **CURAÇAO MOUSSE**
(Refrigerator tray)

Any other kind of liqueur may be substituted, if desired. Follow the directions as indicated for recipe No. 307, Brandy Mousse, using the same amount of ingredients, but substituting curaçao liqueur for brandy.

323 **FRUIT PULP AND FRUIT JUICE MOUSSE**
(Hand freezer or refrigerator tray)

Almost any kind of fresh, dried or canned fruit pulp or fruit juice may be used for making delicious mousses. The usual amount of either pulp or fruit juice for 6 servings, is 1 cup. Sugar

[187]

according to sweetness of fruit used, very little or none for canned fruit, and 1 teaspoon granulated gelatine. These mousses may be slightly flavored (optional) with either liqueur or flavoring extract. They are frozen as indicated for recipe No. 319, Coffee Mousse I, using either hand freezer pail with equal parts ice and salt, or refrigerator tray, 2 to 2½ hours if packed into small molds, and 3½ to 4 hours if whole refrigerator tray is used.

1 cup fruit juice and pulp
1 teaspoon granulated gelatine
2 tablespoons cold water
3 tablespoons boiling water

⅛ generous teaspoon salt
1 pint heavy cream, whipped stiff
sugar and flavoring (optional)

The fruit should be sieved. Add granulated gelatine to cold water and let soak for 5 minutes, then dissolve in hot water to which has been added ½ generous cup of granulated sugar, if fresh fruit is used, and according to sweetness. Stir in fruit pulp and juice and cool, until it begins to congeal. Then beat until smooth, fold in heavy cream, whipped stiff with the salt, and freeze as indicated for recipe No. 319, Coffee Mousse I.

324　　　　　　GINGER MOUSE
　　　　　　　(Refrigerator tray)

A favorite Southern recipe.

1⅓ cups heavy cream, whipped stiff
⅛ teaspoon salt

⅓ cup powdered sugar
¼ cup ground ginger (preserved)

1½ tablespoons ginger syrup

Into the stiffly whipped heavy cream, fold in combined salt and powdered sugar gradually, continuing beating gently; then fold in combined ground preserved ginger and ginger syrup. Chill. When well-chilled, mold and freeze in refrigerator tray for 2 to 2½ hours, if small individual molds are used, and for 3½ to 4 hours if large mold.

325 HOLLANDISH MACAROON NUT MOUSSE
(Hand freezer pail or refrigerator tray)

1 cup heavy cream, whipped	¼ teaspoon salt
½ cup macaroon crumbs	½ cup chocolate sauce (No. 315)
4 tablespoons coarsely ground nuts	¾ teaspoon vanilla extract
	¼ teaspoon almond extract

To the stiffly whipped heavy cream, add, folding gently, the combined macaroon crumbs and nut meats; then stir in the chocolate sauce and pour into large or individual molds or paper cases. Freeze as indicated for recipe No. 319, Coffee Mousse I.

326 LEMON MOUSSE
(Refrigerator tray or hand freezer)

2 tablespoons cornstarch	¾ cup granulated sugar
¼ cup granulated sugar	⅓ cup lemon juice
¼ teaspoon salt	2 cups heavy cream, whipped
1 cup cold milk	stiff
3 egg yolks, slightly beaten	

Combine cornstarch, ¼ cup granulated sugar, salt and mix well. Stir in the cold milk and cook in double boiler for 15 minutes, or until mixture thickens, stirring constantly. Remove from hot water and beat in the egg yolks; return to hot water and cook, or rather allow to simmer gently for 1 short minute, stirring constantly. Strain through double cheesecloth, stir in the ¾ cup of granulated sugar and lemon juice, and strain again. Cool. Fold in the heavy cream, whipped stiffly, and place (molded or unmolded) in refrigerator tray. Chill 3 long hours without stirring. Or pack after molding in hand freezer tray, using equal parts ice and salt, and let stand for 2 to 2½ hours. You may pack in paper cases, or individual molds, and freeze as indicated for recipe No. 319, Coffee Mousse I.

327   LOUISE MOUSSE
          (Hand freezer pail)

This method, largely used in France, consists of a fruit pulp and juice to which is added the juice of 2 oranges and 1 medium-sized lemon, same weight of powdered sugar and equal amount of heavy cream stiffly beaten, as there is of fruit and juice mixture. Pack in a wet mold, then in equal parts of ice and salt, and freeze 3½ long hours.

328   LIQUEUR MOUSSE
          (Hand freezer pail)

Another French method of preparing liqueur mousse.

To a Chantilly Mousse No. 309 or 310, add, when ready to mold before packing in equal parts of ice and rock salt, either one of the following liqueurs: Maraschino, Curaçao, Noyau, Anisette, Chartreuse, Creme de Cacao, and in fact any kind of sweet liqueur, using 2 or more tablespoons of the selected liqueur if desired highly flavored.

329   MAPLE MOUSSE
          (Hand freezer pail or refrigerator tray)

1 cup maple syrup
4 egg yolks, beaten until thick
⅛ teaspoon salt

2 cups undiluted evaporated milk, whipped (Recipe No. 8, "General Information")

Boil maple syrup 5 minutes. Remove from the fire, and immediately pour slowly, very slowly over thickly beaten egg yolks with the salt, beating briskly and constantly. Cool. When cold, fold in the whipped undiluted evaporated milk, following the directions given for recipe No. 8, under "General Information." Freeze in refrigerator tray, or mold and freeze either in refrigerator tray for 3½ hours, or in hand freezer pail, using equal parts ice and salt, for 2½ hours.

330   MINT MOUSSE
(Hand freezer pail or refrigerator tray)

1 cup granulated sugar	4 drops oil of peppermint
3 tablespoons cornstarch	Green vegetable coloring to
¼ teaspoon salt	taste
2 tablespoons butter	¾ cup heavy cream, stiffly
2 tablespoons lemon juice	whipped
2 cups boiling water	2 egg whites, stiffly beaten
1 teaspoon mint extract, or	

Combine sugar, cornstarch, salt, butter and lemon juice, and blend thoroughly. Gradually pour over the boiling water, stirring briskly and constantly, and cook, over hot water (double boiler) until mixture is thick and clear, stirring constantly to prevent lumping. Strain while hot, through a fine sieve, cool a little and add mint extract or oil of peppermint and a few drops of green vegetable coloring so as to obtain the desired hue (see No. 11, under "General Information." Chill. Fold in combined stiffly whipped heavy cream and stiffly beaten egg whites. Freeze either in hand freezer pail, after molding, using equal parts ice and rock salt, for 2¾ to 3 hours; or freeze in refrigerator tray, or mold in large or small molds or paper cases, and freeze in refrigerator tray for 2½ hours, if small molds, and 3½ to 4 hours for large mold or directly in refrigerator tray (unmolded). Delicious!

331 MOLASSES MOUSSE
(Hand freezer or refrigerator tray)

4 whole eggs, slightly beaten
1 cup molasses
2 tablespoons orange juice

⅛ teaspoon salt
2 cups heavy cream, stiffly whipped
½ teaspoon ground cinnamon

Stir slightly beaten eggs into the molasses, and cook in double boiler until mixture thickens, stirring constantly. Place the top of double boiler in a pan of ice and stir briskly, until mixture is creamy and cool. Then, add orange juice, ground cinnamon and salt. Blend well. Chill. When thoroughly chilled fold in the stiffly whipped heavy cream. Mold and freeze in hand freezer pail, using 4 parts ice and 1 part rock salt. Do not churn, just pack for 4 hours. A fine frozen party dessert.

332 ORANGE MOUSSE
(Hand freezer or refrigerator tray)

Proceed as indicated for recipe No. 326, Lemon Mousse, substituting ½ cup orange juice, for lemon juice, and using only ¾ cup cold milk. Freeze as directed.

333 OLD-FASHIONED COFFEE MOUSSE
(Hand freezer)

1 pint heavy cream
4 tablespoons powdered sugar

½ teaspoon vanilla extract
⅓ cup very strong black coffee
⅛ teaspoon salt

Combine unwhipped heavy cream, sugar, vanilla extract and salt. Chill thoroughly, then whip stiffly, setting the bowl in a pan of ice water, removing the froth, as it rises, and placing it over a fine sieve. When no more froth will rise, turn the drowned whip carefully into a wet mold, adjust the cover, bind the edges with a strip of muslin dipped in melted butter, and bury in equal parts of ice and rock salt for 3 hours. *(Given here purely as a document, yet this recipe is really wonderful.)*

334   PEACH MOUSSE I
       (Hand freezer pail or refrigerator tray)

This very economical and really delicious mousse requires 4 good sized fresh peaches, gelatine and undiluted evaporated milk, whipped.

⅔ cup granulated sugar
2 cups, peeled, sliced peaches
½ teaspoon granulated gelatine
1 tablespoon cold water
⅓ cup evaporated milk

⅔ cup warm water
½ teaspoon salt
1 tablespoon cornstarch
2 egg yolks, beaten thick
1 teaspoon vanilla extract

⅔ cup undiluted evaporated milk, whipped (Recipe No. 8.)

Sprinkle sugar over sliced peaches and let stand for 30 minutes, then force through a sieve, using a coarse one. Soak granulated gelatine in cold water for 5 minutes. Combine 1/3 cup undiluted evaporated milk and warm water, and scald in the usual way, and pour over the softened gelatine. Then add salt and cornstarch which have been mixed with enough cold water to form a smooth, thin paste. Cook, over hot water, stirring constantly, until mixture coats the spoon; then pour creamy mixture over thickly beaten egg yolks; return to double boiler and cook few minutes longer, or until mixture is thick. Chill. When cool, fold in the sieved peach pulp and juice, alternately with the whipped undiluted evaporated milk. Freeze either in hand freezer pail, using equal parts ice and rock salt for 2½ to 3 hours, or in the refrigerator tray, either molded or right into the tray. If small molds are used, freeze for 2 to 2½ hours; if large mold or mixture is frozen right into the tray, freeze for 3½ to 4 hours.

335   **PEACH MOUSSE II**
(Refrigerator tray)

1 cup fresh peach pulp, sieved	3 tablespoons boiling water
½ cup granulated sugar	⅛ teaspoon almond extract
⅛ teaspoon salt	1 cup heavy cream, whipped
1 teaspoon granulated gelatine	stiff
2 tablespoons cold water	

Combine peach pulp, sugar, salt, and mix thoroughly. Let stand 30 minutes. Then add granulated gelatine soaked in cold water, then dissolved in boiling water, and mix well, adding meanwhile the almond extract. Lastly, fold in the whipped stiff heavy cream, and freeze in hand freezer or refrigerator tray, following the directions for recipe No. 319, Coffee Mousse I.

336   **PEACH MOUSSE III**
(Refrigerator tray)

A fine party dessert using canned peaches and marshmallows. A combination of ice cream and mousse.

1 cup canned peach pulp	20 marshmallows, cut and melted
¼ cup ground pistachio nuts	¼ teaspoon salt
1 cup orange juice	1 cup heavy cream, whipped
Grated rind of ½ orange	stiff
1 teaspoon lemon juice	

To the peach pulp, add ground pistachio nuts, and chill. Heat orange pulp, grated rind of orange and lemon juice, then stir in the marshmallows, cut fine by using a pair of scissors dipped in flour. Stir until mixture is thoroughly blended. Cool, then chill. Lastly fold in the stiffly whipped heavy cream and spread creamy mixture into the two trays. Allow to freeze for 1½ hours, then without stirring, nor scraping, spread over one tray the peach nut mixture which has been thoroughly chilled and is free of juice, and freeze for 3 hours longer. To serve: Place the peach lined tray on to a well-chilled platter, and cover with the other tray, sandwich-like. You may decorate with designs of whipped cream, forced through a pastry bag with a fancy tube.

337   PEACH MOUSSE IV
(Hand freezer pail or refrigerator tray)

This frozen dessert is very smooth, mellow and light. Fresh peaches should be used.

1 cup fresh peach pulp, free of juice	¼ cup powdered sugar
	⅛ teaspoon salt
1 pint heavy cream, whipped stiff	½ scant teaspoon almond extract

To the stiffly whipped heavy cream, add all the other ingredients and pack either in large mold or small molds or paper cases, and freeze as indicated for recipe No. 319, Coffee Mousse I.

338   PEACH MOUSSE BISCUIT
(Refrigerator tray)

To the above recipe, molding in paper cases, add when mixture begins to freeze 1/3 cup of crumbled, sieved macaroons, stir gently, smooth and continue freezing 2½ hours longer without stirring. You may sprinkle over a small pinch of ground, or finely chopped pistachio nut meats.

339 PEANUT BRITTLE MOUSSE I
(Refrigerator tray)

No stirring required. Have ready ¼ cup peanut brittle made as indicated for recipe No. 17, under "General Information," and proceed as follows:

2 whole eggs, slightly beaten
½ cup maple syrup, heated

1 cup heavy cream, whipped stiff
⅛ teaspoon salt
¼ generous cup ground or pin-rolled peanut brittle

Over the slightly beaten whole eggs, pour slowly the hot maple syrup, cook over hot water, until mixture thickens, beating constantly with rotary egg beater. Cool, then chill. Lastly, add stiffly beaten or rather whipped heavy cream into which the salt and ground peanut brittle has been folded. Fill paper cases, or place directly into freezing tray, and freeze until solid. If paper cases are used, freeze from 2 to 2½ hours; if poured directly into the refrigerator tray, freeze 3½ to 4 hours.

Any other kind of nut brittle may be used, if desired.

340 PEANUT BRITTLE MOUSSE II
(Refrigerator tray)

½ lb. ground, sieved peanut brittle
1 teaspoon granulated gelatine

2 tablespoons cold milk
2 cups heavy cream, whipped stiff
¼ scant teaspoon salt

Soak granulated gelatine in cold milk for 5 minutes; soften over hot water, then add to the well-chilled heavy cream with the salt and whip until stiff; fold in sieved peanut brittle, and freeze as above.

[196]

341   PEPPERMINT MOUSSE
     (Hand freezer or refrigerator tray)

On account of the addition of marshmallows, this mousse is much more mellow and light than the Mint Mousse No. 330. No cornstarch is used, neither butter nor lemon juice.

1 cup fresh milk
20 marshmallows, cut small
1 cup heavy cream, whipped
     stiff

⅛ teaspoon salt
4 drops oil of peppermint
Green vegetable coloring

Place milk and marshmallows, which have been cut small, using a pair of scissors dipped in flour, in top of double boiler. Allow to scald, stirring constantly, so as to melt the marshmallows. Remove from hot water, cool, then chill. Lastly fold in the stiffly whipped heavy cream to which has been added the salt and a few drops of green vegetable coloring. Freeze as indicated for recipe No. 330, Mint Mousse.

342   PINEAPPLE MOUSSE   I
     (Refrigerator tray or hand freezer)

In the following recipe, canned pineapple juice is used. If you use fresh pineapple juice, have it boiled first before stirring in the granulated gelatine.

1 teaspoon granulated gelatine
1 tablespoon cold water
2 tablespoons boiling water
¼ teaspoon salt
2 tablespoons lemon juice

½ cup granulated sugar
2 cups heavy cream, whipped
     stiff
1 cup syrup from canned pineapple

Soak granulated gelatine in cold water; dissolve in boiling water and add to canned pineapple syrup combined with lemon

[197]

juice and sugar. Then, heat mixture to the boiling point, strain while hot; chill until mixture begins to congeal, and beat until light. Lastly fold in the stiffly whipped heavy cream. Freeze in refrigerator tray, molded or unmolded, for 3½ to 4 hours. You may freeze, that is pack, after molding in hand freezer pail, using equal parts ice and rock salt, for 3 hours.

343   PINEAPPLE MOUSSE II
(Hand freezer pail or refrigerator tray)

1 pint heavy cream
2 whole eggs, slightly beaten
¼ teaspoon salt

1 cup well-drained crushed pineapple

Whip the heavy cream until fairly stiff, then slowly pour in the cream the slightly beaten eggs with the salt, continuing whipping the mixture until stiff, alternately with the well-drained crushed pineapple. Freeze in refrigerator tray, either right in or molded for 4 hours if large mold, or for 2½ to 3 hours, if individual molds or paper cases; or in hand freezer pail, using equal parts ice and rock salt, for 2½ hours, if large mold, and 1½ hours, if small molds.

344   PINEAPPLE MOUSSE III
(Hand freezer pail or refrigerator tray)

Another good and easy recipe using crushed pineapple and undiluted whipped evaporated milk. The stabilizer used is melted marshmallows with the syrup of the canned pineapple.

2¼ cups (1 No. 2 can) crushed
    pineapple thoroughly drained
    The syrup from canned pine-
    apple

¼ cup lemon juice
¼ teaspoon (scant) salt
1 can undiluted evaporated
    milk, whipped (see No. 8.)

2 dozen quartered marshmallows

Drain the pineapple; place the syrup in top of double boiler; add the quartered marshmallows and melt, over hot water, stirring constantly until mixture is thoroughly blended; then stir in the salt, drained crushed pineapple and lemon juice. Cool, then chill. Lastly fold in the whipped undiluted evaporated milk, as per recipe No. 8, under "General Information." Freeze molded or unmolded, in refrigerator tray for 4 hours if large mold, or right in the tray, 2½ to 3 hours, if individual molds or paper cases. If hand freezer pail is used, pack in equal parts ice and rock salt, and freeze for 3 long hours, for a large mold, and 1½ to 2 hours, if individual molds.

345   PISTACHIO CHERRY MOUSSE
        (Hand freezer pail or refrigerator tray)

2 cups heavy cream, whipped to   2 egg whites, stiffly beaten with
  a custard-like consistency with   ¼ teaspoon (scant) salt
⅓ cup light corn syrup   ⅓ cup blanched, chopped pis-
½ teaspoon pistachio extract   tachio nuts
   1 small bottle green maraschino cherries, drained and chopped

To the heavy cream, whipped to a custard-like consistency, fold in the light corn syrup with the pistachio extract. Fold in the stiffly beaten egg whites with the salt, alternately with chopped pistachio nut meats and the chopped, well-drained green maraschino cherries. Freeze in refrigerator tray for 2½ hours, if individual molds or paper cups are used, and 3½ to 4 hours, if large mold or mixture is frozen right in the tray. If hand freezer pail method is used, pack in equal parts ice and rock salt, and freeze 1½ to 2 hours for individual molds and 2½ to 3 hours for large mold.

346 PRUNE MOUSSE
(Refrigerator tray or hand freezer)

1 cup heavy cream, whipped to a custard-like consistency
1 can sieved prunes

2 tablespoons powdered sugar
1 egg white, stiffly beaten
⅛ teaspoon salt

4 drops almond extract

When the heavy cream is partially whipped to a custard-like consistency, add salt and sugar and beat until stiff. Then fold in the sieved prunes, alternately with the stiffly beaten egg white into which has been stirred the almond extract. Freeze in refrigerator tray, or mold, for 3½ to 4 hours; if individual molds, or paper cases are used, freeze 2 to 2½ hours. If hand freezer tray pail is used, pack, using equal parts of ice and salt, and let stand 2 hours for individual molds, and 3 hours for large mold. The children like this way to serve them prunes.

347 RASPBERRY MOUSSE I
(Hand freezer pail or refrigerator tray)

1 cup fresh strawberry pulp and juice, sieved
¼ teaspoon salt
¾ cup powdered sugar

1 teaspoon granulated gelatine
1 tablespoon cold water
2 cups heavy cream, whipped stiff

Combine strawberry pulp and juice, salt and powdered sugar. Soak gelatine in cold water for 5 minutes, then dissolve over hot water and add to strawberry mixture; then fold in the stiffly whipped heavy cream. Freeze as indicated for recipe No. 346, Prune Mousse.

348 **RASPBERRY MOUSSE II**
(Hand freezer pail or refrigerator tray)

A very smooth, mellow raspberry mousse resulting from the combination of evaporated milk, egg yolk and heavy cream which makes it fluffy and melt in the mouth. This frozen delicacy may be made in the hand freezer pail, or in the refrigerator tray, molded or right in the tray. If you want to enhance the beauty of the color of the cream, garnish, when unmolded, with a few whole, ripe raspberries.

1 cup fresh, ripe raspberries	4 tablespoons undiluted, evaporated milk
⅛ generous teaspoon salt	rated milk
½ cup granulated sugar	¾ cup heavy cream
1 egg white, unbeaten	4 drops lemon extract

Sprinkle sugar over fresh raspberries, then the salt, and let stand 10 minutes. Crush them, then strain through a fine sieve to remove the seeds. Combine unbeaten egg white, undiluted evaporated milk and heavy cream, and whip until stiff, then folding in the lemon extract. Combine raspberry pulp and juice and cream-egg mixture; mix well. Freeze into refrigerator tray, either molded or right into the tray for 3½ to 4 hours. Or, mold and freeze in hand freezer pail, using equal parts ice and rock salt, for 3 hours.

349 **RASPBERRY MOUSSE III**
(Hand freezer pail or refrigerator tray)

A very appropriate mousse for the budgeteers, as undiluted evaporated milk and gelatine, which are obtainable at low cost, are used.

[201]

1 cup undiluted evaporated milk scalded	1½ cups fresh, ripe raspberries
	1 scant cup powdered sugar
½ teaspoon granulated gelatine	⅛ generous teaspoon salt
2 teaspoons cold water	¾ teaspoon vanilla extract

To the hot scalded milk, add the softened gelatine in cold water and stir until dissolved. Chill well. To the fresh ripe raspberries, add sugar and salt, let stand 10 minutes, then crush and strain through a fine sieve to remove the seeds. Whip the scalded, chilled evaporated milk-gelatine mixture until stiff (see recipe No. 8, under "General Information"). Fold in the vanilla extract, then the raspberry pulp and juice. Freeze, either in hand freezer pail, or in refrigerator tray, following directions for recipe No. 346, Prune Mousse.

350   STRAWBERRY MOUSSE I
(Hand freezer pail or refrigerator tray)

4 cups whole, fresh strawberries	¼ teaspoon salt
1 cup granulated sugar	1 cup undiluted evaporated
2 tablespoons cornstarch	milk whipped stiff
2 tablespoons cold water	2 egg whites, whipped stiff
6 drops vanilla extract	

Wash, stem and press fresh, ripe strawberries through a sieve; add sugar, and heat to the boiling point. Combine, and mix well, cornstarch, salt and cold water to form a smooth thin paste, and add to hot mixture stirring constantly, while pouring, to prevent lumping. Cook, continuing stirring constantly until mixture thickens, that is, coats a spoon. Strain, while hot, through a fine sieve. Chill; then fold in milk that has been whipped as indicated for recipe No. 8, under "General Information" alternately with the stiffly beaten egg whites. Freeze according to directions for recipe No. 346, Prune Mousse.

351   STRAWBERRY MOUSSE II
        (Hand freezer pail or refrigerator tray)

Of course, the amount of sugar may be less or more, according to sweetness of the berries.

1 cup strained strawberry pulp   ¼ teaspoon salt
   and juice   1 pint heavy cream, whipped
1 teaspoon lemon juice   stiff
                ¾ cup powdered sugar

Combine fresh strawberry pulp and juice, which have been strained through a fine sieve, lemon juice, powdered sugar (more or less) and salt. Mix thoroughly and chill. Then fold in the stiffly whipped heavy cream and freeze 3½ to 4 hours in refrigerator tray, or 3 hours in hand freezer pail (when molded).

352   STRAWBERRY MOUSSE III
        (Hand freezer pail or refrigerator tray)

One of the simplest, easy to make, out-of-season strawberry ice creams:

1 cup preserved strawberries   1 cup heavy cream, whipped
                                      stiff
        A few drops of vanilla extract or lemon juice

To the stiffly whipped heavy cream to which has been added a few drops of vanilla extract or a little lemon juice (about 1 teaspoon) fold in the entire content of the cup of preserved strawberries. Chill and freeze as directed for recipe No. 346, Prune Mousse.

353 SHERRY WINE MOUSSE

Proceed as indicated for recipe No. 307, Brandy Mousse, substituting good sherry wine for brandy. Freeze as directed.

354 TEA MOUSSE
(Hand freezer tray or refrigerator tray)

3 tablespoons of your favorite good tea	2 cups heavy cream, or undiluted evaporated milk, whipped stiff
1¼ cups boiling water	
¾ scant cup granulated sugar	¼ scant teaspoon salt
6 egg yolks, unbeaten	3 drops lemon extract

¼ cup assorted, chopped fine (not ground) candied fruits

Prepare an infusion with the tea and water in the usual way, letting it stand until very strong. Strain through double cheesecloth, and off the fire stir in the granulated sugar until thoroughly dissolved. Cook over a gentle flame for 5 long minutes. Strain again while hot and allow to cool a little, then beat in egg yolks, one at a time, beating well after each addition. The mixture should be almost white. Then fold in the heavy cream or undiluted evaporated milk, whipped stiff, alternately with salt, lemon extract and chopped fine, but not ground, candied fruits. Freeze as directed for recipe No. 346, Prune Mousse. Remarkably delicious. You may, if desired, add 1 tablespoon of good rum or brandy, when folding in the whipped cream or milk.

355 VANILLA (or other flavorings) MOUSSE
(Hand freezer or refrigerator tray)

1 cup heavy cream whipped stiff	⅛ teaspoon salt
	½ generous teaspoon vanilla extract
¼ scant cup powdered sugar	

1 egg white, stiffly beaten

Fold into the stiffly whipped heavy cream, the powdered sugar, salt and vanilla extract; then fold in the stiffly beaten egg white. Freeze as indicated for recipe No. 346, Prune Mousse.

356   VANILLA TAPIOCA MOUSSE
(Hand freezer or refrigerator tray)

2 cups rich milk, scalded
3 tablespoons   quick-cooking tapioca
¼ teaspoon salt
½ scant teaspoon grated lemon rind

½ cup granulated sugar
3 tablespoons corn syrup or honey
1 cup heavy cream, whipped stiff
1½ teaspoons vanilla extract

Let fall, rain-like, the quick-cooking tapioca into the scalded milk, into which has been stirred the sugar, corn syrup or honey, salt and grated lemon rind. Cook over hot water, stirring almost constantly until mixture is thick. Now, while hot, rub through a fine strainer, chill, then beat well until creamy and light. Fold in the whipped heavy cream and vanilla, and freeze as directed for recipe No. 346, Prune Mousse.

SECTION VIII

Parfait Recipes

⫸⫸⫸⫸⫸⫸⫸⫸⫸⫸⫸⫷⫷⫷⫷⫷⫷⫷⫷⫷⫷⫷⫷

The final touch of a perfect parfait is the topping with whipped cream, forced through a pastry bag with a small fancy tube. This may be then, topped with either a candied cherry, or a piece of nut, or candied fruit. For effect and contrast, the whipped cream may be colored, according to occasion.

357   **WHAT IS A PARFAIT?**

Parfait, which means "perfect" in French, differs from ice cream in that it is less cold and more creamy, which makes this French creation more delicate. The name "PARFAIT", which used to apply exclusively to "Coffee Parfait", has become very popular in America. Sometimes parfaits are called "Bombes" when their composition is of only one kind of flavoring, their preparation is similar to the bombes, which consist of a thick creamy mixture, in which the same amount of whipped cream is incorporated, before being frozen.

Parfaits may be molded or served in special chilled glasses. They are much appreciated because they do not require special treatment, and are classed among the light ice creams. They may be made with almost any kind of fruit, canned, fresh or dried, as well as with almost any kind of sweet cordials or liqueurs or dessert wines. Whisky, however, is not recommended.

To freeze a parfait in mechanical refrigerator, pack in tray, or mold and place in tray and freeze until firm, or about 2½ hours. To freeze in hand freezer pail, fill mold or molds to overflowing. Cover with buttered paper, then with buttered muslin or cheesecloth around the rim, to prevent salt water from entering into the creamy mixture; or rub butter around rim of the mold or molds, and let stand for about two hours if in small molds, and 3 to 3½ hours if large molds. Use equal parts of ice and rock salt, over and around the molds, turning off the salt water as it accumulates, before it reaches the top of the molds.

In almost every parfait recipe, the basic foundation is a sugar syrup cooked to the indicated stage or degree, egg whites, cream or undiluted whipped evaporated milk, flavoring, and in some granulated gelatine is used as a stabilizer.

358 ALMOND CHERRY ANGEL PARFAIT
(Hand freezer pail or refrigerator tray)

In this recipe egg whites, which hold air bubbles and prevent coarse texture, and gelatine, to help keep ice crystals apart, are used, while cream prevents formation of ice crystals.

½ cup granulated sugar	½ cup blanched, chopped almonds
½ cup water	
2 egg whites, stiffly beaten	1 cup heavy cream, whipped stiff
2 tablespoons cold water	
1½ teaspoons granulated gelatine	1 scant teaspoon almond extract
½ cup chopped maraschino cherries	¼ teaspoon salt

Stir granulated sugar into ½ cup water until dissolved. Boil over a gentle flame, until syrup is at the soft ball stage (238 deg. F.). Immediately pour in a fine stream on to the stiffly beaten egg whites, beating briskly and constantly until mixture is cool.

Then add soaked gelatine in the 2 tablespoons of cold water, dissolve over hot water, and stir until thoroughly blended. Continue beating for 1 minute, placing the pan in cold or ice water. Then add chopped, slightly squeezed maraschino cherries and almonds, and fold in the stiffly whipped heavy cream with almond extract and salt. Freeze as directed for recipe No. 357.

359 ANGEL PARFAIT I
(Hand freezer pail or refrigerator tray)

Same as recipe No. 358, Almond Cherry Angel Parfait, omitting maraschino cherries and blanched chopped almonds. Freeze as directed for recipe No. 357.

360 ANGEL PARFAIT II
(Hand freezer pail or refrigerator tray)

¾ cup water
⅔ cup granulated sugar
3 egg whites, stiffly beaten

¼ scant teaspoon salt
2 cups (1 pint) heavy cream, whipped stiff

1 scant teaspoon vanilla extract

Stir sugar into water and boil until syrup spins a thread when dropped from tip of spoon. Immediately pour in a fine stream on to stiffly beaten egg whites, beating briskly and constantly until mixture is cool. Lastly fold in the stiffly whipped heavy cream with salt and vanilla extract. Freeze as directed for recipe No. 357.

361 ANGEL FOOD PARFAIT
(Hand freezer pail or refrigerator tray)

In this remarkably rich and delicious parfait, called in French "Parfait des Anges", or perfect angel food, the energy-giving quality of candy is included.

[208]

1 teaspoon granulated gelatine
2 tablespoons cold water
½ cup water
½ cup granulated sugar
2 egg whites, stiffly beaten
½ teaspoon almond extract

1½ cups heavy cream, whipped stiff
3 tablespoons orange juice
¼ cup each of candied cherries, candied pineapple, candied citron and candied apricots

¼ scant teaspoonful salt

Soak granulated gelatine in the 2 tablespoons of cold water for 5 minutes. Make a sugar-syrup with water and granulated sugar, boiling until syrup spins a thread when dropped from tip of a spoon. Immediately pour in a fine stream on to stiffly beaten egg whites, beating briskly and constantly, then beat in the soaked gelatine and continue beating until mixture is cool and begins to set. Fold in the stiffly whipped heavy cream, alternately with orange juice and candied fruit, cut fine (not ground), and lastly add the flavoring extract. Freeze as directed for recipe No. 357.

362   APRICOT PARFAIT
(Hand freezer pail or refrigerator tray)

In the following recipe dried cooked apricots are used. The binding is made with cornstarch added to the custard, and undiluted evaporated milk, whipped stiff, adds smoothness, since its butterfat and solid substances hold air bubbles and prevent crystallization.

16 dried, cooked apricots, sieved
⅓ cup evaporated milk, diluted with
⅔ cup hot water
1 tablespoon cornstarch
A little cold water
2 egg yolks, stiffly beaten

⅔ cup granulated sugar
¼ teaspoon salt
½ teaspoon granulated gelatine
1 tablespoon cold water
⅔ cup undiluted evaporated milk, whipped stiff
4 to 5 drops almond extract

Wash dried apricots, rinse, add ½ cup cold water, and let soak overnight, after cutting into small pieces. Cook to a mush, and put through a sieve. Combine 1/3 cup undiluted evaporated milk and hot water in a double boiler, stir in the cornstarch which has been mixed with a little cold water, then stir in the thickly beaten egg yolks with the granulated sugar. Cook over hot water until mixture coats the spoon, stirring constantly. Then, add gelatine which has been soaked in 1 tablespoon cold water and continue cooking until gelatine is dissolved. Pour through a double cheesecloth, then over sieved apricots and mix thoroughly. Chill. Add stiffly whipped undiluted evaporated milk (see recipe No. 8) to which has been added the salt and almond extract. Freeze as directed for recipe No. 357.

363   BUTTERSCOTCH PARFAIT
(Hand freezer pail or refrigerator tray)

½ cup brown sugar
3 tablespoons butter
½ cup hot water
1½ generous teaspoons vanilla extract

2 egg yolks, beaten until very light
2 cups heavy cream, whipped stiff
¼ scant teaspoon salt

Place brown sugar and butter in a skillet and stir over a gentle fire until thoroughly blended and melted, then cook for 1 short minute, and add hot water. Mix well and boil for 5 short minutes. Immediately pour in a fine stream onto beaten egg yolks, beaten briskly and constantly. Return to hot water and cook until mixture is very light. Strain through double cheesecloth, and chill. Then add stiffly whipped heavy cream, vanilla extract and salt. Freeze as directed for recipe No. 357.

364   A BUTTERSCOTCH ANGEL
              FOOD PARFAIT

In the above recipe, you may substitute ¼ teaspoon almond extract for ½ teaspoon of vanilla extract. This will give an added
flavor. You may, also, add ½ cup candied fruit, cut fine, before
freezing, if desired.

365   CHOCOLATE MARRON PARFAIT
              (Hand freezer pail or refrigerator tray)

To a chocolate Parfait mixture, add, before freezing, ½ gener-
ous cup of marrons (chestnuts) prepared as indicated for recipe
No. 191, Marron Glacé Ice Cream. Freeze as directed for recipe
No. 357.

366   CHOCOLATE PARFAIT I
              (Hand freezer pail or refrigerator tray)

½ cup water	2 tablespoons cold water
½ cup granulated sugar	2 egg yolks, well-beaten
¼ teaspoon salt	1 cup heavy cream, whipped
1 scant teaspoon granulated	stiff
gelatine	1½ teaspoons vanilla extract

2 squares bitter chocolate

Boil the ½ cup water, sugar and salt until syrup spins a thread
when dropped from the tip of a spoon. Then stir in the grated
bitter chocolate which has been melted over hot water, and
immediately pour chocolate syrup in a fine stream on to well-
beaten egg yolks, beating briskly and constantly. Then add
granulated gelatine which has been soaked in the 2 tablespoons
of cold water, and continue beating until gelatine is dissolved.

Cool, stirring occasionally. Fold in stiffly whipped heavy cream and vanilla extract. Freeze as directed for recipe No. 357.

367 CHOCOLATE PARFAIT II
(Hand freezer pail or refrigerator tray)

¾ cup granulated sugar
⅓ cup boiling water
2 squares chocolate melted over hot water
¼ scant teaspoon salt

2 cups heavy cream, whipped stiff
1½ generous teaspoons vanilla extract

3 egg yolks, beaten until light

Combine sugar and boiling water, and stir until sugar is dissolved, then cook until syrup spins a thread from the tip of a spoon (230 deg. F.). Then add salt and melted chocolate. Blend well, and immediately pour chocolate syrup in a fine stream into beaten egg yolks, beating briskly and constantly until thoroughly blended. Chill. Add stiffly whipped heavy cream and vanilla extract and freeze as directed for recipe No. 357.

368 COFFEE CARAMEL PARFAIT
(Hand freezer pail or refrigerator tray)

2 egg yolks, beaten with
½ cup granulated sugar, and
¼ scant teaspoon salt
1½ cups heavy cream, whipped stiff

1½ cups milk, scalded with
2 generous tablespoons ground good coffee
½ cup granulated sugar, caramelized

1 teaspoon vanilla extract

TO CARAMELIZE SUGAR: Place ½ cup of granulated sugar in skillet over a gentle flame and stir constantly until melted and dark brown. Remove from the fire and add immediately to coffee-milk mixture.

Scald milk with ground coffee in double boiler and allow to stand, removed from hot water, 5 short minutes. Then strain through double cheesecloth, add caramelized sugar and stir well. Beat egg yolks with remaining ½ cup of granulated sugar and salt and slowly pour scalded milk mixture over egg mixture, stirring briskly and constantly until blended. Return to double boiler and cook, stirring constantly until mixture coats the spoon. Cool. Fold in stiffly whipped heavy cream and vanilla, and freeze as directed for recipe No. 357.

369   COFFEE PARFAIT I
(Hand freezer pail or refrigerator tray)

1½ cups rich milk, scalded	¼ scant teaspoon salt, and
1½ cups extra strong coffee liquid	½ generous cup granulated sugar
4 egg yolks beaten with	½ teaspoon vanilla extract
¼ scant cup of good rum	

Scald milk, remove from the fire and combine with strong coffee liquid. Place egg yolks in a saucepan with salt and sugar and beat mercilessly until thoroughly blended and almost white. Then pour hot milk mixture in a fine stream into beaten egg yolk mixture, beating briskly and constantly. Return this mixture to the fire, and cook, stirring constantly, until mixture coats the spoon. Strain through double cheesecloth. Fill a melon mold to overflowing with the creamy mixture and freeze, either in hand freezer pail or refrigerator tray, according to directions for recipe No. 357, until mushy. Then add and stir in the vanilla extract combined with the rum (curaçao liqueur, or brandy may be substituted for rum, if desired), and continue freezing until solid, or about 2½ hours or longer, according to size of mold. Unmold on to a chilled serving platter, and garnish with plain whipped cream forced through a pastry bag with a fancy tube.

[213]

370 COFFEE PARFAIT II
(Hand freezer pail or refrigerator tray)

1 cup extra strong coffee liquid	3 egg yolks, slightly beaten
1 scant cup granulated sugar	¼ cup cold water
¼ teaspoon salt	1 envelope (tablespoon) granu-
½ teaspoon vanilla extract	lated gelatine

2 cups heavy cream, whipped stiff

Make a custard of extra strong coffee liquid, sugar, salt and egg yolks, in the usual way. Strain while hot, then add gelatine which has been soaked in cold water, and stir until dissolved. Fold in the stiffly whipped heavy cream (or undiluted evaporated milk, if desired) and vanilla, and freeze as directed for recipe No. 357. You may serve, as a side accompaniment, Gingerbread Fingers, made by cutting thin sheet of gingerbread in finger-length strips. Then split and spread with your favorite frosting, and put together sandwich-like. A topping of stiffly whipped, unflavored and unsweetened cream forced through a pastry bag is "de rigueur".

371 CRANBERRY PARFAIT
(Hand freezer pail or refrigerator tray)

A very appropriate parfait for Thanksgiving Day.

½ can cranberry sauce	1 cup heavy cream, whipped
2 tablespoons powdered sugar	stiff
1 egg white, stiffly beaten	½ generous teaspoon almond ex-
⅛ teaspoon salt	tract

6 red or green maraschino cherries

Beat together with a fork cranberry sauce, powdered sugar and salt. Then fold in the stiffly beaten egg white and stiffly beaten heavy cream, folding gently, the cream whipped with almond extract, and add to cranberry mixture. Freeze as directed for recipe No. 357. Top each serving with a rosette of whipped cream, and place a red or green cherry on top of the whipped cream rosette.

372 CRANBERRY RICE PARFAIT
(Hand freezer pail or refrigerator tray)

A very appropriate parfait for children's party, and an excellent accompaniment for roast turkey or chicken. The creamy mixture should be frozen to a mush before adding the cold, grainy cooked rice. Tapicoa may be substituted for rice, if desired.

1 tablespoon granulated gelatine	4 tablespoons lemon juice
2 tablespoons cold water	2 cups granulated sugar
1 quart cranberries, cooked then sieved	¼ teaspoon salt
	1 cup cold, cooked boiled rice

Soak gelatine in cold water, and add to the cooked, sieved, hot cranberries with the sugar. Cool a little, then stir in lemon juice. Chill. Freeze as directed for recipe No. 357, until mushy. Open the mold quickly and fold in lightly, chilled, cooked rice. Return to freezer or refrigerator tray and freeze for ¾ hour longer.

373 FIG PARFAIT
(Hand freezer tray or refrigerator tray)

1 cup fig syrup	3 tablespoons orange juice
1 cup granulated sugar	¼ teaspoon salt
2 egg whites, stiffly beaten	1 cup chopped canned figs (very fine)
1 teaspoon grated orange rind	
1 tablespoon granulated gelatine	1 cup heavy cream, whipped stiff
2 tablespoons cold water	
¼ cup chopped nut meats (optional)	

Combine and boil fig syrup and sugar until syrup spins a thread from the tip of a spoon. Immediately pour in a fine stream on to stiffly beaten egg whites, beating briskly and constantly. Then add granulated gelatine which has been soaked in cold water and dissolved over hot water with orange juice, salt and grated orange rind, continuing beating until mixture is cold. Chill. Then fold in the chopped figs, alternately with whipped cream and chopped nuts (optional). Freeze as directed for recipe No. 357.

374   GOLDEN PARFAIT I
(Hand freezer pail or refrigerator tray)

¾ cup granulated sugar
⅓ cup boiling water
3 egg yolks, beaten until light

⅛ teaspoon salt
2 cups heavy cream, whipped stiff

1¾ teaspoons vanilla extract

Make a sugar syrup with water and sugar, cooking it until it threads (230 deg. F.), that is, spins a thread from tip of a spoon. Immediately pour in a fine stream on to beaten light egg yolks, beating briskly and constantly until mixture is cool. Chill, then fold in stiffly whipped heavy cream and vanilla extract, and freeze as directed for recipe No. 357.

375   GOLDEN PARFAIT II
(Hand freezer pail or refrigerator tray)

½ cup water
½ cup granulated sugar
2 egg yolks, well-beaten
¼ teaspoon salt
1 cup heavy cream, or evaporated milk, whipped stiff

1 generous teaspoon vanilla extract
1 generous teaspoon granulated gelatine
2 tablespoons cold water

Boil sugar, water and salt until syrup spins a thread from the tip of a spoon (230 deg. F.). Immediately pour in a fine stream on to beaten egg yolks, beating constantly and briskly until well blended and cool. Then, add gelatine which has been soaked 5 minutes in cold water and dissolved over hot water, and beat for 1 long minute. Cool, stirring occasionally, then fold in whipped cream or milk with vanilla extract. Freeze as directed for recipe No. 357.

376   IMPERATRICE PARFAIT
(Hand freezer pail only)

This formula may seem laborious and complicated, but it is an easy one. You need a melon mold, having a partition in the center, or you may make one by using a thin piece of tin and placing it in the middle of the melon mold. Each side of the mold is then filled with a different parfait, flavored with different liqueur, then packed in hand freezer pail, using equal parts of ice and rock salt. For example one side will or may contain Brandy Parfait, or a coffee parfait made as indicated for recipe No. 369, Coffee Parfait I, and the other side a Lalla Rookh Parfait, which was very popular before prohibition. Or, one side may contain a parfait mixture, while the other side a liqueur flavored ice cream. The frozen dessert is then unmolded on to a block of colored ice (recipe No. 24, under "General Information") and the block of ice may be decorated according to fancy, with candied fruits, fresh fruits and the like. A real party frozen dessert.

377 ITALIAN MERINGUE PARFAIT
(Hand freezer pail or refrigerator tray)

¼ cup water
½ cup granulated sugar
3 egg whites, stiffly beaten with
¼ teaspoon salt

¼ teaspoon granulated gelatine
¾ cup heavy cream, whipped
stiff
1½ teaspoons vanilla extract

Make a sugar syrup with water and sugar, and boil 5 minutes or until syrup spins a thread when dropped from the tip of a spoon (230 deg. F.). Immediately pour in a fine stream on to stiffly beaten egg whites, beating briskly and constantly, having the pan in ice water and beating until cold. Then add granulated gelatine, which has been dissolved in a small amount of boiling water, by straining gelatine mixture into the mixture. Lastly, add stiffly whipped heavy cream and vanilla extract and freeze as lirected for recipe No. 357.

378 LALLA ROOKH PARFAIT

Put French Vanilla Ice Cream or your favorite vanilla ice cream recipe in a small size parfait glass. Scoop out the center and fill with either sherry wine or cognac (brandy), cover the top of the glass with whipped cream forced through a pastry bag with a small fancy tube.

379 MACAROON PARFAIT
(Hand freezer or refrigerator tray)

To a recipe No. 358, Almond Cherry Angel Parfait, add 1 cup dried pounded macaroons instead of almonds. Freeze as indicated.

380   MAPLE PARFAIT I
(Hand freezer pail or refrigerator tray)

⅔ cup hot maple syrup   1 pint heavy cream, whipped
4 whole eggs, slightly beaten   stiff
¼ teaspoonful salt

Pour in a fine stream on to the slightly beaten whole eggs, the hot maple syrup, beating briskly and constantly. Return mixture to double boiler and cook, stirring constantly, until mixture coats the spoons. Cool, then add stiffly whipped heavy cream with the salt. Freeze as directed for recipe No. 357.

381   MAPLE PARFAIT II
(Hand freezer pail or refrigerator tray)

1 cup hot maple syrup   2 cups heavy cream, whipped
3 egg yolks, beaten until light   stiff
⅛ teaspoon salt   1 teaspoon desired flavoring

Pour the hot maple syrup in a fine stream on to the egg yolks beaten with the salt, beating briskly and constantly. Return mixture to double boiler and cook, stirring constantly, until mixture coats the spoon. Cool, then add stiffly whipped heavy cream and desired flavoring extract. Freeze as directed for recipe No. 357.

382   MAPLE PARFAIT III
(Hand freezer pail or refrigerator tray)

This recipe requires less maple sugar, and butter is used. A very fluffy and rich mixture.

¼ cup maple syrup   ⅛ teaspoon salt
1 tablespoon butter   1 teaspoon vanilla extract
2 egg yolks, beaten until light   ¼ cup assorted candied fruit, cut
2 egg whites, stiffly beaten   very fine or ground
1 cup heavy cream whipped stiff

Add maple syrup to butter in double boiler, and stir over low flame until thoroughly blended. Do not allow to boil. Then pour in fine stream the beaten egg yolks over the hot syrup, beating briskly and constantly until mixture coats the spoon, is light and fluffy. Now stir in the stiffly beaten egg whites, beating rapidly. Cool, then chill. Lastly fold in the stiffly whipped heavy cream, salt, vanilla extract and cut fine candied fruit. Freeze as directed for recipe No. 357. You may freeze in refrigerator tray, for at least 3 hours, and serve in chilled parfait glasses, topping each glass with a rosette of whipped cream (unsweetened and un-flavored) forced through a pastry bag with a small tube.

383 MARRON GLACÉ PARFAIT
(Hand freezer pail or refrigerator tray)

¼ cup water
⅔ cup granulated sugar
6 egg yolks, thickly beaten
1 cup marrons, cut in small pieces (See recipe No. 191, Marron Glacé Ice Cream I.)

3 generous teaspoons vanilla ex-tract
2 cups heavy cream, whipped stiff

Make a sugar syrup with water and sugar, stir until sugar is dissolved, bring to the boiling point, and let boil for 5 long minutes without stirring, or until syrup spins a thread from tip of the spoon. Immediately pour in fine stream over the thickly beaten egg yolks, while beating briskly and constantly. Return to double boiler and cook, over hot water, stirring constantly until mixture coats the spoon. Remove from hot water and beat until cold. Then, add cooked marrons, as indicated for recipe No. 191, which have been cut in small pieces and soaked in the vanilla extract for at least 30 minutes after being cooked and drained. Do not add the vanilla extract remaining in the bowl, reserve it for other use, if any, because the chestnuts will have absorbed the greater part of it. Fold in the stiffly whipped heavy cream, and freeze as directed for recipe No. 357.

If fresh chestnuts are not available, or are out of season use dried ones, or you may substitute chopped nuts, or macaroon crumbs.

384 MARSHMALLOW RASPBERRY PARFAIT
(Refrigerator tray only)

15 marshmallows, quartered	⅛ teaspoon salt
1 cup rich milk, scalded	1¼ cups heavy cream, whipped
1 teaspoon vanilla extract	stiff
Raspberry sauce	

Add quartered marshmallows to the scalded milk. Beat with rotary egg beater, until thoroughly blended, then chill until slightly thickened. Stir in the salt, vanilla extract and stiffly whipped heavy cream. Place in refrigerator tray and freeze for 3½ hours. When ready to serve, have ready one of the following raspberry sauces:

RASPBERRY SAUCE I.

Cook together 1 cup fresh or canned raspberries and 1/3 cup of granulated sugar until mixture is syrupy. Chill. Serve.

RASPBERRY SAUCE II.

Mix 1 cup raspberry juice and ½ tablespoon lemon juice and bring to the boiling point. Dissolve scant ½ tablespoon cornstarch in a little cold water and add to the hot raspberry juice, stirring constantly. Then, add 1/3 cup (more or less, according to sweetness of fruit) and bring to the boiling point. Chill, or serve hot.

RASPBERRY SAUCE III.

Fold 4 tablespoons raspberry jam into ½ cup light cream, or undiluted evaporated milk, or still better into whipped evaporated milk or cream, using ½ cup of either. Chill.

[221]

Place a generous tablespoon of the raspberry sauce desired, in bottom of chilled parfait glass. Over this place 2 or 3 tablespoons of the frozen parfait, and top with more raspberry sauce. Or you may alternate layer of sauce, parfait mixture, and so on, until chilled glasses are full. Top each glass, if desired, with either a fresh or a canned or preserved raspberry.

385   MINT PARFAIT
(Hand freezer pail or refrigerator tray)

1 cup granulated sugar	2 cups heavy cream, stiffly
½ cup water	whipped
1 cup chopped fresh mint	2 or 3 drops green vegetable
2 egg whites, stiffly beaten	coloring
⅛ teaspoon salt	Chocolate sauce

Make a sugar syrup with sugar and water, bring to the boiling point, then boil for 10 minutes. Immediately pour this hot syrup over chopped mint, cover and let stand 1 hour. Then strain through double cheesecloth, and heat, but do not boil the mint syrup. While hot, pour over stiffly beaten egg whites, into fine stream, beating briskly and constantly, until mixture is cold. Now add salt and green vegetable coloring, combined with the heavy cream, stiffly whipped. Mold, and freeze as directed for recipe No. 357. Serve with your favorite chocolate sauce or cold chocolate syrup, if desired.

386   MOCHA PARFAIT (French method)
(Hand freezer only)

Place in a mixing bowl 8 egg yolks with ¼ teaspoon salt and ¼ cup cold water, and using rotary egg beater, beat the eggs until almost white. Then, continuing beating, pour in fine stream 1 cup of extra strong coffee liquid which has been heated to the boiling point. Beat rapidly and constantly, while adding gradually ½ generous cup of powdered sugar. Cook, over hot water, stirring constantly until mixture begins to coat the spoon. Remove from the fire, and stir in rapidly and briskly 1½ to 2 bitter chocolate squares, melted over hot water. Chill, then fold in 2 cups heavy cream stiffly whipped with 1½ teaspoons vanilla extract. Mold; bury in equal parts of ice and salt and let stand for 2 long hours. This parfait should be mellow and very light. Unmold onto a chilled platter, and decorate with small rosettes of whipped cream, forced through a pastry bag with a small fancy tube; or spoon into chilled parfait glasses, and top with whipped cream, also forced through a pastry bag.

387   ORANGE PARFAIT
        (Refrigerator tray or hand freezer)

1 egg yolk, slightly beaten	¼ cup cold water
¾ cup granulated sugar	¾ cup boiling water
Grated rind of 2 oranges	1 cup heavy cream, whipped to
¾ cup orange juice	a custard-like consistency
½ cup lemon juice	1 egg white, stiffly beaten
½ tablespoon granulated gelatine	¼ cup powdered sugar
¼ teaspoon salt	

Combine slightly beaten egg yolk with granulated sugar, orange rind, orange juice and lemon juice, and stir well until sugar is thoroughly dissolved. Then, add granulated gelatine which has been soaked in cold water and dissolved in boiling water, and stir well. Pour mixture in refrigerator tray and freeze until mushy. Then scrape bottom and sides and stir in the heavy cream, whipped to a custard-like consistency, into which has been folded the egg white stiffly beaten with the salt. Return to tray, and freeze again until mushy, then scrape bottom and sides, beat 1 short minute, return to tray and continue freezing, without stirring, for 3 hours.

Parfait Recipes

You may, after the second stirring, mold the creamy mixture, either in large mold or individual ones, and freeze in refrigerator tray, or pack in equal parts of ice and rock salt, and freeze as indicated for recipe No. 357.

388   ORANGE PINEAPPLE PARFAIT

1 pint orange ice cream
½ cup canned crushed pineapple and juice
¼ cup granulated sugar
⅛ teaspoon salt

Grated rind of ½ orange and juice
¼ cup blanched, chopped almonds

Cook crushed pineapple and juice with sugar and salt and orange rind and juice for 5 short minutes, stirring occasionally. Cool, then chill. To serve: Arrange layers of pineapple syrup and orange ice in chilled parfait glasses, and sprinkle with almonds.

389   PEACH PARFAIT
(Hand freezer or refrigerator tray)

1½ teaspoons granulated gelatine
2 tablespoons cold water
¼ cup water
½ cup granulated sugar
2 egg whites, stiffly beaten
¼ teaspoon salt

1 cup sieved peaches (canned or fresh
¼ cup orange juice
1 cup heavy cream, whipped stiff
½ teaspoon vanilla extract

Boil the ¼ cup water and sugar until syrup spins a thread when dropped from the tip of a spoon. Immediately pour in fine stream on to the stiffly beaten egg whites, while beating briskly and constantly until almost cold. Then add gelatine which has been soaked in cold water and softened over boiling water, and stir until thoroughly blended and gelatine is dissolved. Continue beating until mixture is cold and begins to set, then fold in the sieved peaches combined with orange juice, alternately with the stiffly whipped heavy cream with vanilla and salt. Freeze as directed for recipe No. 357.

390   PINEAPPLE PARFAIT I
(Hand freezer pail or refrigerator tray)

1½ teaspoons granulated gelatine	2 egg yolks, slightly beaten, with
2 tablespoons cold water	¼ scant teaspoon salt
½ cup canned pineapple juice	1 cup heavy cream, whipped stiff
5 tablespoons granulated sugar	

¾ teaspoon vanilla extract

Boil canned pineapple juice and sugar until syrup spins a thread when dropped from tip of a spoon. Immediately pour syrup in fine stream over slightly beaten egg yolks and salt, while beating briskly and constantly. Then add gelatine which has been soaked in cold water and dissolved over boiling water, and continue beating until mixture is cold and begins to set. Then fold in the stiffly whipped heavy cream with vanilla, and freeze as directed for recipe No. 357. For effect, and to add flavor, you may serve over chilled pineapple slices.

391   PINEAPPLE PARFAIT II
(Hand freezer or refrigerator tray)

The following formula does not require gelatine. The molding may be decorated with small pieces of canned pineapple and lady fingers, or any other kind of cookies or candied fruits.

1 cup canned pineapple juice	¼ scant teaspoon salt
⅓ cup granulated sugar	½ cup crushed canned pineapple
4 egg yolks, slightly beaten with	1 pint heavy cream, whipped stiff

4 drops almond extract (optional)

Make a sugar syrup with pineapple juice and sugar and boil until syrup spins a thread when dropped from the tip of a spoon (or 230 deg. F.). Immediately pour hot syrup in fine stream over the egg yolks which are in a container placed over a pan containing warm water, while beating briskly and constantly, until thick. Chill; add well-drained crushed pineapple, alternately with the stiffly whipped heavy cream and almond extract. Freeze as directed for recipe No. 357.

392   PINEAPPLE RICE PARFAIT

Proceed as indicated for recipe No. 391, Pineapple Parfait II, above, folding in, alternately with the whipped cream, 1 cup of well-grained cooked rice. Freeze as directed.

393   PISTACHIO PARFAIT I
(Hand freezer or refrigerator tray)

¼ cup water
1 cup granulated sugar
3 egg whites, stiffly beaten
¼ teaspoon salt
2 teaspoons vanilla extract
¾ teaspoon almond extract

2 cups heavy cream, whipped stiff and colored with
2 or 3 drops green vegetable coloring
½ cup coarsely ground pistachio nut meats

Make a sugar syrup with water and sugar, and boil until syrup spins a thread when dropped from the tip of a spoon, then immediately pour hot syrup in fine stream over stiffly beaten egg whites, while beating briskly and constantly, until mixture is cold. Then add combined vanilla and almond extracts. Add stiffly whipped heavy cream which has been colored with green vegetable coloring to the desired tender hue (see No. 11, under General Information), alternately with the coarsely ground pistachio nut meats. Freeze as directed for recipe No. 357.

394   PISTACHIO PARFAIT II
(*Hand freezer or refrigerator tray*)

As in the above recipe, the color should be a tender green. This formula includes granulated gelatine.

½ cup water
½ cup granulated sugar
2 egg whites, stiffly beaten
1½ teaspoons granulated gelatine
2 tablespoons cold water
¾ cup ground pistachio nut meats

1 cup heavy cream, whipped stiff
½ teaspoon pistachio extract
¼ teaspoon vanilla extract
¼ teaspoon salt

Make a sugar syrup with water (½ cup) and sugar, and boil until syrup spins a thread when dropped from the tip of a spoon. Immediately pour in a fine stream onto the stiffly beaten egg whites with the salt, while beating briskly and constantly, until mixture stands in peaks. Then stir in the granulated gelatine which has been soaked in the 2 tablespoons of cold water and dissolved over boiling water, and continue beating until well blended, and mixture begins to set. Then, fold in the heavy cream, stiffly beaten with the combined flavorings, alternately with the ground pistachio nut meats. Freeze as directed for recipe No. 357.

395   RASPBERRY PARFAIT I
(*Hand freezer pail or refrigerator tray*)

2 pints fresh raspberries
1 cup granulated sugar
2 teaspoons lemon juice
2 egg whites

⅛ generous teaspoon salt
1 cup heavy cream, whipped stiff

Wash, drain, and rub fresh raspberries through a sieve. Sprinkle over the sieved raspberries the granulated sugar and lemon juice, and let stand 30 minutes. Strain through a double cheesecloth, and bring the raspberry juice to a boil. Let boil until syrup spins a thread when dropped from the tip of a spoon. Immediately pour in a fine stream onto stiffly beaten egg whites, while beating briskly and constantly, until cold and mixture holds its peaks. Then fold in the stiffly whipped heavy cream with the salt, and freeze as directed for recipe No. 357.

IMPORTANT.—You may, if desired, proceed thus: To the sieved raspberries add ¾ cup of the sugar and lemon juice. Beat egg whites with the salt and remaining ¼ cup of granulated sugar, a small amount at a time. Then fold in this meringue, alternately with the stiffly whipped cream into the strained raspberry juice, blending thoroughly. Freeze as indicated above. This method, called the meringue method, eliminates cooking of the syrup. Yet, the smoothness is not the same.

396   RASPBERRY PARFAIT II
(Hand freezer pail or refrigerator tray)

1½ teaspoons granulated gelatine
2 tablespoons cold water
½ cup water
½ cup granulated sugar
2 egg whites, stiffly beaten with
¼ scant teaspoon salt

1 cup heavy cream (or evaporated milk) whipped stiff
2 pints fresh raspberries, washed, drained, then sieved and strained through cheesecloth
1 teaspoon vanilla extract

Make a sugar syrup with water and sugar, and boil until syrup spins a thread when dropped from the tip of a spoon. Immediately pour in a fine stream onto the stiffly beaten egg whites, while beating briskly and constantly. Then add gelatine which has been soaked in the 2 tablespoons of cold water, then dissolved over boiling water, and continue beating until mixture holds its peaks and begins to congeal. Fold in the stiffly whipped heavy cream or evaporated milk, (see recipe No. 8), alternately with strained raspberries, salt and vanilla extract. Freeze as directed for recipe No. 357.

A combination of equal parts of raspberries and strawberries, or equal parts of raspberries, strawberries and red currants, gives a delicious flavor.

397   SNOW BALL PARFAIT
            (A French recipe)

Have ready, molded melon-shaped, a Coffee Parfait made as indicated for recipe No. 369, Coffee Parfait I. When ready to serve, unmold onto a well-chilled platter, covered with a large paper lace doily. Then, using a pastry bag with a small fancy rose tube, cover the entire surface of the melon-shaped Coffee Parfait with small rosettes of unsweetened and unflavored whipped cream, each rosette, the size of a nickel, and close to one another so there is no uncovered spot. Onto each rosette, or dot, press very gently a small piece of candied angelica. (Angelica is the crystallized stalk of a plant of the rhubarb family growing extensively where rhubarb is found. It is a delicate green color.) Serve at once with a side dish of soft custard sauce flavored with maraschino liqueur, and another side dish of "Tuiles", a kind of very light wafer, usually served on the Continent with all sorts of ice creams, mousses, sherbets and parfaits (See recipe No. 401).

Simple, isn't it, and how delicious! Try this for your next party.

398   STRAWBERRY PARFAIT I
            (Hand freezer pail or refrigerator tray)

Proceed exactly as indicated for recipe No. 395, Raspberry Parfait I, substituting fresh strawberries for raspberries. Freeze as directed.

399 STRAWBERRY PARFAIT II
(Hand freezer pail or refrigerator tray)

Proceed exactly as indicated for recipe No. 396, Raspberry Parfait II, substituting fresh strawberries for fresh raspberries. Freeze as directed.

400 TRAILER PARFAIT
(Refrigerator tray only)

3 cups milk scalded	½ teaspoon salt
¾ cups rice	½ teaspoon vanilla extract
¾ cup white corn syrup	1 cup heavy cream, whipped
2 squares melted chocolate,	stiff
melted over hot water	¼ scant teaspoon almond extract
1 tablespoon grated bitter chocolate	

Scald milk in double boiler; add the rice which has been washed and well drained, and cook for about 1 hour, or until rice is tender and the milk is absorbed, stirring occasionally. Then stir in the corn syrup, melted chocolate and salt, and heat thoroughly, but do not allow to boil. Remove from hot water. Stir in the vanilla extract, and immediately fill 6 sherbet glasses with the mixture. Place in refrigerator tray and let stand 3½ to 4 hours. When ready to serve, top each parfait with plain whipped cream, forced through a pastry bag with a small fancy tube and sprinkle lightly with grated chocolate. Serve at once.

401 TUILES

Not a parfait, but delicious little French wafers, easy to prepare, and economical at that. They are usually served, on the Continent, with all sorts of frozen desserts, as well as champagne and sweet dessert wines. They may be kept a long time when packed in a container and kept in a dry cool place.

2½ tablespoons powdered sugar	A small pinch salt
1 whole egg, slightly beaten	Thin slices of blanched
¼ scant teaspoon vanilla extract	almonds
1 tablespoon pastry flour, sifted	Fine granulated sugar

Combine sugar, egg, vanilla and salt and mix well, but do not beat. Then add gradually the flour which has been sifted, and mix thoroughly. Place this soft paste onto the floured board and roll as thinly as possible. Cut into 3 x 3 inch squares, with the large spatula, place onto a buttered baking sheet and sprinkle with fine granulated sugar; then dot here and there with thin slices of blanched almonds (thin slices of pistachio nuts may be used), and bake 5 or 6 minutes, in a moderate oven (350 deg. F.). Remove and immediately roll each wafer around the handle of a wooden spoon. Cool until dry, pack or serve.

402   TUTTI-FRUTTI PARFAIT
(Hand freezer pail or refrigerator tray)

Two delicious methods here present themselves. The ingredients are the same, except that one formula requires the soaking of the cut fine candied fruit (French method) into your favorite liqueur, while the second one demands that the fruit should be soaked in fruit juice, maple syrup or honey. Hostess may select the one she prefers.

1½ teaspoons granulated gelatine	1 cup heavy cream, whipped stiff
2 tablespoons cold water	1 teaspoon vanilla extract
½ cup water	¼ teaspoon salt
½ cup granulated sugar	1 cup assorted candied fruits,
2 egg whites, stiffly beaten	in equal parts, chopped fine
Fruit juice, syrup, or liqueur	

Make a sugar syrup with the sugar and the ½ cup of water, and boil until syrup spins a thread when dropped from the tip of a spoon (230 deg. F.). Immediately pour in a fine stream onto the stiffly beaten egg whites with the salt, while beating briskly and constantly until stiff. Then add gelatine which has been soaked in the 2 tablespoons of cold water and dissolved over boiling water. Continue beating until mixture is thoroughly blended and stands in peaks. Then fold in the stiffly whipped heavy cream, alternately with the cut fine candied fruit, which has been soaked either in fruit juice, syrup or liqueur for 15 minutes, then gently squeezed through a clean dry cloth. Lastly stir in the vanilla extract. Freeze as directed for recipe No. 357. Or fill 6 parfait glasses and let stand in refrigerator tray for 3½ to 4 hours. Serve with a topping of whipped cream.

403   VANILLA WAFER PARFAIT
(Refrigerator tray only)

¾ cup heavy cream, whipped stiff

⅛ teaspoon salt

1½ dozens crumbled vanilla wafers

2 tablespoons powdered sugar

2 egg whites, stiffly beaten

6 red or green maraschino cherries

Fold into the stiffly whipped heavy cream, salt and powdered sugar; then combine crumbled, sieved vanilla wafers with stiffly beaten egg whites and add to whipped cream. Fill 6 sherbet glasses which have been well-chilled with the creamy mixture; top each glass with a maraschino cherry, cut rose or daisy-like, and freeze in refrigerator tray for 3½ hours.

SECTION IX

Sherbet Recipes

❯❯❯ ❯❯❯ ❯❯❯ ❯❯❯ ❯❯❯ ❯❯❯ ❯❯❯ ❯❯❯ ❯❯❯ ❯❯❯ ❯❯❯ ❮❮❮ ❮❮❮ ❮❮❮ ❮❮❮ ❮❮❮ ❮❮❮ ❮❮❮ ❮❮❮ ❮❮❮ ❮❮❮ ❮❮❮ ❮❮❮

404   WHAT IS A SHERBET?

SHERBET originated in Turkey where it is very popular. In a sherbet there is a very large proportion of liquid or fruit juice, hence special treatment is required to keep the texture solid and smooth. Beaten egg whites, marshmallow and gelatine are used most as stabilizers. As in ice cream, parfaits, ices and mousses, there is no limit to the varieties of sherbets.

Like refrigerator ice cream, sherbets should be stirred once, or twice while freezing, before they get too hard and after they are about half frozen or mushy. They should be scraped up from the sides and bottom of the tray, or molded with a large spoon and then returned to the refrigerator tray to continue freezing until solid. If they are stirred too soon, they will infallibly return to their original liquid state. If they freeze too hard, it will be difficult to stir them to a very smooth mush without beating so hard that the air which was included with the stabilizer—whipped cream, beaten egg whites, marshmallows or gelatine—is irredeemably lost. This operation is not required when using a hand crank freezer.

The mixture should be thoroughly chilled for this saves time in freezing. Whichever method of freezing is used, hand freezer or refrigerator tray, the mold or tray should not be more than

¾ full, as the constant stirring during the freezing process beats in air, causing the mixture to increase in bulk.

The reason that the freezing process takes longer in a refrigerator tray than in the hand freezer is because of the temperature of the ice chamber. (26 to 30 deg. F.)

Sherbets are usually served in special sherbet glasses, always chilled before filling, yet they may be molded in large or individual molds. Seldom is a sauce served with a sherbet. The sherbet may be served either as an appetizer, a digestive or a dessert. If served to help digestion, this should be done immediately after the roast, and it should be eaten very slowly. For this purpose, sherbets have no equal.

Almost any sherbet, as well as water or fruit ice, may be made into a delicious flavored beverage, especially when the mixture is made with a syrup base. And, any water or fruit ice may be made into sherbets by the addition of two stiffly beaten egg whites or 1½ teaspoons of granulated gelatine which has been soaked in cold water and dissolved over hot water or steam.

You may color almost any kind of sherbet to the desired hue, using vegetable coloring. See No. 11 "How to tint Ice Cream", under General Information.

405 APPLE CINNAMON SHERBET
(Hand freezer or refrigerator tray)

This very appropriate dessert for a children's party or supper, contains all the desired elements required for a child, especially during hot days. The undiluted evaporated milk may be changed and thin cream used. Apricots, pears, and in fact all the fresh, canned or dried fruits, may be prepared likewise, when cooked and sieved.

6 medium-sized apples	1½ cups water
¼ cup red cinnamon candies	½ cup undiluted evaporated
⅔ cup granulated sugar	milk
¼ teaspoon salt	

Cook pared, cored apples which have been sliced, with cinnamon candies, granulated sugar, salt and water until tender. While hot, put through a sieve, adding gradually the evaporated milk, or thin cream. Mix well, chill, then freeze for 3 hours, without stirring. When ready to serve, scrape up thin layers of the frozen mixture, using an inverted spoon. Stir rapidly to blend together again, and fill chilled sherbet glasses. Serve at once.

406   APPLEJACK SHERBET
(Hand freezer or refrigerator tray)

A fine digestive sherbet which may be served right after the fish or roast in a dinner party, formal or informal.

2½ cups apple juice   1 tablespoon lemon juice
¼ cup (more or less) granu-   ¼ scant cup applejack
   lated sugar   2 egg whites, stiffly beaten
                    ⅛ teaspoon salt

Simmer apple juice, (made by cooking enough apples, in cold water to cover) sugar and lemon juice for 10 minutes. Strain. Chill, then pour into tray or hand freezer and allow to freeze until firm. Remove to an ice cold mixing bowl, and beat with chilled egg beater gradually adding the applejack, until light. Return to tray or hand freezer and freeze again until mushy. Again beat, using rotary egg beater, until light. Fold in salted egg whites beaten till stiff, but not dry. Return to tray or hand freezer and continue freezing, without stirring anymore and freeze 3 hours, if refrigerator tray is used, and 2 hours, if hand freezer.

Any other kind of pulpy, juicy fruit may be used this way.

407   APPLE GRAPE SHERBET
(Refrigerator tray only)

2 lbs. purple grapes   1½ cups granulated sugar
3 lbs. apples, cored and peeled   ¼ teaspoon salt
                    1 cup heavy cream, whipped stiff

Wash grapes and pick from the stems. Peel and core, then slice the apples (you may leave the peel, if desired) and combine grapes, sliced apples and sugar and salt. Cook, over a gentle flame until tender; then while hot force through a sieve. Cool and chill. Place in refrigerator tray and freeze for 4 hours without stirring. When ready to serve, scrape up thin layers of the frozen mixture, using an inverted spoon. Stir rapidly to blend together again, and fill chilled sherbet glasses with alternate layers of frozen mixture and unsweetened, unflavored whipped cream. You may top with a rosette of whipped cream, if desired, and place a cherry in center.

408   BANANA SHERBET
(Refrigerator tray only)

2 cups sieved bananas   ¼ scant teaspoon salt
6 tablespoons lemon juice   1 egg white, stiffly beaten, but
½ cup granulated sugar   not dry
¼ cup white corn syrup (light)   2 cups milk (cold)

Combine sieved bananas with lemon juice and mix thoroughly; then add sugar, light corn syrup and salt, and mix well. Fold in the stiffly beaten egg white gently; then very slowly, pouring in a stream, stir in the cold milk. Freeze in refrigerator tray until beginning to mush. Then scrape bottom and sides and beat gently for ½ minute. Return to refrigerator tray, and repeat scraping and beating as soon as mixture is mushy again; then freeze without stirring anymore for 3 hours. Serve in chilled sherbet glasses.

409   **BLACKBERRY SHERBET**
(Hand freezer method)

A delicious sherbet very appropriate with roast dark meat. It may be served in orange cup, or scooped and placed over a well-chilled canned pineapple slice.

½ cup water
1 cup granulated sugar
¼ scant teaspoon salt
2⅓ cups undiluted evaporated milk, chilled

1 No. 2 can or fresh blackberries, sieved

Make a sugar syrup with water, sugar and salt, and cook until syrup spins a thin thread when poured from the tip of a spoon. Cool a little and stir in the sieved, strained blackberry juice. Cool, then chill. Stir in chilled undiluted evaporated milk, and freeze in hand freezer, using 6 parts ice and 1 part rock salt, until mixture is solid. Pack, using 4 parts ice and 1 part rock salt for 1 hour. Serve in chilled sherbet glasses, or orange cup, or placed over a well-chilled canned pineapple slice.

410   **CHAMPAGNE SHERBET I**
(Hand freezer only)

Very appropriate for a dinner party of 12 people, and to be served right after the roast. For 6 servings, use half of the ingredients and serve in chilled sherbet glasses.

½ cup granulated sugar
1 cup water
Grated rind of ½ lemon
Grated rind of 1 orange
1 (extra) pint dry champagne, chilled

¼ teaspoon salt
1 pint dry champagne, chilled
Juice of 1 lemon
Juice of 4 oranges

Make a sugar syrup with sugar and water, and boil until syrup spins a thin thread when dropped from the tip of a spoon; then stir in the lemon and orange rinds and salt. Let stand 10 long minutes. Then stir in the previously chilled pint of champagne, juices of lemon and orange. Stir, chill, then freeze in hand freezer, using 5 parts ice and 1 part salt, until mushy. Stir and add the second pint of chilled champagne, stirring constantly. Pack and allow to stand in 6 parts ice and 1 part rock salt for 1 hour. Serve in chilled sherbet glasses.

A less expensive method is the following:

411 CHAMPAGNE SHERBET II
(Hand freezer only)

1½ cups water	¼ teaspoon salt
¾ cup granulated sugar	1 pint chilled champagne
Grated rind of ½ orange	1 pony brandy (about 1½ table-
Juice of 2 lemons	spoons)
Juice of 2 oranges	½ cup chilled champagne

Make a sugar syrup with the water and sugar, and cook until syrup spins a thread when dropped from the tip of a spoon. Remove from the fire and add grated orange rind and the fruit juices. Strain through a double cheesecloth. Chill. When well-chilled, combine syrup mixture with the chilled pint of champagne and freeze, using 5 parts ice and 1 part rock salt, until almost solid. Pack, using equal parts of ice and salt, for 1 hour, and when ready to serve, stir in the combined pony of brandy and the ½ cup of chilled champagne. Serve in sherbet glasses.

412   CHAMPAGNE PINEAPPLE SHERBET
(Hand freezer only)

1 pint champagne, chilled
4 tablespoons lemon juice
¼ teaspoon salt

1 No. 2 can (2½ cups) crushed
pineapple, juice and pulp

1⅓ cups (1 can) sweetened condensed milk

Add lemon juice to juice and pulp of crushed pineapple, and blend thoroughly with sweetened condensed milk and salt. Freeze in 2-quart hand freezer until mushy. Add champagne, which has been chilled, stir to blend well; remove dasher from hand freezer, and pack in equal parts ice and rock salt for 1 hour or more, or until solid. Serve in chilled sherbet glasses or in champagne coupes.

413   CIDER SHERBET
(Hand freezer only)

Proceed as indicated for recipe No. 411, Champagne Sherbet II, substituting cider for champagne, and applejack for brandy. Freeze as directed.

414   CITRUS BANANA SHERBET
(Hand freezer only)

Juice of 3 oranges
Juice of 3 lemons
Pulp of 3 bananas
¼ scant teaspoon salt

2 cups (scant) granulated sugar
5 cups undiluted evaporated
milk

Stir the combined orange and lemon juices into the banana pulp (sieved bananas); then stir in the sugar, alternately with the milk to which the salt has been added. Freeze in hand freezer, using 5 parts ice and 1 part rock salt, until almost solid. Pack, remove the dasher from hand freezer, and let stand for 1 hour, using equal parts of ice and rock salt.

415 CITRUS SHERBET
(Hand freezer or refrigerator tray)

The following sherbet, in great favor on the Pacific Coast as well as in Florida, if prepared as indicated, is one of the most digestive and delicious of the sherbet family. You may use blood oranges, if a beautiful color effect is desired.

3 cups granulated sugar	¼ scant teaspoon salt
3 cups water	Juice of 3 oranges
Grated rind of 1 orange	Juice of 3 lemons
3 bananas, sieved	3 egg whites, stiffly beaten

·Make a sugar syrup with sugar, water and grated rind of 1 orange. Boil for 5 minutes. Chill. Add banana pulp (sieved) combined and thoroughly blended with the fruit juices and salt. Then, fold in the stiffly beaten egg whites. Freeze either in refrigerator tray, without stirring, for 3 hours, or in hand freezer, using 3 parts ice and 1 part rock salt until almost solid. Pack, remove dasher, and let stand 1 hour, using equal parts of ice and salt. Serve in chilled sherbet glasses.

416 COFFEE SHERBET
(Hand freezer only)

Here's one of those special sherbets that does special things for your hostess' reputation. It is a French method, rich, with the tasty flavor of good coffee—it will make a hit with everyone. Fine for formal teas or parties . . . equally fine for a special treat at home meals.

1¼ cups granulated sugar 2 cups very strong coffee liquid
1½ cups heavy cream ¾ cup heavy cream, whipped
¼ teaspoon salt stiff
5 drops vanilla extract

Place sugar and 1½ cups unwhipped heavy cream in a sauce-pan, and heat to the boiling point, stirring almost constantly. Remove from the fire and cool, then add salt and strong coffee liquid. Freeze in hand freezer, using 3 parts ice and 1 part rock salt, until mushy; then stir in very gently the stiffly whipped heavy cream with the vanilla extract and freeze until solid. Pack into 4 parts ice and 1 part rock salt, after removing the dasher, for 1 hour. Serve in sherbet glasses which have been thoroughly chilled.

417   CRANBERRY SHERBET I
(Hand freezer only)

1 lb. fresh cranberries ¼ scant teaspoon salt
2 cups water Juice of a medium-sized lemon
1¼ cups granulated sugar Grated rind of 1 orange
1 cup orange juice 2 egg whites, stiffly beaten

Cook washed, picked over cranberries and water for 10 min-utes, or until berries pop. While hot rub through a fine sieve. There should be 2 cups of juice, if not add enough hot water to compensate. To the still hot cranberry juice add sugar and stir until dissolved. Boil once, remove from the fire, and strain through a double cheesecloth. Then, add orange juice, salt, lemon juice and grated rind of 1 orange. Fold in stiffly beaten egg whites and freeze in hand freezer, using 6 parts ice and 1 part rock salt, turning crank slowly and steadily to insure smooth fine grained mixture. Freeze until almost solid. Remove dasher, let the water run, and pack in 4 parts ice and 1 part rock salt for 1 hour. Serve in chilled sherbet glasses.

418 CRANBERRY SHERBET II
(Hand freezer or refrigerator tray)

1 can cranberry sauce
Grated rind and juice of 1 lemon
Juice of 1 orange

⅛ teaspoon (generous) salt
2 egg whites, stiffly beaten
1 cup heavy cream, whipped stiff

Crush chilled cranberry sauce, or still better, rub through a fine sieve, adding lemon juice and orange juice which have been combined. Then stir in the grated rind, chill and freeze until mushy, either in hand freezer, using 4 parts ice and 1 part rock salt, or in refrigerator tray. When mushy, scrape bottom and sides, and stir in the stiffly beaten egg whites and salt and the stiffly whipped heavy cream or evaporated milk. Return to either hand freezer or tray and freeze until almost solid. Pack (if hand freezer is used) in 4 parts ice and 1 part salt for 1 hour. If refrigerator tray is used, freeze for 3 hours.

419 CRANBERRY SHERBET III
(Refrigerator tray only)

1 tablespoon granulated gelatine
½ cup cold water
2 cups hot water
1½ cups granulated sugar

¼ teaspoon salt
1 cup unsweetened, thick cranberry sauce or juice
1 tablespoon grated orange rind
1 large banana, sieved

2 egg whites, stiffly beaten

Boil sugar and hot water until syrup spins a thread when dropped from the tip of a spoon. While hot add gelatine which has been soaked in cold water for 5 minutes, and stir until gelatine is entirely and thoroughly dissolved. Cool until mixture begins to congeal, then beat in the thick cranberry sauce or juice combined with the grated orange rind and sieved banana. Chill; then stir in, gently but thoroughly, the egg whites stiffly beaten with the salt. Freeze in refrigerator tray until mushy, or about after 30 minutes; scrape bottom and sides, beat ½ minute, return to refrigerator tray, for another 20 minutes, then scrape and beat smooth, operating rapidly, lest the mixture soften. Return to refrigerator and freeze for 2½ to 3 hours. Serve in chilled sherbet glasses.

420 CRANBERRY SHERBET IV
(Refrigerator tray only)

This method results in a fine product.

4 cups fresh cranberries	½ cup orange juice
3 cups boiling water	Grated rind of ½ lemon
¼ teaspoon salt	2 teaspoons brandy or rum
3 tablespoons corn syrup	2 egg whites stiffly beaten

1¼ cups granulated sugar

Wash and pick over the berries, add boiling water and salt and cook until skins pop. Put through a sieve, stir in the corn syrup and sugar until melted and thoroughly blended. Strain through a fine sieve and chill. Then add the sieved cranberry pulp and juice, combined with brandy or rum and orange juice and lemon rind, and freeze in refrigerator tray, until mushy. Scrape bottom and sides; fill either paper cases, chilled orange shells or cantaloupe halves, also chilled, and return to refrigerator tray to freeze harder for 1 hour.

421 GRAPEFRUIT MINT SHERBET
(Hand freezer only)

Very appropriate to serve on Saint Patrick's Day, right after the roast, or at Thanksgiving Dinner, omitting green coloring if desired and substituting another tint.

2 tablespoons bruised fresh mint leaves
2 cups granulated sugar
4 cups hot water
¼ teaspoon salt

3 drops green vegetable coloring
2 cups grapefruit juice (fresh or canned)
½ cup lemon juice

2 egg whites, stiffly beaten

Place bruised fresh mint leaves on a saucepan; sprinkle with the sugar, then pour over the hot water. Bring to a boil and let boil for 5 minutes. Strain through a double cheesecloth, cool and stir in 3 drops (more if a stronger hue is desired) of green vegetable coloring, the chilled grapefruit juice and lemon juice. Freeze in hand freezer, using 5 parts ice and 2 parts rock salt, until mushy. Then stir in the stiffly beaten egg whites, and continue freezing until almost solid. Pack in 4 parts ice and 1 part rock salt for 1 hour. Serve in chilled sherbet glasses.

422 GRAPE JUICE SHERBET I
(Hand freezer or refrigerator tray)

1 cup of grape (fresh) juice
1 cup boiling water
½ cup granulated sugar
⅛ teaspoon salt

1 teaspoon gelatine (granulated
1 tablespoon cold water
2 cups milk, chilled

Make a sugar syrup of boiling water and sugar and boil for 5 short minutes. Remove from the fire and add gelatine which has been soaked for 5 minutes in cold water, and stir until mixture is well-blended. Strain. Cool and chill. Lastly add combined fresh grape juice and chilled milk. Freeze, if using hand freezer, with 3 parts ice and 1 part rock salt, for 1½ to 2 hours. Pack, using 5 parts ice and 1 part rock salt, for 1 short hour to mellow and ripen. If using refrigerator tray, freeze, without stirring for 3 hours. Serve in chilled sherbet glasses.

423   GRAPE JUICE SHERBET II
        (Hand freezer or refrigerator tray)

This second formula has more piquancy resulting from the addition of lemon and orange juices. You may garnish the filled sherbet glasses with almost any kind of small pieces of candied fruits, such as candied or crystallized violets, which may be purchased from confectioner's stores, small pieces of angelica, or candied apricots or candied pineapple.

1½ cups boiling water   ½ cup cold water
 1 cup granulated sugar   4 tablespoons lemon juice
 ¼ scant teaspoon salt   1 pint bottled grape juice
 1 tablespoon granulated gela-   ⅓ cup orange juice
   tine

Make a sugar syrup by boiling hot water and sugar 10 long minutes. Stir in salt and granulated gelatine which has been soaked in cold water for 5 minutes, until thoroughly dissolved. Cool slightly, then add combined lemon, grape juice and orange juices. Freeze as indicated for recipe No. 422, Grape Juice Sherbet I. Serve in sherbet glasses which have been chilled and garnish with candied fruits.

424   GRAPE JUICE (fresh) SHERBET III
        (Hand freezer only)

A very delicious French recipe, requiring fresh muscat grapes (during season) or Muscatel wine, found in almost any wine store.

Proceed as indicated for recipe No. 423, above, Grape Juice Sherbet II, substituting strained muscat grapes, which should be very ripe, for bottled grape juice. Freeze as directed. You may add 1 tablespoon of rum to the mixture, before freezing, if desired. The delicate flavor of the muscatel grapes will be greatly enhanced. Serve in well-chilled sherbet glasses.

425   **HAWAIIAN SHERBET**
(Hand freezer or refrigerator tray)

½ cup shredded pineapple
½ cup granulated sugar
1 cup pineapple juice
2 tablespoons lemon juice

2 cups cold milk
1½ teaspoons granulated gelatine
2 tablespoons cold water

Make a sugar syrup of sugar and pineapple juice. Boil 10 minutes. While hot add the gelatine which has been soaked in cold water, and stir until gelatine is thoroughly dissolved, then add lemon juice, shredded pineapple to which has been added a few grains of salt, alternately with the milk. Chill. Freeze as indicated for recipe No. 422, Grape Juice Sherbet I. Serve in well-chilled sherbet glasses.

426   **HUCKLEBERRY SHERBET**
(Refrigerator tray only)

It is very easy to tell huckleberries because they are smaller than the blues and they are bright without the powdery frost-like film, which overlies the cool, grayed color of the blueberries. The huckleberry seeds are larger, harder and more objectionable.

2 quarts washed, picked over huckleberries
3 cups hot water
1 cup granulated sugar

2 tablespoons lemon juice
2 egg whites, stiffly beaten with
¼ teaspoon salt

Add washed, picked over huckleberries to hot water and bring to the boiling point. Let simmer for 10 minutes, then stir in the sugar, and allow to simmer 5 minutes longer, stirring gently occasionally. Rub mixture through a fine sieve while hot, cool a little, and stir in the lemon juice. Chill. Freeze in refrigerator tray until mushy, or about 30 minutes; then remove from the tray, fold in the stiffly beaten egg whites and salt. Freeze again for 30 minutes, scrape bottom and sides, then beat ½ minute, return to refrigerator and continue freezing for 2 to 2½ hours. You may serve in chilled glasses, orange shells, or still better in chilled, ripe cantaloupe halves.

427   KIRSCH SHERBET
        (*Hand freezer or refrigerator tray*)

Almost any kind of liqueur may be prepared in this way:

¾ cup granulated sugar   Grated rind of ½ lemon
2 cups water   Juice of 1 lemon
¼ teaspoon salt   ¼ scant cup kirsch liqueur
         2 egg whites, stiffly beaten

Make a sugar syrup with sugar and water and salt; boil 10 minutes, add grated lemon rind and lemon juice, and let stand for 30 minutes. Strain through double cheesecloth. Chill, then freeze as indicated for recipe No. 422, Grape Juice Sherbet I, until mushy. Add kirsch liqueur, alternately with stiffly beaten egg whites, mixing well, but gently. Then freeze until solid. Serve in sherbet glasses which have been chilled.

428   LEMON SHERBET I
        (*Hand freezer or refrigerator tray*)

2 cups water   4 tablespoons cold water
¾ cup granulated sugar   ⅛ teaspoon salt (generous)
1 teaspoon grated lemon rind   ⅓ cup lemon juice
2 teaspoons granulated gelatine   2 egg whites, stiffly beaten

[247]

Combine water, sugar and grated lemon rind; bring to the boiling point, then let simmer for 10 minutes. Remove from the fire and stir in the granulated gelatine which has been soaked in cold water; add the salt, stir, then strain through double cheesecloth and chill. When well chilled stir in the lemon juice, and freeze as indicated for recipe No. 422, Grape Juice Sherbet I, until mushy. Then stir well and fold in the stiffly beaten egg whites and freeze again until creamy mixture begins to solidify, and stir again to break up the ice crystals. Return to freezer or tray, and continue freezing until solid. Serve in chilled sherbet glasses.

429   LEMON SHERBET II
(Hand freezer or refrigerator tray)

Does not require any stirring.

⅔ cup granulated sugar
   Grated rind of 1 lemon
   Juice of 2 lemons
1 cup of rich milk
2 egg whites, stiffly beaten

1 cup undiluted evaporated milk or thin cream
⅓ cup well-drained maraschino cherries chopped fine
¼ teaspoon salt

Dissolve sugar, grated lemon rind and juice of 2 lemons thoroughly. Gradually stir in sugar mixture the cup of rich milk; then beat, using rotary egg beater, until thoroughly blended. To this slowly add while stirring constantly, the evaporated milk or thin cream alternately with the chopped maraschino cherries, well-drained, or rather squeezed through a dry clean towel. Freeze either in hand freezer or refrigerator as indicated for recipe No. 422, Grape Juice Sherbet I. Serve in chilled sherbet glasses.

Try adding ½ teaspoon of good rum to the sherbet when chilled glasses have been filled, by making a small hole with a teaspoon, and pouring the rum, or any other kind of desired liqueur in the hole.

430   LEMON MARSHMALLOW SHERBET III
(Hand freezer or refrigerator tray)

⅔ cup granulated sugar
Grated rind of 1 lemon
2½ cups water

½ cup lemon juice
2 egg whites, stiffly beaten
¼ scant teaspoon salt

4 whole marshmallows, quartered

Combine sugar, lemon rind, water and quartered marshmallows and bring to the boiling point; then let simmer very gently for 10 minutes, stirring once or twice. Add this syrup slowly to the lemon juice. (Note that I do not say "strained lemon juice"). Strain through double cheesecloth and chill. Freeze either method, as indicated for recipe No. 422, Grape Juice Sherbet I, until mushy; remove from refrigeration beat ½ minute, fold in the stiffly beaten egg whites with the salt. Return to the freezer or tray and freeze until set. Serve in chilled sherbet glasses or orange cups or cantaloupe halves, also well chilled.

431   LEMON MILK SHERBET IV
(Hand freezer or refrigerator tray)

1 quart milk
1½ cups granulated sugar
¼ teaspoon salt

2 teaspoons granulated gelatine
¾ cup lemon juice

Soak gelatine in ½ cup of cold milk and dissolve over hot water. When thoroughly dissolved, add to remaining milk; then add combined lemon juice, sugar and salt. Mix thoroughly, then freeze as indicated for recipe No. 422, Grape Juice Sherbet I. Serve in well-chilled sherbet glasses.

You may substitute buttermilk for fresh milk if desired.

432   LEMON MINT SHERBET V

Proceed as indicated for recipe No. 428, Lemon Sherbet I, using the same amount of indicated ingredients and adding, just before freezing, 2 tablespoons of fresh ground mint leaves.

433   LEMON SNOW SHERBET VI
(Hand freezer or refrigerator tray)

This French method of serving Lemon Sherbet, called in French "La Neige au Cointreau" is very easy to make. Have ready ½ recipe of your favorite Lemon Sherbet mixture, ready to be frozen. To this add 2 extra egg whites, stiffly beaten with 2 tablespoons of praline powder flavoring (see No. 14 under "General Information"), and freeze until solid. Serve in chilled sherbet glasses, make a small hole in the sherbet mixture and pour in 1 scant teaspoon of Cointreau liqueur. Serve at once.

434   LIME SHERBET
(Refrigerator tray only)

This fine sherbet which is very appropriate for roast lamb instead of the traditional mint jelly or sauce.

⅔ cup granulated sugar	4 drops green vegetable coloring
1½ cups water	Juice of 5 fresh limes, strained
1 teaspoon granulated gelatine	or not
1 tablespoon cold water	2 egg whites, stiffly beaten
⅛ generous teaspoon salt	

Combine sugar and water and stir until sugar is thoroughly dissolved; bring to the boiling point and let simmer for 10 minutes. Then add the granulated gelatine, which has been soaked in cold water, and stir until gelatine is dissolved. Cool, then chill. Stir in 4 drops of green vegetable coloring, alternately with the lime juice (strained or unstrained). Freeze in refrigerator tray until mushy; remove from refrigerator and beat until fluffy, folding in at the same time the stiffly beaten egg whites and salt. Return to tray, and freeze again for 30 minutes, beat again, return to tray and freeze for 2½ hours. Serve in chilled sherbet glasses.

435   MARASCHINO LIQUEUR SHERBET
(Hand freezer only)

The following French recipe, in great favor all over the Continent is perhaps the best and most appropriate sherbet for a formal or informal dinner party. It may seem laborious, but it is not, and if the directions are religiously followed, the result will amply repay the labor. The mixture is first frozen to a mush, then a cooked meringue is gently folded into the mushy mixture, and the freezing operation is continued until the mixture is solid.

2 cups water	Juice of 3 oranges
1 cup granulated sugar	¼ cup Maraschino Liqueur
¼ scant teaspoon salt	Italian meringue (cooked meringue)
Juice of 3 lemons	

2 or 3 tablespoons Maraschino liqueur

Boil water, sugar and salt to the soft ball stage. Remove from the fire, cool a little, and stir in the lemon and orange juices, alternately with the maraschino liqueur (the addition of ¼ cup of dry white wine will enhance the flavor, but it is optional). Freeze in hand freezer, using 4 parts ice and 1 part rock salt, until mixture is mushy, but rather solid, then add the Italian meringue made as follows:

3 egg whites, stiffly beaten with   ¼ cup water
¼ scant teaspoon salt   1 cup powdered sugar
4 drops almond extract

Put the sugar, and water in a saucepan; stir until sugar is thoroughly dissolved, then boil without stirring, to the soft ball stage (238 deg. F.), that is, until a little dropped into cold water forms a soft ball. Immediately pour the hot syrup in a fine stream onto the stiffly beaten salted egg whites, while beating briskly and constantly until mixture is almost cold, adding the almond extract with the remaining syrup. The mixture will by this time be almost solid. Fold this delicious meringue into the sherbet frozen to a hard mush, alternately with 2 or 3 (according to strength desired) tablespoons of maraschino liquer. Freeze for a few minutes, and pack for an hour in 6 parts ice and 1 part rock salt. Serve either in sherbet glasses, orange cups or baskets, or in cantaloupe halves, which should be chilled; and serve immediately. Remember that sherbets like any kind of frozen desserts, are like soufflés, they cannot wait, but the guests can.

436   MARSHMALLOW CHERRY SHERBET
(Hand freezer or refrigerator tray)

This delicious sherbet needs to be stirred but once when mushy.

½ lb. marshmallows, quartered
2 tablespoons hot water
1 tablespoon lemon juice
1 cup canned red cherries, drained then coarsely chopped
¼ cup cherry juice

1 cup heavy cream, whipped stiff
¼ teaspoon salt
¼ scant teaspoon almond extract

Melt quartered marshmallows with hot water over hot water, until marshmallows are nearly melted, stirring once or twice. Remove from hot water and beat until smooth. Cool. When cold, add coarsely chopped canned cherries, lemon juice, and cherry juice. Fold in stiffly whipped heavy cream with salt and almond extract. Freeze as indicated for recipe No. 422, Grape Juice Sherbet I. Serve in orange shells or cantaloupe halves, which have been well chilled.

437 MARSHMALLOW GRAPE JUICE SHERBET
(Hand freezer or refrigerator tray)

2 dozen marshmallows, quartered

1 cup unsweetened grape juice

½ cup lemon juice

2 egg whites, stiffly beaten with ¼ scant teaspoon salt, and

1 tablespoon powdered sugar, and

¼ scant teaspoon vanilla extract

Melt quartered marshmallows in top of double boiler with ¾ cup of the unsweetened grape juice, stirring slowly, always in the same way, until nearly melted. Then add remaining ¼ cup grape juice, combined with lemon juice and blend thoroughly. Remove from water, cool a little then fold in the stiffly beaten egg white mixture. Freeze as indicated for recipe No. 422, Grape Juice Sherbet I, until mushy, then stir thoroughly, and continue freezing until solid. Serve in chilled sherbet glasses, or in paper cases, or orange baskets, or in cantaloupe halves.

438 MARSHMALLOW PINEAPPLE SHERBET
(Hand freezer or refrigerator tray)

In the following recipe two kinds of stabilizers are used: (a) marshmallows, and (b) gelatine. This frozen dessert is very

*rich and should be served only for dessert and not as a digestive.
It is rather a frozen pudding than a sherbet.*

2 tablespoons granulated gelatine
2 cups pineapple juice, heated
½ teaspoon salt
2 cups canned crushed pineapple well-drained

½ cup blanched almonds, ground
16 marshmallows, cut into small
pieces
1 cup undiluted evaporated
milk whipped stiff
¼ cup powdered sugar

Sprinkle granulated gelatine over cold pineapple juice, and
allow to soak for 5 minutes; then heat over direct flame, stirring
almost constantly, until gelatine is thoroughly dissolved. Do
not allow to boil. Stir in the salt, then add well-drained crushed
pineapple, ground almonds and cut marshmallows. Stir until
marshmallows are dissolved and cool. To the stiffly beaten undiluted evaporated milk, fold in the powdered sugar, a little
amount at a time, and fold mixture into the pineapple-almond
mixture. Chill. When well-chilled, freeze as indicated for recipe
No. 422, Grape Juice Sherbet I. Serve in chilled sherbet glasses.
You may top each glass with a candied or maraschino cherry.

439 MINT SHERBET
(Hand freezer or refrigerator tray)

To a Lemon Ice (No. 81, or 82), add 4 tablespoons bruised
mint leaves to the boiling syrup. Strain and freeze as directed.
A delicious side dish to hot or cold lamb, or any kind of cut
or assorted cold cuts.

440 ORANGE CREAM SHERBET I
(Hand freezer only)

*A really delicious party sherbet which will serve 12 persons.
For 6, use half of the indicated ingredients.*

½ cup cold water
1 tablespoon granulated gelatine
1½ cups granulated sugar
1½ cups hot water
Grated rind of 2 oranges
1 cup lemon juice
1½ cups orange juice

2 cups heavy cream, whipped
stiff
½ cup powdered sugar
¼ generous teaspoon salt
2 egg yolks, beaten thick
2 egg whites, stiffly beaten
¼ cup heavy cream, whipped
stiff

Orange sections

Pour cold water in a bowl and sprinkle granulated gelatine. Then when gelatine has been soaked for 5 minutes, add combined granulated sugar and water and stir until gelatine and sugar are thoroughly dissolved. Add then, orange rind, lemon juice, combined with orange juice, and stir well. Chill. Freeze in hand freezer, using 4 parts ice and 1 part rock salt, until mushy. Then add whipped cream to which has been added, in small amount the combined powdered sugar and salt, alternately with the thickly beaten egg yolks and stiffly beaten egg whites. Continue freezing until solid, but not too hard. Serve in chilled sherbet glasses, topping each glass with a rosette of the remaining ¼ cup of heavy cream, whipped stiff, and garnish the rosette with a section of orange, free from white skin. Serve at once.

441   ORANGE CREAM SHERBET II
(Hand freezer or refrigerator tray)

This formula is not so rich as the preceding one, and no gelatine is used.

3 cups boiling water
2 cups granulated sugar
¾ cup orange juice
½ cup lemon juice

1 cup heavy cream or undiluted
evaporated milk, whipped
stiff
¼ scant teaspoon salt

Stir sugar in the boiling water until thoroughly dissolved. Chill after cooling, then add combined fruit juices, and fold in the heavy cream or undiluted evaporated milk, whipped stiff with the salt. Freeze until solid either in hand freezer or refrigerator tray, as indicated for recipe No. 422, Grape Juice Sherbet I. Serve in chilled sherbet glasses.

442 ORANGE MILK SHERBET I
(Hand freezer only)

¾ cup undiluted evaporated milk or heavy cream, unwhipped, but thoroughly chilled

1 cup granulated sugar

⅛ generous teaspoon salt

½ cup hot water

1 cup orange juice

1 tablespoon lemon juice

1 teaspoon grated orange rind

Chill milk in refrigerator or a pan of chopped ice. Boil sugar, salt and water for 5 minutes, beginning after boiling point is reached. Remove from the fire and add orange and lemon juice and grated rind of orange. Let stand for 10 minutes, then chill. Pour chilled mixture into chilled cream or evaporated milk and freeze in hand freezer, using 4 parts ice and 1 part salt, until solid but not too hard. Serve in chilled sherbet glasses, orange cups, or cantaloupe halves.

VARIATIONS USING ORANGE MILK SHERBET.
WITH PEACHES AND STRAWBERRIES.—Arrange sliced peaches (fresh or canned) and strawberries in chilled sherbet glasses. Sprinkle over with minced maraschino cherries, green or red, and set in refrigerator until needed. Just before serving, fill the glasses with orange milk sherbet.
WITH PINEAPPLE AND STRAWBERRIES.—Mix 2/3 cup, each, fresh shredded pineapple and strawberries, cut in quarters. Sprinkle with ¼ cup powdered sugar. Cover and let stand in a cold place (refrigerator) for 2 long hours—the longer the

better. When ready to serve, put mixture in equal parts in 6 sherbet glasses, which have been chilled, and cover with orange milk sherbet. You may top with a rosette of unsweetened whipped cream or undiluted evaporated milk, if desired.

443 ORANGE MILK SHERBET II
(Hand freezer only)

A richer Orange Milk Sherbet, yet economical, may be made as follows:

2 cups undiluted, well chilled, evaporated milk	1¾ cups granulated sugar
1 cup boiling water	2 cups orange juice
	4 tablespoons lemon juice

⅛ generous teaspoon salt

Boil sugar and water for 5 long minutes. Cool, then chill. Add orange and lemon juice, mix thoroughly, then combine, while beating gently, with chilled undiluted evaporated milk. Freeze as indicated for recipe No. 442, above. Serve in chilled sherbet glasses.

444 ORANGE SYRUP SHERBET
(Hand freezer only)

1 cup granulated sugar	¼ cup orange juice
⅔ cup boiling water	2 cups heavy cream, whipped
Grated rind of 2 oranges	stiff
⅛ teaspoon salt	2 whole oranges

Boil sugar and water until syrup spins a thread; then add the grated rind and orange juice; cover and allow to infuse in a warm place for ¾ hour; then cool. To the stiffly whipped cream, add slowly the cooled syrup, stirring almost constantly until thoroughly blended. Cut the 2 oranges in halves, crosswise, remove the pulp, and separate into small pieces. Pieces should be free of white skins. Now pour the juice collected from the 2 oranges in to a brick mold; then put in alternate layers of cream mixture and orange pulp until the mold is filled to over-flowing. Place a buttered paper over the mixture, adjust cover hermetically, then bury the mold in 4 parts of ice and 1 part of rock salt, for 3 hours. To serve: unmold on to a chilled platter, and cut into slices. Serve a side dish of assorted cookies, or wafers.

445   PEACH CREAM SHERBET
(Hand freezer or refrigerator tray)

3 cups fresh peach pulp   ¼ teaspoon salt
1½ cups granulated sugar   1 pint heavy cream, unwhipped

Sprinkle sugar over fresh peach pulp; let stand in refrigerator for 2½ to 3 hours; then stir in the unwhipped heavy cream with the salt and freeze as indicated for recipe No. 422, Grape Juice Sherbet I. Serve either in chilled sherbet glasses, orange cups, or cantaloupe halves. Try adding 1 or 2 tablespoons of good brandy before freezing. It is simply delicious.

446   PEACH ORANGE SHERBET
(Hand freezer or refrigerator tray)

3 cups fresh peach pulp   1½ cups granulated sugar
1½ cups orange juice   1 cup cold water
¼ cup lemon juice   ¼ teaspoon salt
2 egg whites, stiffly beaten

Put fresh peach through a sieve or potato ricer after peeling and stoning; sprinkle sugar over the pulp (this should be done rapidly lest the peach pulp blacken) and allow to stand 1½ hour in refrigerator. Stir in the combined orange and lemon juices, water and salt; then freeze as indicated for recipe No. 422, Grape Juice Sherbet I, until mushy. Stir briskly for ½ minute; add stiffly beaten egg whites, and continue freezing until solid. Serve in chilled sherbet glasses.

447   PEACH SHERBET
(Refrigerator tray or hand freezer)

⅔ cup sweetened condensed milk
2 tablespoons lemon juice
2 tablespoons slightly melted butter

½ cup cold water
1 cup sieved peach pulp
⅛ teaspoon salt
2 egg whites, stiffly beaten

Have all the above ingredients well-chilled. Combine milk, lemon juice, melted butter (not chilled, of course), and cold water. Fold in the stiffly beaten egg whites, and freeze as indicated for recipe No. 422, Grape Juice Sherbet I, until mushy; then scrape and beat for 1 minute, or until smooth; return to refrigerator (if using hand freezer, you do not need to remove from the pan, simply scrape and beat until smooth) and freeze until solid. Serve in chilled sherbet glasses.

448   PEANUT CARAMEL SHERBET
(Refrigerator tray only)

1 cup granulated sugar, caramelized
1 cup hot water
1 cup milk, scalded

¼ teaspoon salt
1 teaspoon vanilla extract
1 cup chilled milk
½ cup ground roasted peanuts

3 whole eggs, well-beaten

Caramelize granulated sugar in the usual way, stirring constantly, over a low flame. Add boiling water slowly, while stirring constantly, until caramelized sugar is thoroughly dissolved. Set aside in a warm place. Combine scalded milk, well beaten eggs and salt in top of a double boiler, and pour caramelized mixture in a fine stream onto the egg mixture, stirring constantly, over hot water, until mixture coats the spoon. Remove from hot water and add vanilla extract, combined with chilled milk and roasted ground peanuts. Freeze in refrigerator tray until mushy; then scrape bottom and sides and beat 1 short minute. Return to tray and freeze until solid but not too hard, or about 2½ hours. Serve in chilled sherbet glasses. You may use almonds if desired.

449   PINEAPPLE HONEY SHERBET
(Hand freezer or refrigerator tray)

¾ cup of canned pineapple juice
4 tablespoons lemon juice
⅓ scant cup strained honey, warm

2 egg yolks, thickly beaten
⅛ teaspoon salt
1¼ cups warm milk
2 egg whites, stiffly beaten

Combine pineapple juice, lemon juice and warm honey. Mix well. Slowly pour this mixture over thickly beaten egg yolks alternately with the warm milk, while beating constantly. Chill. Freeze as indicated for recipe No. 422, Grape Juice Sherbet I, until mushy, then fold in the egg whites stiffly beaten with the salt. Return to tray or hand freezer and freeze until solid but not too hard. Serve in chilled sherbet glasses.

450   PINEAPPLE MARASCHINO CHERRY SHERBET
(Hand freezer or refrigerator tray)

2 teaspoons granulated gelatine
¼ cup cold water
½ cup granulated sugar
1¾ cups water

1 cup pineapple juice
½ cup canned crushed pineapple
2 tablespoons lemon juice
¼ scant teaspoon salt

½ cup quartered maraschino cherries (red or green)

Soak granulated gelatine in the ¼ cup cold water for 5 minutes. Make a syrup of sugar and remaining 1¾ cups of water, bring to the boiling point, and allow to boil gently for 5 minutes. Remove from the fire, cool a little, then stir in the combined pineapple juice, crushed pineapple, lemon juice, salt and quartered maraschino cherries. Chill. Freeze in either hand freezer or refrigerator tray as indicated for recipe No. 422, Grape Juice Sherbet I, without stirring until solid, but not too hard. Serve in chilled sherbet glasses, orange cups or cantaloupe halves, also chilled.

451   PINEAPPLE MILK SHERBET
        (Hand freezer or refrigerator tray)

1½ cups pineapple juice (canned)	2 egg whites, stiffly beaten
½ cup granulated sugar	½ cup thin cream or evaporated milk
⅛ generous teaspoon salt	3 tablespoons lemon juice

Combine canned pineapple juice, sugar and salt and bring to the boiling point; then boil for 5 minutes. Pour this hot syrup over the stiffly beaten egg whites, stirring briskly and constantly. Chill. Combine chilled thin cream or undiluted evaporated milk with lemon juice and stir into the chilled pineapple mixture. Freeze either in hand freezer or refrigerator tray as indicated for recipe No. 422, Grape Juice Sherbet I, without stirring, for 3 long hours, if using refrigerator tray, and until solid, but not too stiff, if using hand freezer. Serve in chilled sherbet glasses.

452   PINEAPPLE MINT SHERBET I
(Hand freezer or refrigerator tray)

1 quart hot water
2 cups (more or less, according to sweetness of pineapple) granulated sugar
2 cups drained canned crushed pineapple

Juice of a medium-sized lemon
¼ teaspoon salt
1 or 2 drops oil of peppermint
2 or 3 drops green vegetable coloring
2 egg whites, stiffly beaten

Into the hot water, stir the granulated sugar, bring to a boil, then let boil for 5 long minutes. Add well-drained crushed pineapple and boil once. Pour mixture into a fine sieve and rub, discarding the pulp remaining into the sieve. Cool, then add lemon juice, oil of peppermint and enough green vegetable coloring to obtain a delicate mint green. The oil of peppermint should not be too strong and dominate that of the pineapple. Freeze as indicated for recipe No. 422, Grape Juice Sherbet I, until mushy; then beat in the stiffly beaten egg whites, and continue freezing until mixture is solid, but not too hard. Serve in chilled sherbet glasses.

453   PINEAPPLE MINT SHERBET II
(Hand freezer or refrigerator tray)

1 teaspoon granulated gelatine
½ cup cold water
1 cup canned pineapple juice, scalded
½ cup granulated sugar

1 cup canned crushed pineapple
3 tablespoons lemon juice
1 tablespoon chopped fresh mint
2 egg whites, stiffly beaten
⅛ teaspoon salt

Soak gelatine in cold water five minutes; add the scalded pineapple juice and stir until gelatine is thoroughly dissolved. Now add sugar, crushed canned pineapple, lemon juice and mint, and blend well. Cool, then chill. Freeze, as indicated for recipe No. 422, Grape Juice Sherbet I, until mushy. Then, stir in the egg whites stiffly beaten with the salt, and continue freezing until mixture becomes firm, but not too hard. Serve either in sherbet glasses, orange cups or green pepper cups right after the roast or as a dessert.

454   PINEAPPLE SHERBET I
              (Hand freezer only)

A very economical recipe.

1 cup chilled water
4 tablespoons lemon juice
1 No. 2 can (2½ cups) crushed pineapple

1⅓ cups (1 can) sweetened condensed milk
⅛ teaspoon salt

Add water and lemon juice to crushed pineapple. Blend thoroughly with sweetened condensed milk and salt, and freeze in hand freezer, using 4 parts ice and 1 part rock salt until firm. Pack in 6 parts ice and 1 part salt for 1½ hours. Serve in chilled sherbet glasses.

455   PINEAPPLE SHERBET II
         (Hand freezer or refrigerator tray)

1 cup granulated sugar
3 cups boiling water
1 teaspoon granulated gelatine
¼ teaspoon salt

1½ tablespoons cold water
2 cups canned crushed pineapple
Juice of 1 lemon, rind of half

2 egg whites stiffly beaten

Boil sugar and boiling water for 5 long minutes. Add granulated gelatine which has been softened in cold water, and stir until thoroughly dissolved. Cool, then combine with crushed pineapple, lemon juice and rind, mix well and stir in, very gently, the egg whites stiffly beaten with the salt. Freeze either in hand freezer or refrigerator tray, until solid and without stirring. If hand freezer is used, use 4 parts ice and 1 part of rock salt. Serve either in chilled sherbet glasses, orange cups, cantaloupe halves or in paper cases.

456　　　　　　　PLUM SHERBET

Proceed as indicated for recipe No. 445, Peach Cream Sherbet, substituting plum pulp for peach pulp, and adding, just before freezing 4 or 5 drops of almond extract. Freeze as directed.

457　　　　PRUNE JUICE SHERBET
　　　　　　(Hand freezer only)

1 tablespoon granulated gelatine	2 cups prune juice
½ cup cold water	¼ cup lemon juice
1 cup boiling water	2 cups fresh milk
	⅛ teaspoon salt

Sprinkle gelatine on the cold water, let soak five minutes; then add the boiling water and stir until gelatine is thoroughly dissolved. Now combine prune juice and lemon juice and add to gelatine mixture. Chill; then add fresh milk and salt. Freeze in hand freezer, using 4 parts ice and 1 part rock salt, until solid, but not too hard. You may add ½ cup chopped nuts before freezing, if desired. *A fine sherbet for children's party, or supper, especially during the hot weather.*

458   RASPBERRY MILK SHERBET   I
(Hand freezer only)

A very economical way of making this refreshing frozen dessert when raspberries are out of season is to use canned raspberries, operating as follows:

1 cup canned raspberries	⅛ teaspoon salt
2 cups chilled milk	Juice of 1 lemon
½ cup granulated sugar	1½ teaspoons vanilla extract

Force canned raspberries through a sieve. Add chilled milk, sugar, salt, lemon juice and vanilla extract. Blend thoroughly, and freeze as indicated for recipe No. 422, Grape Juice Sherbet I, until solid but not too hard. Serve in chilled sherbet glasses, or chilled orange cups or cantaloupe halves.

You may use fresh raspberries, if desired.

459   RASPBERRY SHERBET   II
(Hand freezer or refrigerator tray)

This recipe results in a rich, nourishing frozen dessert. The creamy mixture should be stirred, when mushy, or about 30 minutes after being placed in the tray, and 15 minutes after being churned in the hand freezer.

1½ cups granulated sugar	1 tablespoon lemon juice
1 tablespoon corn syrup	1 quart fresh raspberries
⅔ cup boiling water	½ cup heavy cream, whipped
2 egg whites stiffly beaten	stiff
¼ scant teaspoon salt	

Cook sugar, corn syrup and boiling water until syrup spins a fine thread (238 deg. F.). Immediately pour in a fine stream over stiffly beaten egg whites which have been salted, while beating briskly and constantly. Then add lemon juice combined with fresh raspberries, which have been forced through a sieve, alternately with the stiffly whipped heavy cream. Freeze either in hand freezer, or refrigerator tray, until mushy; scrape bottom and sides, then beat for 1 short minute and continue freezing until solid, but not too hard. Serve according to fancy. A good suggestion is to serve this sherbet in fresh scooped yellow apples. The effect is really tempting.

460   RHUBARB SHERBET I
(Hand freezer or refrigerator tray)

½ cup stewed rhubarb

⅓ cup (generous) lemon juice

⅛ teaspoon salt

½ cup granulated sugar

¼ cup light corn syrup

1 cup chilled milk

1 teaspoon granulated gelatine

1 tablespoon cold water

½ cup heavy cream, whipped stiff

To the unmashed cold stewed rhubarb, add lemon juice, salt, sugar and corn syrup. Blend carefully, but thoroughly with the milk. Then add gelatine soaked in cold water for 5 minutes, then dissolved over hot water. Mix well and chill. Lastly fold in the stiffly whipped heavy cream, and freeze as indicated for recipe No. 422, Grape Juice Sherbet I until mushy; stir from bottom and sides, beat ½ minute, then continue freezing until solid, but not too hard. Serve according to fancy, that is either in chilled sherbet glasses, orange cups or cantaloupe halves which have been chilled.

461 **RHUBARB SHERBET II**
(Hand freezer or refrigerator tray)

2½ cups cooked, sieved chilled   1 tablespoon lemon juice
    rhubarb   1 cup granulated sugar
  1 teaspoon granulated gelatine   ¼ teaspoon salt
½ cup cold water   2 egg whites stiffly beaten

To the chilled sieved rhubarb, add granulated gelatine, which has been soaked in cold water for 5 minutes, and dissolved over hot water, stirring briskly until mixture is thoroughly blended. Stir in the lemon juice, sugar and salt. Mix well. Freeze as indicated for recipe No. 422, Grape Juice Sherbet I, until mushy. Scrape bottom and sides, then stir in the stiffly beaten egg whites. Continue freezing until mixture is solid, but not too hard. Serve in sherbet glasses, or for a children's party you may place a scoop of this healthy sherbet in a cold, baked individual tartlet shell.

462 **RHUBARB ORANGE MARMALADE**
SHERBET
(Hand freezer or refrigerator tray)

Another delightful frozen dessert for a children's party, or a bridge, afternoon, or lawn party.

2 cups cooked, sieved rhubarb   1 tablespoon cold water
3 cups boiling water   Juice of 1 lemon, rind of half
1 cup granulated sugar   2 egg whites, stiffly beaten
1 teaspoon granulated gelatine   ½ cup orange marmalade
        ⅛ teaspoon salt

Boil sugar and water for 5 long minutes; add granulated gelatine which has been soaked in cold water for 5 minutes, and stir well. Then add sieved rhubarb, lemon juice and rind, and stir

[267]

well. Lastly fold in the stiffly beaten egg whites to which the orange marmalade has been added, after the beating. Freeze, without stirring, as indicated for recipe No. 422, Grape Juice Sherbet I, until solid, but not too hard. Serve in chilled sherbet glasses.

463   SAUTERNE SHERBET
(Hand freezer only)

2 cups boiling water
1½ cups granulated sugar
¼ scant teaspoon salt
Juice of 2 lemons
Juice of 2 oranges

2 cups of Sauterne wine
Italian meringue (cooked meringue) made as indicated for No. 377
1 cup Sauterne wine

1 generous tablespoon brandy

Boil water, sugar and salt to the soft ball stage. Remove from the fire, cool a little and stir in the lemon and orange juices, alternately with the 2 cups of Sauterne wine. Freeze in 4 parts ice and 1 part rock salt, until mushy, but rather solid. Then add the Italian meringue, made as indicated for recipe No. 435, Maraschino Liqueur Sherbet, which has been folded with the remaining cup of Sauterne wine, combined with the tablespoon of good brandy (more brandy may be added, if desired strong). Continue freezing until solid, but not too hard. Serve in well-chilled sherbet glasses.

464   SHERRY SHERBET
(Hand freezer only)

2 cups boiling water   Juice of 4 lemons
1 cup granulated sugar   Grated rind of 1 lemon
¼ scant teaspoon salt   ¼ cup orange juice
2 teaspoons granulated gelatine   1 cup (scant) sherry wine
2 tablespoons cold water   2 egg whites, stiffly beaten
            Green vegetable coloring (optional)

Boil sugar and boiling water until syrup spins a thread. Remove from the fire and add gelatine which has been soaked in cold water for 5 minutes, and stir until gelatine is thoroughly dissolved. Then add lemon juice and rind, salt, orange juice, and blend well. Strain through double cheesecloth, and chill. Add sherry wine and 3 or 4 drops of vegetable coloring, remembering that freezing or cooking lessens all colors. The mixture should be a pretty pale green when served. Freeze in hand freezer, using 4 parts ice and 1 part rock salt until mushy, then stir in the stiffly beaten egg whites, and continue freezing until solid, but not too hard. Serve in chilled sherbet glasses or orange cups.

465   STRAWBERRY SHERBET I
(Hand freezer or refrigerator tray)

In addition to the following recipes, the various methods of raspberry sherbet preparations may be applied or adapted to strawberries. The following method is a very easy one.

2½ cups strawberry pulp and   ¾ cup granulated sugar
    juice   ⅛ teaspoon salt
          2 egg whites, stiffly beaten

Combine strawberry pulp and juice with sugar and salt, and chill for 1 long hour; then freeze as indicated for recipe No. 422, Grape Juice Sherbet I, until mushy. Stir in the stiffly beaten egg whites, and continue freezing until solid, but not too hard. Serve in chilled sherbet glasses or orange cups or cantaloupe halves.

466   STRAWBERRY SHERBET II
(Hand freezer only)

The following French recipe is rather rich. This recipe will serve 12 persons. For 6, reduce the ingredients to half.

2 quarts fresh strawberries, washed huled, and drained	2 cups heavy cream, un-whipped
1½ cups granulated sugar	1½ cups ice water
½ teaspoon salt	Juice of 1 lemon

Italian meringue (recipe No. 377)

Sprinkle sugar over the prepared fresh strawberries, and let stand in refrigerator for 1 hour. Add the unwhipped heavy cream and rub mixture through a fine sieve. Add salt combined with ice water and lemon juice. Freeze in hand freezer, using 4 parts ice and 1 part rock salt, until mushy; then fold in the Italian meringue, made as indicated for recipe No. 435, Maraschino Liqueur Sherbet, and continue freezing until solid, but not too hard. Serve in chilled sherbet glasses or in orange cups, or in cantaloupe halves, also chilled, topping each serving with a nice, ripe fresh strawberry, dipped or not in melted currant jelly.

467   TOMATO JUICE SHERBET
(Hand freezer or refrigerator tray)

This healthy sherbet may be served as an appetizer, or as a digestive right after the roast.

2 teaspoons granulated gelatine   ½ teaspoon salt
¼ scant cup ice water   ⅛ teaspoon ground nutmeg
4 cups tomato juice   A dash white pepper
Juice of a whole lemon   2 egg whites, stiffly beaten

Soak granulated gelatine in ice water for 5 minutes. Bring tomato juice to the boiling point, but do not boil, and stir in the soaked gelatine, until thoroughly dissolved. Then add lemon juice, salt, nutmeg and white pepper. Chill; then freeze in hand freezer, using 4 parts ice and 1 part rock salt, until mushy; after which fold in the stiffly beaten egg whites, and freeze until solid, but not too hard. If refrigerator tray is used, freeze until mushy, remove from refrigerator to a chilled bowl, and scrape bottom and sides. Then beat for 1 minute or until smooth, and fold in the stiffly beaten egg whites, and continue freezing for 3 hours, or until solid, but not too hard.

Any other kind of vegetable or fruit juice may be prepared in this way. A dash of Worcestershire sauce, enhances the flavor if added when folding in the stiffly beaten egg whites.

468   VENETIAN SHERBET

To recipe No. 455, Pineapple Sherbet II, add, when mixture is frozen to a mush, the combined following ingredients: 1 teaspoon of kirsch liqueur, 1 generous teaspoon of good brandy, and ¼ cup of dry champagne (you may substitute dry white wine for champagne), and continue freezing until solid, but not too hard. Serve in chilled sherbet glasses.

469   WATERMELON CREAM SHERBET
(Refrigerator tray only)

1½ cups hot watermelon water
1 cup granulated sugar
¼ scant teaspoon salt
1 tablespoon granulated gelatine
4 tablespoons cold watermelon water

⅛ generous teaspoon ginger
⅛ generous teaspoon nutmeg
2 tablespoons lemon juice
2 cups ripe watermelon pulp
2 tablespoons maraschino juice
1 cup heavy cream, whipped stiff

Stir in the granulated sugar with hot watermelon water and salt, bring to a boil, and allow to boil 5 long minutes. Remove from the fire and stir in the granulated gelatine, which has been soaked in cold watermelon water, stirring until gelatine is entirely dissolved. Strain through a double cheesecloth, and cool. Add lemon juice, ginger and nutmeg and the thinly shaved watermelon pulp. Chill. Then whip mixture until it begins to thicken and fold in the stiffly beaten heavy cream to which has been added the maraschino juice (from canned maraschino cherries). Now line refrigerator tray with waxed paper, pour in the creamy mixture evenly and let freeze overnight, or at least 7 hours. Serve in chilled sherbet glasses, or better still: cut a chilled watermelon into slices 2 inches thick, cut into rounds about 3½ inches in diameter with large cookie cutter. Remove as many seeds as possible. Scoop out a little watermelon pulp from the center of each round with a teaspoon and fill with watermelon sherbet.

470   WATERMELON MILK SHERBET
            (Refrigerator tray only)

2 tablespoons lemon juice
½ teaspoon grated lemon rind
½ cup granulated sugar
1 quart (4 cups) diced water-
    melon

⅛ generous teaspoon salt
1¼ cups undiluted evaporated
    milk
2 tablespoons sherry wine
    (optional)

2 egg whites, stiffly beaten

Combine lemon juice, grated rind, sugar and watermelon pulp. Mix well and let stand in refrigerator for 30 minutes. Rub this through a sieve; then add well-chilled undiluted evaporated milk slowly to watermelon mixture. Freeze to a mush; remove from tray and scrape bottom and sides, then fold in the stiffly beaten egg whites with the sherry wine. Continue freezing for at least 4 hours. Serve in chilled sherbet glasses.

Index

❯❯❯ ❯❯❯ ❯❯❯ ❯❯❯ ❯❯❯ ❯❯❯ ❯❯❯ ❯❯❯ ❯❯❯ ❮❮❮ ❮❮❮ ❮❮❮ ❮❮❮ ❮❮❮ ❮❮❮ ❮❮❮ ❮❮❮ ❮❮❮ ❮❮❮

SECTION I: GENERAL INFORMATION

Index

Index

[277]

Index

SECTION VII: MOUSSE RECIPES

Index

A CATALOGUE OF SELECTED DOVER BOOKS
IN ALL FIELDS OF INTEREST

AMERICA'S OLD MASTERS, James T. Flexner. Four men emerged unexpectedly from provincial 18th century America to leadership in European art: Benjamin West, J. S. Copley, C. R. Peale, Gilbert Stuart. Brilliant coverage of lives and contributions. Revised, 1967 edition. 69 plates. 365pp. of text.

21806-6 Paperbound $3.00

FIRST FLOWERS OF OUR WILDERNESS: AMERICAN PAINTING, THE COLONIAL PERIOD, James T. Flexner. Painters, and regional painting traditions from earliest Colonial times up to the emergence of Copley, West and Peale Sr., Foster, Gustavus Hesselius, Feke, John Smibert and many anonymous painters in the primitive manner. Engaging presentation, with 162 illustrations. xxii + 368pp.

22180-6 Paperbound $3.50

THE LIGHT OF DISTANT SKIES: AMERICAN PAINTING, 1760-1835, James T. Flexner. The great generation of early American painters goes to Europe to learn and to teach: West, Copley, Gilbert Stuart and others. Allston, Trumbull, Morse; also contemporary American painters—primitives, derivatives, academics—who remained in America. 102 illustrations. xiii + 306pp.   22179-2 Paperbound $3.50

A HISTORY OF THE RISE AND PROGRESS OF THE ARTS OF DESIGN IN THE UNITED STATES, William Dunlap. Much the richest mine of information on early American painters, sculptors, architects, engravers, miniaturists, etc. The only source of information for scores of artists, the major primary source for many others. Unabridged reprint of rare original 1834 edition, with new introduction by James T. Flexner, and 394 new illustrations. Edited by Rita Weiss. 6⅝ x 9⅝.

21695-0, 21696-9, 21697-7 Three volumes, Paperbound $15.00

EPOCHS OF CHINESE AND JAPANESE ART, Ernest F. Fenollosa. From primitive Chinese art to the 20th century, thorough history, explanation of every important art period and form, including Japanese woodcuts; main stress on China and Japan, but Tibet, Korea also included. Still unexcelled for its detailed, rich coverage of cultural background, aesthetic elements, diffusion studies, particularly of the historical period. 2nd, 1913 edition. 242 illustrations. lii + 439pp. of text.

20364-6, 20365-4 Two volumes, Paperbound $6.00

THE GENTLE ART OF MAKING ENEMIES, James A. M. Whistler. Greatest wit of his day deflates Oscar Wilde, Ruskin, Swinburne; strikes back at inane critics, exhibitions, art journalism; aesthetics of impressionist revolution in most striking form. Highly readable classic by great painter. Reproduction of edition designed by Whistler. Introduction by Alfred Werner. xxxvi + 334pp.

21875-9 Paperbound $3.00

VISUAL ILLUSIONS: THEIR CAUSES, CHARACTERISTICS, AND APPLICATIONS, Matthew Luckiesh. Thorough description and discussion of optical illusion, geometric and perspective, particularly; size and shape distortions, illusions of color, of motion; natural illusions; use of illusion in art and magic, industry, etc. Most useful today with op art, also for classical art. Scores of effects illustrated. Introduction by William H. Ittleson. 100 illustrations. xxi + 252pp.

21530-X Paperbound $2.00

A HANDBOOK OF ANATOMY FOR ART STUDENTS, Arthur Thomson. Thorough, virtually exhaustive coverage of skeletal structure, musculature, etc. Full text, supplemented by anatomical diagrams and drawings and by photographs of undraped figures. Unique in its comparison of male and female forms, pointing out differences of contour, texture, form. 211 figures, 40 drawings, 86 photographs. xx + 459pp. 5⅜ x 8⅜.

21163-0 Paperbound $3.50

150 MASTERPIECES OF DRAWING, Selected by Anthony Toney. Full page reproductions of drawings from the early 16th to the end of the 18th century, all beautifully reproduced: Rembrandt, Michelangelo, Dürer, Fragonard, Urs, Graf, Wouwerman, many others. First-rate browsing book, model book for artists. xviii + 150pp. 8⅜ x 11¼.

21032-4 Paperbound $2.50

THE LATER WORK OF AUBREY BEARDSLEY, Aubrey Beardsley. Exotic, erotic, ironic masterpieces in full maturity: Comedy Ballet, Venus and Tannhauser, Pierrot, Lysistrata, Rape of the Lock, Savoy material, Ali Baba, Volpone, etc. This material revolutionized the art world, and is still powerful, fresh, brilliant. With *The Early Work*, all Beardsley's finest work. 174 plates, 2 in color. xiv + 176pp. 8⅛ x 11.

21817-1 Paperbound $3.00

DRAWINGS OF REMBRANDT, Rembrandt van Rijn. Complete reproduction of fabulously rare edition by Lippmann and Hofstede de Groot, completely reedited, updated, improved by Prof. Seymour Slive, Fogg Museum. Portraits, Biblical sketches, landscapes, Oriental types, nudes, episodes from classical mythology—All Rembrandt's fertile genius. Also selection of drawings by his pupils and followers. "Stunning volumes," *Saturday Review*. 550 illustrations. lxxviii + 552pp. 9⅛ x 12¼.

21485-0, 21486-9 Two volumes, Paperbound $10.00

THE DISASTERS OF WAR, Francisco Goya. One of the masterpieces of Western civilization—83 etchings that record Goya's shattering, bitter reaction to the Napoleonic war that swept through Spain after the insurrection of 1808 and to war in general. Reprint of the first edition, with three additional plates from Boston's Museum of Fine Arts. All plates facsimile size. Introduction by Philip Hofer, Fogg Museum. v + 97pp. 9⅜ x 8¼.

21872-4 Paperbound $2.00

GRAPHIC WORKS OF ODILON REDON. Largest collection of Redon's graphic works ever assembled: 172 lithographs, 28 etchings and engravings, 9 drawings. These include some of his most famous works. All the plates from *Odilon Redon: oeuvre graphique complet*, plus additional plates. New introduction and caption translations by Alfred Werner. 209 illustrations. xxvii + 209pp. 9⅛ x 12¼.

21966-8 Paperbound $4.50

DESIGN BY ACCIDENT; A BOOK OF "ACCIDENTAL EFFECTS" FOR ARTISTS AND DESIGNERS, James F. O'Brien. Create your own unique, striking, imaginative effects by "controlled accident" interaction of materials: paints and lacquers, oil and water based paints, splatter, crackling materials, shatter, similar items. Everything you do will be different; first book on this limitless art, so useful to both fine artist and commercial artist. Full instructions. 192 plates showing "accidents," 8 in color. viii + 215pp. 8⅜ x 11¼. 21942-9 Paperbound $3.75

THE BOOK OF SIGNS, Rudolf Koch. Famed German type designer draws 493 beautiful symbols: religious, mystical, alchemical, imperial, property marks, runes, etc. Remarkable fusion of traditional and modern. Good for suggestions of timelessness, smartness, modernity. Text. vi + 104pp. 6⅛ x 9¼. 20162-7 Paperbound $1.25

HISTORY OF INDIAN AND INDONESIAN ART, Ananda K. Coomaraswamy. An unabridged republication of one of the finest books by a great scholar in Eastern art. Rich in descriptive material, history, social backgrounds; Sunga reliefs, Rajput paintings, Gupta temples, Burmese frescoes, textiles, jewelry, sculpture, etc. 400 photos. viii + 423pp. 6⅜ x 9¾. 21436-2 Paperbound $5.00

PRIMITIVE ART, Franz Boas. America's foremost anthropologist surveys textiles, ceramics, woodcarving, basketry, metalwork, etc.; patterns, technology, creation of symbols, style origins. All areas of world, but very full on Northwest Coast Indians. More than 350 illustrations of baskets, boxes, totem poles, weapons, etc. 378 pp. 20025-6 Paperbound $3.00

THE GENTLEMAN AND CABINET MAKER'S DIRECTOR, Thomas Chippendale. Full reprint (third edition, 1762) of most influential furniture book of all time, by master cabinetmaker. 200 plates, illustrating chairs, sofas, mirrors, tables, cabinets, plus 24 photographs of surviving pieces. Biographical introduction by N. Bienenstock. vi + 249pp. 9⅞ x 12¾. 21601-2 Paperbound $4.00

AMERICAN ANTIQUE FURNITURE, Edgar G. Miller, Jr. The basic coverage of all American furniture before 1840. Individual chapters cover type of furniture—clocks, tables, sideboards, etc.—chronologically, with inexhaustible wealth of data. More than 2100 photographs, all identified, commented on. Essential to all early American collectors. Introduction by H. E. Keyes. vi + 1106pp. 7⅞ x 10¾. 21599-7, 21600-4 Two volumes, Paperbound $11.00

PENNSYLVANIA DUTCH AMERICAN FOLK ART, Henry J. Kauffman. 279 photos, 28 drawings of tulipware, Fraktur script, painted tinware, toys, flowered furniture, quilts, samplers, hex signs, house interiors, etc. Full descriptive text. Excellent for tourist, rewarding for designer, collector. Map. 146pp. 7⅞ x 10¾. 21205-X Paperbound $2.50

EARLY NEW ENGLAND GRAVESTONE RUBBINGS, Edmund V. Gillon, Jr. 43 photographs, 226 carefully reproduced rubbings show heavily symbolic, sometimes macabre early gravestones, up to early 19th century. Remarkable early American primitive art, occasionally strikingly beautiful; always powerful. Text. xxvi + 207pp. 8⅜ x 11¼. 21380-3 Paperbound $3.50

ALPHABETS AND ORNAMENTS, Ernst Lehner. Well-known pictorial source for decorative alphabets, script examples, cartouches, frames, decorative title pages, calligraphic initials, borders, similar material. 14th to 19th century, mostly European. Useful in almost any graphic arts designing, varied styles. 750 illustrations. 256pp. 7 x 10. 21905-4 Paperbound $4.00

PAINTING: A CREATIVE APPROACH, Norman Colquhoun. For the beginner simple guide provides an instructive approach to painting: major stumbling blocks for beginner; overcoming them, technical points; paints and pigments; oil painting; watercolor and other media and color. New section on "plastic" paints. Glossary. Formerly *Paint Your Own Pictures*. 221pp. 22000-1 Paperbound $1.75

THE ENJOYMENT AND USE OF COLOR, Walter Sargent. Explanation of the relations between colors themselves and between colors in nature and art, including hundreds of little-known facts about color values, intensities, effects of high and low illumination, complementary colors. Many practical hints for painters, references to great masters. 7 color plates, 29 illustrations. x + 274pp.
20944-X Paperbound $2.75

THE NOTEBOOKS OF LEONARDO DA VINCI, compiled and edited by Jean Paul Richter. 1566 extracts from original manuscripts reveal the full range of Leonardo's versatile genius: all his writings on painting, sculpture, architecture, anatomy, astronomy, geography, topography, physiology, mining, music, etc., in both Italian and English, with 186 plates of manuscript pages and more than 500 additional drawings. Includes studies for the Last Supper, the lost Sforza monument, and other works. Total of xlvii + 866pp. 7⅞ x 10¾.
22572-0, 22573-9 Two volumes, Paperbound $11.00

MONTGOMERY WARD CATALOGUE OF 1895. Tea gowns, yards of flannel and pillow-case lace, stereoscopes, books of gospel hymns, the New Improved Singer Sewing Machine, side saddles, milk skimmers, straight-edged razors, high-button shoes, spittoons, and on and on . . . listing some 25,000 items, practically all illustrated. Essential to the shoppers of the 1890's, it is our truest record of the spirit of the period. Unaltered reprint of Issue No. 57, Spring and Summer 1895. Introduction by Boris Emmet. Innumerable illustrations. xiii + 624pp. 8½ x 11⅝.
22377-9 Paperbound $6.95

THE CRYSTAL PALACE EXHIBITION ILLUSTRATED CATALOGUE (LONDON, 1851). One of the wonders of the modern world—the Crystal Palace Exhibition in which all the nations of the civilized world exhibited their achievements in the arts and sciences—presented in an equally important illustrated catalogue. More than 1700 items pictured with accompanying text—ceramics, textiles, cast-iron work, carpets, pianos, sleds, razors, wall-papers, billiard tables, beehives, silverware and hundreds of other artifacts—represent the focal point of Victorian culture in the Western World. Probably the largest collection of Victorian decorative art ever assembled— indispensable for antiquarians and designers. Unabridged republication of the Art-Journal Catalogue of the Great Exhibition of 1851, with all terminal essays. New introduction by John Gloag, F.S.A. xxxiv + 426pp. 9 x 12.
22503-8 Paperbound $5.00

A HISTORY OF COSTUME, Carl Köhler. Definitive history, based on surviving pieces of clothing primarily, and paintings, statues, etc. secondarily. Highly readable text, supplemented by 594 illustrations of costumes of the ancient Mediterranean peoples, Greece and Rome, the Teutonic prehistoric period; costumes of the Middle Ages, Renaissance, Baroque, 18th and 19th centuries. Clear, measured patterns are provided for many clothing articles. Approach is practical throughout. Enlarged by Emma von Sichart. 464pp. 21030-8 Paperbound $3.50

ORIENTAL RUGS, ANTIQUE AND MODERN, Walter A. Hawley. A complete and authoritative treatise on the Oriental rug—where they are made, by whom and how, designs and symbols, characteristics in detail of the six major groups, how to distinguish them and how to buy them. Detailed technical data is provided on periods, weaves, warps, wefts, textures, sides, ends and knots, although no technical background is required for an understanding. 11 color plates, 80 halftones, 4 maps. vi + 320pp. 6⅛ x 9⅛. 22366-3 Paperbound $5.00

TEN BOOKS ON ARCHITECTURE, Vitruvius. By any standards the most important book on architecture ever written. Early Roman discussion of aesthetics of building, construction methods, orders, sites, and every other aspect of architecture has inspired, instructed architecture for about 2,000 years. Stands behind Palladio, Michelangelo, Bramante, Wren, countless others. Definitive Morris H. Morgan translation. 68 illustrations. xii + 331pp. 20645-9 Paperbound $3.00

THE FOUR BOOKS OF ARCHITECTURE, Andrea Palladio. Translated into every major Western European language in the two centuries following its publication in 1570, this has been one of the most influential books in the history of architecture. Complete reprint of the 1738 Isaac Ware edition. New introduction by Adolf Placzek, Columbia Univ. 216 plates. xxii + 110pp. of text. 9½ x 12¾. 21308-0 Clothbound $12.50

STICKS AND STONES: A STUDY OF AMERICAN ARCHITECTURE AND CIVILIZATION, Lewis Mumford.One of the great classics of American cultural history. American architecture from the medieval-inspired earliest forms to the early 20th century; evolution of structure and style, and reciprocal influences on environment. 21 photographic illustrations. 238pp. 20202-X Paperbound $2.00

THE AMERICAN BUILDER'S COMPANION, Asher Benjamin. The most widely used early 19th century architectural style and source book, for colonial up into Greek Revival periods. Extensive development of geometry of carpentering, construction of sashes, frames, doors, stairs; plans and elevations of domestic and other buildings. Hundreds of thousands of houses were built according to this book, now invaluable to historians, architects, restorers, etc. 1827 edition. 59 plates. 114pp. 7⅞ x 10¾. 22236-5 Paperbound $3.50

DUTCH HOUSES IN THE HUDSON VALLEY BEFORE 1776, Helen Wilkinson Reynolds. The standard survey of the Dutch colonial house and outbuildings, with constructional features, decoration, and local history associated with individual homesteads. Introduction by Franklin D. Roosevelt. Map. 150 illustrations. 469pp. 6⅝ x 9¼. 21469-9 Paperbound $5.00

THE ARCHITECTURE OF COUNTRY HOUSES, Andrew J. Downing. Together with Vaux's *Villas and Cottages* this is the basic book for Hudson River Gothic architecture of the middle Victorian period. Full, sound discussions of general aspects of housing, architecture, style, decoration, furnishing, together with scores of detailed house plans, illustrations of specific buildings, accompanied by full text. Perhaps the most influential single American architectural book. 1850 edition. Introduction by J. Stewart Johnson. 321 figures, 34 architectural designs. xvi + 560pp.

22003-6 Paperbound $4.00

LOST EXAMPLES OF COLONIAL ARCHITECTURE, John Mead Howells. Full-page photographs of buildings that have disappeared or been so altered as to be denatured, including many designed by major early American architects. 245 plates. xvii + 248pp. 7⅞ x 10¾.

21143-6 Paperbound $3.50

DOMESTIC ARCHITECTURE OF THE AMERICAN COLONIES AND OF THE EARLY REPUBLIC, Fiske Kimball. Foremost architect and restorer of Williamsburg and Monticello covers nearly 200 homes between 1620-1825. Architectural details, construction, style features, special fixtures, floor plans, etc. Generally considered finest work in its area. 219 illustrations of houses, doorways, windows, capital mantels. xx + 314pp. 7⅞ x 10¾.

21743-4 Paperbound $4.00

EARLY AMERICAN ROOMS: 1650-1858, edited by Russell Hawes Kettell. Tour of 12 rooms, each representative of a different era in American history and each furnished, decorated, designed and occupied in the style of the era. 72 plans and elevations, 8-page color section, etc., show fabrics, wall papers, arrangements, etc. Full descriptive text. xvii + 200pp. of text. 8⅜ x 11¼.

21633-0 Paperbound $5.00

THE FITZWILLIAM VIRGINAL BOOK, edited by J. Fuller Maitland and W. B. Squire. Full modern printing of famous early 17th-century ms. volume of 300 works by Morley, Byrd, Bull, Gibbons, etc. For piano or other modern keyboard instrument; easy to read format. xxxvi + 938pp. 8⅜ x 11.

21068-5, 21069-3 Two volumes, Paperbound $10.00

KEYBOARD MUSIC, Johann Sebastian Bach. Bach Gesellschaft edition. A rich selection of Bach's masterpieces for the harpsichord: the six English Suites, six French Suites, the six Partitas (Clavierübung part I), the Goldberg Variations (Clavierübung part IV), the fifteen Two-Part Inventions and the fifteen Three-Part Sinfonias. Clearly reproduced on large sheets with ample margins; eminently playable. vi + 312pp. 8⅛ x 11.

22360-4 Paperbound $5.00

THE MUSIC OF BACH: AN INTRODUCTION, Charles Sanford Terry. A fine, nontechnical introduction to Bach's music, both instrumental and vocal. Covers organ music, chamber music, passion music, other types. Analyzes themes, developments, innovations. x + 114pp.

21075-8 Paperbound $1.50

BEETHOVEN AND HIS NINE SYMPHONIES, Sir George Grove. Noted British musicologist provides best history, analysis, commentary on symphonies. Very thorough, rigorously accurate; necessary to both advanced student and amateur music lover. 436 musical passages. vii + 407 pp.

20334-4 Paperbound $2.75

JOHANN SEBASTIAN BACH, Philipp Spitta. One of the great classics of musicology, this definitive analysis of Bach's music (and life) has never been surpassed. Lucid, nontechnical analyses of hundreds of pieces (30 pages devoted to St. Matthew Passion, 26 to B Minor Mass). Also includes major analysis of 18th-century music. 450 musical examples. 40-page musical supplement. Total of xx + 1799pp.
(EUK) 22278-0, 22279-9 Two volumes, Clothbound $17.50

MOZART AND HIS PIANO CONCERTOS, Cuthbert Girdlestone. The only full-length study of an important area of Mozart's creativity. Provides detailed analyses of all 23 concertos, traces inspirational sources. 417 musical examples. Second edition. 509pp.
21271-8 Paperbound $3.50

THE PERFECT WAGNERITE: A COMMENTARY ON THE NIBLUNG'S RING, George Bernard Shaw. Brilliant and still relevant criticism in remarkable essays on Wagner's Ring cycle, Shaw's ideas on political and social ideology behind the plots, role of Leitmotifs, vocal requisites, etc. Prefaces. xxi + 136pp.
(USO) 21707-8 Paperbound $1.75

DON GIOVANNI, W. A. Mozart. Complete libretto, modern English translation; biographies of composer and librettist; accounts of early performances and critical reaction. Lavishly illustrated. All the material you need to understand and appreciate this great work. Dover Opera Guide and Libretto Series; translated and introduced by Ellen Bleiler. 92 illustrations. 209pp.
21134-7 Paperbound $2.00

BASIC ELECTRICITY, U. S. Bureau of Naval Personel. Originally a training course, best non-technical coverage of basic theory of electricity and its applications. Fundamental concepts, batteries, circuits, conductors and wiring techniques, AC and DC, inductance and capacitance, generators, motors, transformers, magnetic amplifiers, synchros, servomechanisms, etc. Also covers blue-prints, electrical diagrams, etc. Many questions, with answers. 349 illustrations. x + 448pp. 6½ x 9¼.
20973-3 Paperbound $3.50

REPRODUCTION OF SOUND, Edgar Villchur. Thorough coverage for laymen of high fidelity systems, reproducing systems in general, needles, amplifiers, preamps, loudspeakers, feedback, explaining physical background. "A rare talent for making technicalities vividly comprehensible," R. Darrell, *High Fidelity.* 69 figures. iv + 92pp.
21515-6 Paperbound $1.35

HEAR ME TALKIN' TO YA: THE STORY OF JAZZ AS TOLD BY THE MEN WHO MADE IT, Nat Shapiro and Nat Hentoff. Louis Armstrong, Fats Waller, Jo Jones, Clarence Williams, Billy Holiday, Duke Ellington, Jelly Roll Morton and dozens of other jazz greats tell how it was in Chicago's South Side, New Orleans, depression Harlem and the modern West Coast as jazz was born and grew. xvi + 429pp.
21726-4 Paperbound $3.00

FABLES OF AESOP, translated by Sir Roger L'Estrange. A reproduction of the very rare 1931 Paris edition; a selection of the most interesting fables, together with 50 imaginative drawings by Alexander Calder. v + 128pp. 6½x9¼.
21780-9 Paperbound $1.50

AGAINST THE GRAIN (A REBOURS), Joris K. Huysmans. Filled with weird images, evidences of a bizarre imagination, exotic experiments with hallucinatory drugs, rich tastes and smells and the diversions of its sybarite hero Duc Jean des Esseintes, this classic novel pushed 19th-century literary decadence to its limits. Full unabridged edition. Do not confuse this with abridged editions generally sold. Introduction by Havelock Ellis. xlix + 206pp.   22190-3 Paperbound $2.50

VARIORUM SHAKESPEARE: HAMLET. Edited by Horace H. Furness; a landmark of American scholarship. Exhaustive footnotes and appendices treat all doubtful words and phrases, as well as suggested critical emendations throughout the play's history. First volume contains editor's own text, collated with all Quartos and Folios. Second volume contains full first Quarto, translations of Shakespeare's sources (Belleforest, and Saxo Grammaticus), Der Bestrafte Brudermord, and many essays on critical and historical points of interest by major authorities of past and present. Includes details of staging and costuming over the years. By far the best edition available for serious students of Shakespeare. Total of xx + 905pp.
21004-9, 21005-7, 2 volumes, Paperbound $7.00

A LIFE OF WILLIAM SHAKESPEARE, Sir Sidney Lee. This is the standard life of Shakespeare, summarizing everything known about Shakespeare and his plays. Incredibly rich in material, broad in coverage, clear and judicious, it has served thousands as the best introduction to Shakespeare. 1931 edition. 9 plates. xxix + 792pp.   21967-4 Paperbound $3.75

MASTERS OF THE DRAMA, John Gassner. Most comprehensive history of the drama in print, covering every tradition from Greeks to modern Europe and America, including India, Far East, etc. Covers more than 800 dramatists, 2000 plays, with biographical material, plot summaries, theatre history, criticism, etc. "Best of its kind in English," New Republic. 77 illustrations. xxii + 890pp.
20100-7 Clothbound $10.00

THE EVOLUTION OF THE ENGLISH LANGUAGE, George McKnight. The growth of English, from the 14th century to the present. Unusual, non-technical account presents basic information in very interesting form: sound shifts, change in grammar and syntax, vocabulary growth, similar topics. Abundantly illustrated with quotations. Formerly Modern English in the Making. xii + 590pp.
21932-1 Paperbound $3.50

AN ETYMOLOGICAL DICTIONARY OF MODERN ENGLISH, Ernest Weekley. Fullest, richest work of its sort, by foremost British lexicographer. Detailed word histories, including many colloquial and archaic words; extensive quotations. Do not confuse this with the Concise Etymological Dictionary, which is much abridged. Total of xxvii + 830pp. 6½ x 9¼.
21873-2, 21874-0 Two volumes, Paperbound $7.90

FLATLAND: A ROMANCE OF MANY DIMENSIONS, E. A. Abbott. Classic of science-fiction explores ramifications of life in a two-dimensional world, and what happens when a three-dimensional being intrudes. Amusing reading, but also useful as introduction to thought about hyperspace. Introduction by Banesh Hoffmann. 16 illustrations. xx + 103pp.   20001-9 Paperbound $1.00

POEMS OF ANNE BRADSTREET, edited with an introduction by Robert Hutchinson. A new selection of poems by America's first poet and perhaps the first significant woman poet in the English language. 48 poems display her development in works of considerable variety—love poems, domestic poems, religious meditations, formal elegies, "quaternions," etc. Notes, bibliography. viii + 222pp.

22160-1 Paperbound $2.50

THREE GOTHIC NOVELS: THE CASTLE OF OTRANTO BY HORACE WALPOLE; VATHEK BY WILLIAM BECKFORD; THE VAMPYRE BY JOHN POLIDORI, WITH FRAGMENT OF A NOVEL BY LORD BYRON, edited by E. F. Bleiler. The first Gothic novel, by Walpole; the finest Oriental tale in English, by Beckford; powerful Romantic supernatural story in versions by Polidori and Byron. All extremely important in history of literature; all still exciting, packed with supernatural thrills, ghosts, haunted castles, magic, etc. xl + 291pp.

21232-7 Paperbound $2.50

THE BEST TALES OF HOFFMANN, E. T. A. Hoffmann. 10 of Hoffmann's most important stories, in modern re-editings of standard translations: Nutcracker and the King of Mice, Signor Formica, Automata, The Sandman, Rath Krespel, The Golden Flowerpot, Master Martin the Cooper, The Mines of Falun, The King's Betrothed, A New Year's Eve Adventure. 7 illustrations by Hoffmann. Edited by E. F. Bleiler. xxxix + 419pp. 21793-0 Paperbound $3.00

GHOST AND HORROR STORIES OF AMBROSE BIERCE, Ambrose Bierce. 23 strikingly modern stories of the horrors latent in the human mind: The Eyes of the Panther, The Damned Thing, An Occurrence at Owl Creek Bridge, An Inhabitant of Carcosa, etc., plus the dream-essay, Visions of the Night. Edited by E. F. Bleiler. xxii + 199pp. 20767-6 Paperbound $1.50

BEST GHOST STORIES OF J. S. LEFANU, J. Sheridan LeFanu. Finest stories by Victorian master often considered greatest supernatural writer of all. Carmilla, Green Tea, The Haunted Baronet, The Familiar, and 12 others. Most never before available in the U. S. A. Edited by E. F. Bleiler. 8 illustrations from Victorian publications. xvii + 467pp. 20415-4 Paperbound $3.00

MATHEMATICAL FOUNDATIONS OF INFORMATION THEORY, A. I. Khinchin. Comprehensive introduction to work of Shannon, McMillan, Feinstein and Khinchin, placing these investigations on a rigorous mathematical basis. Covers entropy concept in probability theory, uniqueness theorem, Shannon's inequality, ergodic sources, the E property, martingale concept, noise, Feinstein's fundamental lemma, Shanon's first and second theorems. Translated by R. A. Silverman and M. D. Friedman. iii + 120pp. 60434-9 Paperbound $2.00

SEVEN SCIENCE FICTION NOVELS, H. G. Wells. The standard collection of the great novels. Complete, unabridged. *First Men in the Moon, Island of Dr. Moreau, War of the Worlds, Food of the Gods, Invisible Man, Time Machine, In the Days of the Comet.* Not only science fiction fans, but every educated person owes it to himself to read these novels. 1015pp. (USO) 20264-X Clothbound $6.00

LAST AND FIRST MEN AND STAR MAKER, TWO SCIENCE FICTION NOVELS, Olaf Stapledon. Greatest future histories in science fiction. In the first, human intelligence is the "hero," through strange paths of evolution, interplanetary invasions, incredible technologies, near extinctions and reemergences. Star Maker describes the quest of a band of star rovers for intelligence itself, through time and space: weird inhuman civilizations, crustacean minds, symbiotic worlds, etc. Complete, unabridged. v + 438pp. (USO) 21962-3 Paperbound $2.50

THREE PROPHETIC NOVELS, H. G. WELLS. Stages of a consistently planned future for mankind. *When the Sleeper Wakes,* and *A Story of the Days to Come,* anticipate *Brave New World* and *1984,* in the 21st Century; *The Time Machine,* only complete version in print, shows farther future and the end of mankind. All show Wells's greatest gifts as storyteller and novelist. Edited by E. F. Bleiler. x + 335pp. (USO) 20605-X Paperbound $2.50

THE DEVIL'S DICTIONARY, Ambrose Bierce. America's own Oscar Wilde—Ambrose Bierce—offers his barbed iconoclastic wisdom in over 1,000 definitions hailed by H. L. Mencken as "some of the most gorgeous witticisms in the English language." 145pp. 20487-1 Paperbound $1.25

MAX AND MORITZ, Wilhelm Busch. Great children's classic, father of comic strip, of two bad boys, Max and Moritz. Also Ker and Plunk (Plisch und Plumm), Cat and Mouse, Deceitful Henry, Ice-Peter, The Boy and the Pipe, and five other pieces. Original German, with English translation. Edited by H. Arthur Klein; translations by various hands and H. Arthur Klein. vi + 216pp. 20181-3 Paperbound $2.00

PIGS IS PIGS AND OTHER FAVORITES, Ellis Parker Butler. The title story is one of the best humor short stories, as Mike Flannery obfuscates biology and English. Also included, That Pup of Murchison's, The Great American Pie Company, and Perkins of Portland. 14 illustrations. v + 109pp. 21532-6 Paperbound $1.25

THE PETERKIN PAPERS, Lucretia P. Hale. It takes genius to be as stupidly mad as the Peterkins, as they decide to become wise, celebrate the "Fourth," keep a cow, and otherwise strain the resources of the Lady from Philadelphia. Basic book of American humor. 153 illustrations. 219pp. 20794-3 Paperbound $2.00

PERRAULT'S FAIRY TALES, translated by A. E. Johnson and S. R. Littlewood, with 34 full-page illustrations by Gustave Doré. All the original Perrault stories—Cinderella, Sleeping Beauty, Bluebeard, Little Red Riding Hood, Puss in Boots, Tom Thumb, etc.—with their witty verse morals and the magnificent illustrations of Doré. One of the five or six great books of European fairy tales. viii + 117pp. 8⅛ x 11. 22311-6 Paperbound $2.00

OLD HUNGARIAN FAIRY TALES, Baroness Orczy. Favorites translated and adapted by author of the *Scarlet Pimpernel.* Eight fairy tales include "The Suitors of Princess Fire-Fly," "The Twin Hunchbacks," "Mr. Cuttlefish's Love Story," and "The Enchanted Cat." This little volume of magic and adventure will captivate children as it has for generations. 90 drawings by Montagu Barstow. 96pp. (USO) 22293-4 Paperbound $1.95

THE RED FAIRY BOOK, Andrew Lang. Lang's color fairy books have long been children's favorites. This volume includes Rapunzel, Jack and the Bean-stalk and 35 other stories, familiar and unfamiliar. 4 plates, 93 illustrations x + 367pp.
21673-X Paperbound $2.50

THE BLUE FAIRY BOOK, Andrew Lang. Lang's tales come from all countries and all times. Here are 37 tales from Grimm, the Arabian Nights, Greek Mythology, and other fascinating sources. 8 plates, 130 illustrations. xi + 390pp.
21437-0 Paperbound $2.50

HOUSEHOLD STORIES BY THE BROTHERS GRIMM. Classic English-language edition of the well-known tales — Rumpelstiltskin, Snow White, Hansel and Gretel, The Twelve Brothers, Faithful John, Rapunzel, Tom Thumb (52 stories in all). Translated into simple, straightforward English by Lucy Crane. Ornamented with headpieces, vignettes, elaborate decorative initials and a dozen full-page illustrations by Walter Crane. x + 269pp.
21080-4 Paperbound **$2.00**

THE MERRY ADVENTURES OF ROBIN HOOD, Howard Pyle. The finest modern versions of the traditional ballads and tales about the great English outlaw. Howard Pyle's complete prose version, with every word, every illustration of the first edition. Do not confuse this facsimile of the original (1883) with modern editions that change text or illustrations. 23 plates plus many page decorations. xxii + 296pp.
22043-5 Paperbound $2.50

THE STORY OF KING ARTHUR AND HIS KNIGHTS, Howard Pyle. The finest children's version of the life of King Arthur; brilliantly retold by Pyle, with 48 of his most imaginative illustrations. xviii + 313pp. 6⅛ x 9¼.
21445-1 Paperbound $2.50

THE WONDERFUL WIZARD OF OZ, L. Frank Baum. America's finest children's book in facsimile of first edition with all Denslow illustrations in full color. The edition a child should have. Introduction by Martin Gardner. 23 color plates, scores of drawings. iv + 267pp.
20691-2 Paperbound $2.50

THE MARVELOUS LAND OF OZ, L. Frank Baum. The second Oz book, every bit as imaginative as the Wizard. The hero is a boy named Tip, but the Scarecrow and the Tin Woodman are back, as is the Oz magic. 16 color plates, 120 drawings by John R. Neill. 287pp.
20692-0 Paperbound $2.50

THE MAGICAL MONARCH OF MO, L. Frank Baum. Remarkable adventures in a land even stranger than Oz. The best of Baum's books not in the Oz series. 15 color plates and dozens of drawings by Frank Verbeck. xviii + 237pp.
21892-9 Paperbound $2.25

THE BAD CHILD'S BOOK OF BEASTS, MORE BEASTS FOR WORSE CHILDREN, A MORAL ALPHABET, Hilaire Belloc. Three complete humor classics in one volume. Be kind to the frog, and do not call him names . . . and 28 other whimsical animals. Familiar favorites and some not so well known. Illustrated by Basil Blackwell. 156pp.
(USO) 20749-8 Paperbound $1.50

EAST O' THE SUN AND WEST O' THE MOON, George W. Dasent. Considered the best of all translations of these Norwegian folk tales, this collection has been enjoyed by generations of children (and folklorists too). Includes True and Untrue, Why the Sea is Salt, East O' the Sun and West O' the Moon, Why the Bear is Stumpy-Tailed, Boots and the Troll, The Cock and the Hen, Rich Peter the Pedlar, and 52 more. The only edition with all 59 tales. 77 illustrations by Erik Werenskiold and Theodor Kittelsen. xv + 418pp. 22521-6 Paperbound $3.50

GOOPS AND HOW TO BE THEM, Gelett Burgess. Classic of tongue-in-cheek humor, masquerading as etiquette book. 87 verses, twice as many cartoons, show mischievous Goops as they demonstrate to children virtues of table manners, neatness, courtesy, etc. Favorite for generations. viii + 88pp. 6½ x 9¼.
22233-0 Paperbound $1.25

ALICE'S ADVENTURES UNDER GROUND, Lewis Carroll. The first version, quite different from the final *Alice in Wonderland,* printed out by Carroll himself with his own illustrations. Complete facsimile of the "million dollar" manuscript Carroll gave to Alice Liddell in 1864. Introduction by Martin Gardner. viii + 96pp. Title and dedication pages in color. 21482-6 Paperbound $1.25

THE BROWNIES, THEIR BOOK, Palmer Cox. Small as mice, cunning as foxes, exuberant and full of mischief, the Brownies go to the zoo, toy shop, seashore, circus, etc., in 24 verse adventures and 266 illustrations. Long a favorite, since their first appearance in St. Nicholas Magazine. xi + 144pp. 6⅝ x 9¼.
21265-3 Paperbound $1.75

SONGS OF CHILDHOOD, Walter De La Mare. Published (under the pseudonym Walter Ramal) when De La Mare was only 29, this charming collection has long been a favorite children's book. A facsimile of the first edition in paper, the 47 poems capture the simplicity of the nursery rhyme and the ballad, including such lyrics as I Met Eve, Tartary, The Silver Penny. vii + 106pp. (USO) 21972-0 Paperbound
$1.25

THE COMPLETE NONSENSE OF EDWARD LEAR, Edward Lear. The finest 19th-century humorist-cartoonist in full: all nonsense limericks, zany alphabets, Owl and Pussycat, songs, nonsense botany, and more than 500 illustrations by Lear himself. Edited by Holbrook Jackson. xxix + 287pp. (USO) 20167-8 Paperbound $2.00

BILLY WHISKERS: THE AUTOBIOGRAPHY OF A GOAT, Frances Trego Montgomery. A favorite of children since the early 20th century, here are the escapades of that rambunctious, irresistible and mischievous goat—Billy Whiskers. Much in the spirit of *Peck's Bad Boy,* this is a book that children never tire of reading or hearing. All the original familiar illustrations by W. H. Fry are included: 6 color plates, 18 black and white drawings. 159pp. 22345-0 Paperbound $2.00

MOTHER GOOSE MELODIES. Faithful republication of the fabulously rare Munroe and Francis "copyright 1833" Boston edition—the most important Mother Goose collection, usually referred to as the "original." Familiar rhymes plus many rare ones, with wonderful old woodcut illustrations. Edited by E. F. Bleiler. 128pp. 4½ x 6⅜. 22577-1 Paperbound $1.00

TWO LITTLE SAVAGES; BEING THE ADVENTURES OF TWO BOYS WHO LIVED AS INDIANS AND WHAT THEY LEARNED, Ernest Thompson Seton. Great classic of nature and boyhood provides a vast range of woodlore in most palatable form, a genuinely entertaining story. Two farm boys build a teepee in woods and live in it for a month, working out Indian solutions to living problems, star lore, birds and animals, plants, etc. 293 illustrations. vii + 286pp.

20985-7 Paperbound $2.50

PETER PIPER'S PRACTICAL PRINCIPLES OF PLAIN & PERFECT PRONUNCIATION. Alliterative jingles and tongue-twisters of surprising charm, that made their first appearance in America about 1830. Republished in full with the spirited woodcut illustrations from this earliest American edition. 32pp. 4½ x 6⅜.

22560-7 Paperbound $1.00

SCIENCE EXPERIMENTS AND AMUSEMENTS FOR CHILDREN, Charles Vivian. 73 easy experiments, requiring only materials found at home or easily available, such as candles, coins, steel wool, etc.; illustrate basic phenomena like vacuum, simple chemical reaction, etc. All safe. Modern, well-planned. Formerly *Science Games for Children*. 102 photos, numerous drawings. 96pp. 6⅛ x 9¼.

21856-2 Paperbound $1.25

AN INTRODUCTION TO CHESS MOVES AND TACTICS SIMPLY EXPLAINED, Leonard Barden. Informal intermediate introduction, quite strong in explaining reasons for moves. Covers basic material, tactics, important openings, traps, positional play in middle game, end game. Attempts to isolate patterns and recurrent configurations. Formerly *Chess*. 58 figures. 102pp. (USO) 21210-6 Paperbound $1.25

LASKER'S MANUAL OF CHESS, Dr. Emanuel Lasker. Lasker was not only one of the five great World Champions, he was also one of the ablest expositors, theorists, and analysts. In many ways, his Manual, permeated with his philosophy of battle, filled with keen insights, is one of the greatest works ever written on chess. Filled with analyzed games by the great players. A single-volume library that will profit almost any chess player, beginner or master. 308 diagrams. xli x 349pp.

20640-8 Paperbound $2.75

THE MASTER BOOK OF MATHEMATICAL RECREATIONS, Fred Schuh. In opinion of many the finest work ever prepared on mathematical puzzles, stunts, recreations; exhaustively thorough explanations of mathematics involved, analysis of effects, citation of puzzles and games. Mathematics involved is elementary. Translated by F. Göbel. 194 figures. xxiv + 430pp.

22134-2 Paperbound $3.50

MATHEMATICS, MAGIC AND MYSTERY, Martin Gardner. Puzzle editor for Scientific American explains mathematics behind various mystifying tricks: card tricks, stage "mind reading," coin and match tricks, counting out games, geometric dissections, etc. Probability sets, theory of numbers clearly explained. Also provides more than 400 tricks, guaranteed to work, that you can do. 135 illustrations. xii + 176pp.

20335-2 Paperbound $1.75

MATHEMATICAL PUZZLES FOR BEGINNERS AND ENTHUSIASTS, Geoffrey Mott-Smith. 189 puzzles from easy to difficult—involving arithmetic, logic, algebra, properties of digits, probability, etc.—for enjoyment and mental stimulus. Explanation of mathematical principles behind the puzzles. 135 illustrations. viii + 248pp.
20198-8 Paperbound $1.75

PAPER FOLDING FOR BEGINNERS, William D. Murray and Francis J. Rigney. Easiest book on the market, clearest instructions on making interesting, beautiful origami. Sail boats, cups, roosters, frogs that move legs, bonbon boxes, standing birds, etc. 40 projects; more than 275 diagrams and photographs. 94pp.
20713-7 Paperbound $1.00

TRICKS AND GAMES ON THE POOL TABLE, Fred Herrmann. 79 tricks and games— some solitaires, some for two or more players, some competitive games—to entertain you between formal games. Mystifying shots and throws, unusual caroms, tricks involving such props as cork, coins, a hat, etc. Formerly *Fun on the Pool Table*. 77 figures. 95pp.
21814-7 Paperbound $1.25

HAND SHADOWS TO BE THROWN UPON THE WALL: A SERIES OF NOVEL AND AMUSING FIGURES FORMED BY THE HAND, Henry Bursill. Delightful picturebook from great-grandfather's day shows how to make 18 different hand shadows: a bird that flies, duck that quacks, dog that wags his tail, camel, goose, deer, boy, turtle, etc. Only book of its sort. vi + 33pp. 6½ x 9¼. 21779-5 Paperbound $1.00

WHITTLING AND WOODCARVING, E. J. Tangerman. 18th printing of best book on market. "If you can cut a potato you can carve" toys and puzzles, chains, chessmen, caricatures, masks, frames, woodcut blocks, surface patterns, much more. Information on tools, woods, techniques. Also goes into serious wood sculpture from Middle Ages to present, East and West. 464 photos, figures. x + 293pp.
20965-2 Paperbound $2.00

HISTORY OF PHILOSOPHY, Julián Marías. Possibly the clearest, most easily followed, best planned, most useful one-volume history of philosophy on the market; neither skimpy nor overfull. Full details on system of every major philosopher and dozens of less important thinkers from pre-Socratics up to Existentialism and later. Strong on many European figures usually omitted. Has gone through dozens of editions in Europe. 1966 edition, translated by Stanley Appelbaum and Clarence Strowbridge. xviii + 505pp. 21739-6 Paperbound $3.50

YOGA: A SCIENTIFIC EVALUATION, Kovoor T. Behanan. Scientific but non-technical study of physiological results of yoga exercises; done under auspices of Yale U. Relations to Indian thought, to psychoanalysis, etc. 16 photos. xxiii + 270pp.
20505-3 Paperbound $2.50